T0305256

Import Safety

Import Safety

Regulatory Governance in the Global Economy

Edited by
Cary Coglianese, Adam M. Finkel,
and David Zaring

PENN

UNIVERSITY OF PENNSYLVANIA PRESS

PHILADELPHIA

Published by
University of Pennsylvania Press
Philadelphia, Pennsylvania 19104-4112

Printed in the United States of America on acid-free paper
10 9 8 7 6 5 4 3 2 1

A Cataloging-in-Publication record is available from the Library of Congress.

ISBN 978-0-8122-4222-5

Contents

Preface

For centuries, governments have imposed legal obligations on businesses in order to protect consumers from harmful products. Bavaria's Purity Law of 1516, one of the first consumer safety statutes in Europe, purported to protect consumers from unsafe beer. Throughout the seventeenth and eighteenth centuries, British judges and legislators developed principles of tort and fraud that provided more general protections. Today, consumer protection around the world depends significantly on domestic laws and institutions established after the rapid expansion of industrialization at the turn of the last century and on others created in response to social movements in the 1960s and 1970s.

We have now entered a new era that calls out for further legal change. Existing regulatory structures arose within a business climate much different from that of today's globalized economy. Protecting consumers through proactive regulation has never been easy, but now such regulatory efforts face new challenges because of expansive growth in trade and rapid changes in technologies and economic conditions. Each year, more food products, drugs, and other goods move across national borders than any single government alone can inspect and test. Government officials face a growing set of regulatory targets abroad. Just identifying producers of ingredients and products in other countries poses daunting challenges; holding such foreign companies accountable for unsafe products presents still further administrative and legal obstacles.

If products entering the domestic marketplace from foreign countries are harder to regulate through traditional means, will consumer safety risks increase in an era of global trade? It seems likely they will. If foreign firms are harder to regulate, then the law's deterrent effect will presumably also be diminished for such firms, making safety problems more likely at the margin. With trillions of dollars worth of goods crossing international borders each year, even a slight reduction in deterrence could lead to hundreds, if not thousands, of additional injuries or fatalities annually. If nothing changes, the recent spate of import safety crises—from lead-painted toys to melamine in milk—could mark just the beginning of a dangerous trend.

Of course, changes are in fact occurring in how governments approach import safety. Each new crisis over unsafe imports generates calls for reform by politicians, regulators, and publics around the world. Governments are now beginning to respond with new policy proposals and initiatives. Some of these efforts seek to strengthen existing inspection and enforcement capabilities within importing countries; others seek to establish bilateral and multilateral regulatory coordination and cooperation; and still others seek to create incentives for private actors, such as retailers, insurance companies, trade associations, and consumer groups, to serve as surrogate regulators. *Import Safety: Regulatory Governance in the Global Economy* offers important scholarly analyses of these and other innovative ideas for improving product safety governance around the world. Its varied disciplinary perspectives on import safety deserve particular attention at this time of economic change and global transformation.

Admittedly, the most salient transformation at the present time centers on the restoration and reconfiguration of global financial markets. As this book was being written, the world endured—and is still reeling from the effects of—its worst economic collapse in several generations. One risk in publishing a book on regulatory governance at this time is that some readers might wonder why its authors entertain any solution other than strengthening the exercise of traditional authority by strong, central regulatory authorities. After all, conventional wisdom places the blame for the economic collapse on the excesses of private-sector institutions and on an unhealthy relaxation of central regulatory oversight.

Yet the current economic crisis does not diminish the vital need for a book like this, at a time like this. Hard economic times are likely to accentuate the competitive pressures that lead firms to cut corners on safety. At the same time, there is simply no getting around the need to consider the role of private-sector institutions in maintaining product safety. After all, no single, central regulatory authority exists that could be strengthened when it comes to policing international trade. Furthermore, the achievement of any regulatory goal ultimately depends on what private-sector institutions do. The challenge is, and always has been, to alter the incentives of private actors so that they better align with public goals.

Conventional forms of oversight clearly remain important avenues for trying to accomplish regulatory objectives, and this book accordingly provides ideas for enhancing traditional import-related inspections. But even when applied in the most efficient manner possible, central regulatory approaches run up against clear limits, especially when addressing the kind of vexing challenges that policy analysts sometimes call "wicked" problems. In this case, the problem of import safety is actually a steady stream of diffuse problems arising from a set of constantly changing products generated through complex, decentralized supply chains.

Rather than accepting the status quo, *Import Safety* is motivated by a search for better solutions. If the old ways cannot adequately protect consumers, then new ways deserve policy makers' and scholars' serious consideration.

Cary Coglianese
Penn Program on Regulation

Part I
Perspectives on the Problem

Chapter 1
Consumer Protection in an Era of Globalization

Cary Coglianese, Adam M. Finkel, and David Zaring

Society has long tolerated some risk in the products consumers buy, especially when the risks are understood to be inherent in the products' use. By their very nature, for example, cigarettes and fat-laden desserts pose risks to consumers, and, although some car models may be more crashworthy than others, driving any automobile introduces a degree of risk. But when two identical products sit side by side on a shelf, and one of them might be deadly and the other benign, we have a recipe for serious public health problems as well as major economic consequences from diminishing consumer trust.

The problem of unsafe food, pharmaceuticals, and consumer products coexisting with goods the public assumes to be safe has recently become more acute as a consequence of the boom in global trade. For example, in the span of just two recent years, consumers in a number of countries have endured a series of health crises from products imported from China:

- In 2006, Panama imported from China syrup for cough medicine that contained diethylene glycol—a chemical compound used in antifreeze—instead of glycerin. More than 250,000 bottles of cold medicine were manufactured from the toxic syrup, which fatally poisoned more than 100 people (Bogdanich and Koster 2008). The same poisonous ingredient also made its way into more than 6,000 imported tubes of toothpaste sold in Panama in 2007 (Bogdanich and McLean 2007).
- Multinational toy manufacturers recalled tens of millions of toys in 2007 in response to the discovery of lead paint or unsafe magnetic parts on many popular toys—from Barbie to Thomas the Tank Engine—that were produced in China and sold worldwide (Story 2007).

- A toy product manufactured in China and marketed in the United States as "Aqua Dots" and in Australia as "Bindeez" was found in 2007 to contain beads manufactured with a glue that, when ingested, converted to an analog of the so-called date rape drug, putting at least several children into comas (Bradsher 2007).
- In 2008, milk and milk products from China, including infant formula, were found to contain melamine, a chemical used as a fire retardant that had been illegally added as a thickening agent to increase and mask the protein content of diluted milk. Melamine contamination led to hundreds of thousands of illnesses and numerous deaths in China, as well as to massive product recalls throughout Asia, the Americas, and Europe (Oster et al. 2008). A similar scare in 2007 involved imported pet food contaminated with melamine (Nestle 2008).
- Nearly 150 deaths have occurred globally from the contamination of Chinese-manufactured heparin, a blood thinner used for patients undergoing certain types of kidney dialysis and cardiovascular surgeries (Powell 2008). The heparin manufactured in China was found by the U.S. Food and Drug Administration (FDA) to contain a lower-cost substance—oversulfated chondroitin sulfate—that mimics the anticoagulant effects of pure heparin but may have lethal side effects (Powell 2008).
- An estimated 100,000 homes throughout the United States may contain Chinese-manufactured drywall linked to indoor air pollution—specifically "rotten egg" odors—and to the corrosion of copper piping and air-conditioner coils (CPSC 2009; Lee and Semuels 2009; Schmit 2009). Residents and public health officials are concerned about eye, skin, and respiratory irritation, as well as other health and safety risks, including the possibility of fire or shock from corroded piping and wiring.

China is not the only source of alarm about unsafe products. Government officials around the world have raised safety concerns about products imported from other countries. In 2008, for example, the U.S. FDA barred for safety reasons the importation of more than thirty generic drugs produced by Ranbaxy Laboratories Ltd., an Indian pharmaceutical manufacturer (Dooren and Favole 2009).

The need to protect consumers from unsafe food, drugs, and other products is a persistent one—and is certainly not limited to imported products. As with the Chinese deaths resulting from the recent melamine contamination of milk products, the citizens of the countries that export unsafe products can be just as much affected as those in the importing country (Powell 2008). Moreover, national regulatory apparatuses for monitoring domestic producers have been in place around the world for most of the last century to address the same kind of risks that arise from unsafe imports (Vogel 2007). Even in developed countries with long-standing regulatory regimes, domestic products can be as dangerous as any import (Moss and Martin 2009). The same market pressures and consumer demands for cheap goods that may lead some producers to cut corners on safety apply whether products are made at home or abroad: the expansive recall of peanut-based products throughout the United States in early 2009, for example, targeted a Georgia-based processing facility of the Peanut Corporation of America (Zhang 2009). When in 2007 the U.S. National Highway Traffic Safety Administration (NHTSA) sought to recall defective tires manufactured in China (sold by the aptly named Foreign Tire Sales), the underlying concern was not much different from when NHTSA took action in 2000 against the U.S.-based Firestone company for defective tires produced at a plant in Decatur, Illinois (Aeppel 2007).

Nevertheless, the challenge of protecting consumers from unsafe imports deserves special and intensive analysis at this time of expanding globalization. Not only are safety crises from imported products not going to disappear, but they are likely to increase with international trade. When the world recovers from its recent economic downturn, the flow of goods moving across borders will continue to expand. Already the U.S. economy depends on more than $2 trillion worth of imported goods per year, with more than half coming from Canada, China, Mexico, Japan, and Germany (HHS 2007a). The sheer volume of international trade creates a vast and complex network of the sources of safety problems. More than 825,000 different exporting companies bring products into the United States through more than 300 airports, seaports, and border crossings (HHS 2007a), straining the capacity of national regulatory authorities to inspect products at the borders and monitor facilities at the site of manufacture.

The benefits of international trade are clear: the lowering of trade barriers creates new market opportunities and enhances welfare by lowering costs to consumers. But global trade also contributes to added vulnerabilities. The Indian pharmaceutical company cited by U.S. regulators in 2008 for safety problems was reportedly the sole source of a key children's antibiotic supplied to the New Zealand health system (Das 2008). Even a country such as the United States, which has long placed restrictions on the importation of drugs produced from outside its borders (ostensibly for safety reasons), currently relies on imports for more than 80 percent of the active pharmaceutical ingredients used by its drug manufacturers (GAO 1998). In addition to the vulnerabilities citizens face from goods manufactured in parts of the world not subject to their common "social contract," the combination of global trade with modern technology's constant innovation in manufacturing techniques, product designs, and formulas makes the challenge all the greater for the regulator of imported products. As Professor Li Shaomin has observed, "When millions of people experiment with new ways to make money without moral self-constraint, the chance of new products that can evade existing testing methods is pretty high" (Xin and Stone 2008: 1311).

The challenge of import safety calls for new policy ideas and analysis. The former U.S. Secretary of Health and Human Services, Michael Leavitt, noted that "just as the volume of trade has changed, so must the strategies to regulate safety. Simply scaling up our current inspection strategy will not work" (Leavitt 2008: 4).

This book is premised on the view that global trade poses both quantitatively and qualitatively distinct problems for consuming publics around the globe and for those governments charged with protecting them. Although consumers can be harmed just as much by domestic products as by imports, the import safety problem raises a variety of jurisdictional, legal, cultural, political, and practical issues that are not present with domestic product regulation. The research in this book casts a needed light on the distinct nature of the import safety problem, analyzes a variety of innovative solutions to it, and addresses the implications these solutions hold for important social values, ranging from accountability to efficiency.

This book also treats the problem as a general one confronting the food industry, the pharmaceutical industry, and all other industries that manufacture consumer products of all kinds, from tires to toys. In much of the world, separate regulatory laws and institutions have been created to deal with safety problems in different industries. Policy research has often tracked these divisions, with distinct communities of experts focused on food safety, drug regulation, and consumer safety. In editing this volume, we have certainly been mindful of these divisions of expertise, as well as of the varied industrial processes, economic conditions, and sources of safety problems that exist across these domains. The contamination of food products from the *E. coli* bacterium is obviously quite a different policy problem than the risks of tread separation in automobile tires. The risks to different subpopulations of the public may also vary depending on the type of product, ranging from children with toys to the elderly and immunocompromised populations with pharmaceuticals. Yet, as much as we recognize these differences, we also resist dividing the import safety issue into separate problems of regulating the safety of imported food, drugs, and consumer products. Decision makers and analysts in each of these domains confront the same fundamental policy choices and, broadly speaking, the same kinds of challenges. Those with a particular interest in one domain can learn from the experiences in other domains and from efforts, such as this book represents, to generalize across different domains.

The Import Safety Problem

We begin with a straightforward understanding of the problem of import safety. The ultimate concern is to avoid the adverse health effects that arise from lapses in safe practices. Such lapses could arise from a variety of possible sources, some intentional, others simply accidental. The schematic shown in Figure 1 provides a highly simplified model of the various links in the causal chain that leads to consumer harm from imported products. At each step along the way there is the possibility for tampering and contamination—from the initial creation of ingredients or other product inputs to the manufacturing, shipment, and sale of the product. As the schematic shows, protecting import safety requires oversight of a complex welter of inputs on both sides of the border.

The actual causal chain for unsafe imports is much more complex. Ingredient and input production is often undertaken by entities separate from those involved in manufacturing itself (Neef 2004). Con-

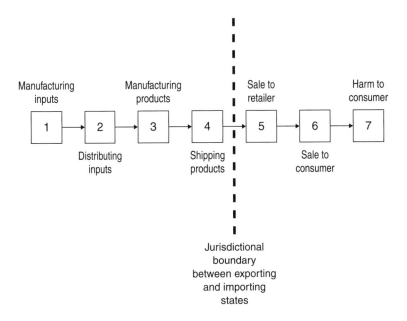

Figure 1. Causal steps to import safety problems.

sumer products can contain many components, drugs often include numerous different ingredients, and food products comprise the outputs of numerous farmers and ranchers. Supply chains, especially in countries as large as China, can be vast and complicated. The schematic in Figure 1 fails to represent this complexity. Furthermore, in reality, the vertical jurisdictional line in the figure can be placed at more than one step in the more complex chain that leads to real consumer harm. Manufacturing can even take place in the importing state, with just product components imported. Large manufacturers and large retail operations, such as "big box" stores, rely on many different sources around the world. As a result, the number of individuals who could tamper with or contaminate a product can be quite substantial. For any given imported product, each step in the causal chain can involve numerous different actors, each with their own incentives, constraints, knowledge, capacity, and motivations.

At some point from the initial ingredient production to the sale and use by consumers, an imported product moves from one jurisdiction to another. That movement over a jurisdictional border—from the exporting state to the importing one—qualitatively distinguishes the problem of import safety from the "ordinary" problems all governments face in policing the safety of food, drug, and consumer products within their borders. What the dotted vertical line in Figure 1 represents is the qualitatively different problem of import safety, one that brings with it an additional set of regulatory challenges. These challenges can be legal, cultural, and even practical. Just identifying who manufactured an ingredient can sometimes be difficult when records are kept in another country and in another language. For example, in 2001 a pair of FDA inspectors were reportedly unable to conduct an inspection of a Chinese facility producing acetaminophen imported into the United States because they simply could not find where the facility was located (Harris 2008). Even when harm can be practically traced back to sources in other countries, regulatory and legal liability may not extend overseas, effectively giving importers a "free ride" on the harm that their products impose on consumers.

In addition to the challenges of monitoring and enforcing safety abroad, international trade complicates consumer protection still further when nations exhibit different cultural postures toward risk and place different domestic priorities on the use of government regulatory resources (Douglas and Wildavsky 1982; GAO 2008b). Even if some cross-cultural risk threshold exists above which no consumer should be expected to suffer, it is still undoubtedly the case that the consuming publics in wealthy importing nations will often have different expectations for safety than consumers in developing countries. Even wealthy publics in different parts of the world—Europe versus the United States, for example—can differ in their perceptions of what product safety means, both across countries and within them (Ansell and Vogel 2006; Hanrahan 2001; Meijer and Stewart 2004). These differences factor not only into differences in government-imposed safety standards, but also into political and institutional choices about what types of domestic regulatory organizations to create and how to fund them, choices that are affected by competing priorities for scarce government resources.

Policy Challenges

As with any regulatory problem, import safety can be addressed by attending to the various links on the causal chain that lead to consumer risk. Of course, if it were possible to test each and every individual pill, product, or morsel of food just before it came into contact with the ultimate consumer, then in principle the regulator could address risk only at that end point and not worry about the causal chain leading up to it. But it is obviously impossible for any government to have the equivalent of a "royal taster" (or other inspector) to check each consumer's intake or purchase in advance. Moreover, import safety is simply not an achievable goal absent some form of international cooperation or interaction. If nothing else, it is that interaction, in the form of international trade, that gives rise to imports, and hence to the problem of ensuring their safety. Because the traditional tools of domestic regulation cannot, alone, address the totality of the problem, any proposal for innovative new protections must not only overcome domestic regulatory hurdles but also survive in the international environment as well.

It is possible, of course, to impose tort liability when consumers are harmed by products, but such liability by itself will be insufficient for several reasons. Although the threat of ex post imposition of liability can create incentives for manufacturers to ensure safety ex ante (Moore and Viscusi 2001), the incentives from tort liability are usually below the socially optimal level because of the costs and practical difficulties in assigning responsibility when consumers are harmed. Consider someone who gets sick or injured from a product with different components—say, even something as simple as a hamburger: it will often not be possible to identify which specific component caused the problem. Was it the meat, the bun, the ketchup, the pickles? Even if the specific component can be identified, when supply chains are long and complex, with suppliers entering and exiting the market, it will often be difficult to trace back the source of the harm to hold the appropriate party liable. Even if the retailer or manufacturer were to be held strictly liable for any harm from products within its purview, that still means that the direct incentives from such liability arise only *after* consumers have been harmed—when the ideal objective would be to prevent such harm from occurring in the first place (Bamberger and Guzman 2008). To the extent that the decision makers at retail and manufacturing firms underestimate the risk of being held liable, or to the extent that the impact of tort liability is reduced to below the socially optimal level because of the existence of insurance, the possibility of bankruptcy, or the ability to negotiate damage awards downward, the need for preventive regulation remains.

Each of the various steps along the causal chain then becomes a potential target of regulatory intervention. At each of these steps, at least three types of decisions about regulatory intervention must be made:

1. What is the appropriate level of safety to strive for? In other words, how safe is safe enough (WTO 1998)?
2. What form should regulatory standards take? Regulators can specify the end point to achieve by adopting performance standards (e.g., from general standards such as "drugs shall be safe" to specific standards such as "foods shall contain no more than 0.01 ppm [parts per million] residues of each listed pesticide"). Another option would be to impose requirements that firms adopt certain safety practices or use specified technologies ("pasteurize milk to a temperature of 161 degrees Fahrenheit for at least two separate 15-second periods," or "keep fish refrigerated at or below 34 degrees Fahrenheit"). A still further, more recent alternative would be to impose management standards that essentially require firms to develop their own performance and technology standards (Coglianese and Lazer 2003).
3. How should compliance with the applicable standards be monitored and enforced? Possibilities range from record-keeping and reporting requirements by businesses to inspections by third-party auditors or government officials.

To be sure, these decisions apply to the regulation of products produced domestically as well as to those imported from another country. However, when regulation seeks to protect against harm experienced in one country but caused by manufacturing and shipping practices in another country, there will be jurisdictional choices.

One choice for the importing country might be simply to rely on the exporting country to set the safety standards and to enforce them. Another choice for the importing nation is to screen products when they cross the border and enter its jurisdiction—but then, since only the product itself is observed, the only option available to the importing nation is to apply performance standards and assess whether the product is unsafe, rather than dictating anything about how it was manufactured (Sullivan 2007). Of course, in an era of expanding global trade, the task of inspecting and testing each product entering from international trade would be monumental, if not Sisyphean. Yet another option, then, would be for exporting and importing countries to share regulatory responsibilities, cooperating in standard-setting, enforcement, or both. Importing and exporting countries could harmonize their standards, or at least enter into mutual recognition treaties on the substantive standards to apply to products available in both countries (Horton 1998; Merrill 1998; Nicolaïdis 1996; Shaffer 2002). They could share enforcement intelligence and monitoring reports, or even allow each other's government inspectors to visit production plants inside the others' borders. And, of course, they could also combine several of these or other approaches into a portfolio of interventions.

International cooperation over import safety poses important, even at times novel, challenges. The challenges are greatest when the exporting and importing countries do not share the same substantive safety standards. If the exporting country will accept foods that contain higher pesticide levels, for example, to what extent should it be permissible for the importing country to enforce more stringent standards? If such differences in standards grow out of real differences in risk tolerances, and are not just a cover for protectionism, they will be permissible under global rules, but nevertheless they might still affect the willingness of an exporting country to engage in forms of regulatory cooperation with an importing country.

In addition to bilateral regulatory cooperation between exporting and importing countries, other institutional arrangements could involve the creation of transnational institutions that would possess standard-setting authority or enforcement powers (or both). Or perhaps such arrangements could involve attempts to leverage private-sector institutions to address product safety, either through greater reliance on private standard-setting and auditing bodies, through trade associations, or even through large manufacturers or retailers that could use their purchasing power to impose safety-related demands on their suppliers.

In considering the appropriate form of intervention, a further question arises concerning the consequences that should be imposed on those who violate safety standards. Some of these consequences may be imposed by the marketplace itself. If Europeans want to avoid foods with genetically modified organisms (GMOs), and they know that U.S. foods have GMO ingredients, they may simply avoid buying foods produced in the United States. When it comes to nonmarket or government consequences, though, these can be blunt instruments, such as applying trade sanctions or product bans against the exporting country rather than specific manufacturers—effectively punishing responsible producers in the same industry from the same country along with the offending manufacturers of the dangerous products. More specific consequences might involve targeted penalties or liability judgments against the specific actors who created and sold unsafe products (Bamberger and Guzman 2008).

New Directions in Domestic Regulatory Strategy

In the wake of the recent safety scares and scandals, both importing and exporting countries stand at a crossroads. As the subsequent chapters in this book demonstrate, solving the import safety problem will require new ideas. It will also require careful analysis by a broad range of scholars from a variety of disciplines such as those represented in this volume. Import safety is a regulatory problem as well as a trade problem, a domestic problem as well as an international problem.

The range of solutions available to policy makers is a testament to the size and scope of the import safety problem. A country might try to improve its enforcement program by deploying limited resources more effectively. Or it might try to improve outcomes by encouraging consumers themselves to take more care—and ensuring that they can do so by requiring more and better labeling on products, highlighting their risks, their origins, and their ingredients. Countries might improve safety by turning away, to some degree, from border interdiction and facilitated consumer self-help and turning instead toward improving the government's responsiveness when outbreaks of unsafe products are identified. Probably no small part of the solution to import safety problems will continue to be responsive and reactive in form—though more effectively than at present—rather than purely preventive.

Effective policies will require smart, well-functioning regulatory institutions to carry them out. In the United States, this kind of institutional support is widely thought to be hamstrung by the extensive patchwork of agencies with overlapping and incomplete jurisdictions (GAO 2007; O'Reilly 2004). Nearly a dozen different entities at the federal level bear responsibility for food safety alone (GAO 2008a). General principles for reorganization might include: (1) centralizing authority (e.g., the same agency should inspect "the entire pizza," not just the cheese underneath the pepperoni); (2) establishing robust, shared databases and integrated communications systems in which multiple agencies must be involved; and (3) separating organizational units that promote and subsidize industries from those that manage risks.

However difficult to achieve, institutional reform may not be enough. Hoffmann (2007: 15) argues that in the realm of food safety "incremental solutions like restoring funding, appointing a food safety czar, consolidating agencies, and even eliminating the 'silos' around regulation of different food products, will not do the job." Hoffmann, like others, emphasizes the need for the implementation of Hazard Analysis and Critical Control Point (HACCP) systems, through which companies essentially develop their own internal regulatory systems (Coglianese and Lazer 2003). HACCP regulations require companies to identify the potential hazards associated with their processing operations and to identify methods for addressing these hazards. Companies must identify all "critical control points" in their operations at which risks can be monitored and addressed, and then they must create internal plans and procedures for ensuring that risks can be minimized. Under an approach like HACCP, any importer of food, drugs, or consumer products could be required to develop its own plan for monitoring its suppliers and ensuring that any products sold within the importing nation meet that country's standards. Such a management-based approach holds much promise for conditions like those that apply to imports, where product performance is costly for the government to measure and where one-size-fits-all solutions do not apply (Bennear 2007; Coglianese and Lazer 2003).

The sheer volume, heterogeneity, and changing nature of products that pass through the global trade network make it virtually impossible for the government to regulate products through more conventional means. Thus, imposing mandates or otherwise encouraging importers to develop their own private forms of regulation holds great appeal. Of course, the same vastness and complexity that make it difficult for governments to impose and enforce traditional regulatory standards will also undoubtedly hamper to some extent efforts to ensure that firms' management systems are operating well and that other forms of public-private partnerships are delivering substantive results rather than just symbolism (Coglianese and Lazer 2003).

Toward a Global Consumer Protection System

That so many import safety responses are located at the international level presents a paradox. Although imports can come from the other side of the globe, the goal in any safety regime is to protect the most local of experiences—the relationship between individuals and the food they eat, the drugs that keep them healthy, and the products that enrich their lives. Taking the very personal and making it multinational is hard enough as a matter of institutional design. But doing so without fostering alienation and discouraging the security of relationships between people and what they consume may be especially daunting (Esty 2006).

Managing the very local within the very global is what makes some of the otherwise most promising international import safety ideas particularly challenging. In the United States, the possibility that personal safety could be delegated to an international regime that would evolve on its own to respond to new threats, with new tools of its own devising, has raised fears about the delegation of power and authority that last held prominence when the Supreme Court gave the nondelegation doctrine its one good year in the 1930s (*A.L.A. Schechter Poultry Corp. v. United States* 1935; *Panama Refining Co. v. Ryan* 1935). Despite predictable fears and resistance to the delegation of regulatory authority to international institutions, the creation of such institutions, or other forms of international cooperation, either through formal treaty or informal networking, would appear nevertheless inevitable. After all, in a world of food scares, drug poisonings, and producers who do not have to bear the cost of the injuries they inflict on the other side of the world, certainly the marketplace by itself does not seem equipped to handle the problem, and, as noted above, national governments cannot hope to patrol all the goods entering their borders.

In developing regulatory responses to import safety problems, critical issues will also arise over how to manage the relationship between the goal of global free trade and the safety demanded by domestic publics. The WTO was designed to encourage freer trade among its members (Nedzel 2008), but the imposition of domestic safety requirements on imported products would seem antithetical to the WTO's raison d'être—even when such requirements are consistent with General Agreement on Tariffs and Trade (GATT) exceptions to the general ban on barriers to free trade. How can the WTO reconcile its recognition that countries have legitimate differences in risk tolerance (WTO 2000–2001) with its emphasis on harmonizing regulatory standards so as to facilitate international trade (WTO 1994)? Will it still be possible for the WTO to accept local *tastes* on safety and health protections if such protections must be based on common transnational standards of scientific evidence and risk analysis, as the WTO also expects?

International solutions also need to take into account the various steps in the causal chain leading to consumer harm. Where on that chain should international efforts aim? Should they aim to stop dangerous products from being created in the first place, to identify unsafe products before they reach the consumer, or both? Although interdiction at the borders would appear to be most compatible with a traditional international system based on sovereignty, some promising international institutions are starting to focus on prevention of unsafe products at their source, even when doing so means crossing jurisdictional lines. The United Nations Technical Capacity Program, for example, is designed to develop the abilities of regulators in the developing world (WHO 2003).

Other recognizably international solutions to the problems of import safety turn more on the prospect of using international resources to enhance domestic responses to dangerous imports. For example, law enforcement cooperation does not require international harmonization at all; it only facilitates the ability of government regulators to oversee the safety of foreign imports and to investigate injuries even if the causal chain reaches across borders. The United States has avidly pursued this sort of cooperation with China, concluding food, drug, medical device, and animal feed agreements with Chinese regulators in the past decade or so (HHS 2007b). Importing nations have also sought to build capacity among the regulators of exports in other similar jurisdictions. For example, the FDA has made efforts to educate foreign food regulators on food safety, again with particular attention paid to China (Fan 2008).

International networks exemplify an increasingly salient approach in which domestic regulators play the central role (Slaughter 2005). Regulatory networks of varying types are now being put to the task of regulating import risks, including the Codex Alimentarius Commission (an international organization that has become the authorized entity for global food safety standards) and the International Consumer Product Safety Caucus (a transnational organization comprising representatives from domestic regulatory agencies) (DeWaal and Brito 2005). These networks, and other forms of soft law and so-called new governance strategies, all raise advantages and disadvantages that merit full consideration in addressing import safety (Abbott and Snidal 2006).

The various international strategies for addressing consumer protection in a globalized economy raise at least three major sets of questions. The first set focuses on efficacy. How effective are the varied strategies and under what conditions? When should international hard or binding law, and even the creation of supranational institutions, be deployed? When should soft, nonbinding law, or more collaborative forms of governance, be pursued? When are domestic responses more effective than international responses, and vice versa?

The second set of questions focuses on equity. There are, after all, winners and losers to all domestic and international solutions. Who benefits? And who suffers? How should the demands of the developed world be reconciled with the realities of the developing world? Is it morally just to have the costs of new regulation imposed disproportionately on those who are already struggling in order to reap benefits for consumers in the wealthiest parts of the world? As the global exchange of goods continues to gather momentum, these sorts of questions will only continue to arise.

The final set of questions focuses on accountability. Who exactly are the publics to be served by any international import safety regime? Is it the public in exporting countries, the public in importing countries, or both? How are all of their voices to be heard or represented in the process of setting and enforcing international standards? Solving the market failures inherent in import safety will only give rise to worries about creating failures in democratic governance.

Framing the Discussion

To begin to answer these questions, this book is organized into four sections, followed by a concluding chapter. In the first section, the chapters provide broad perspectives on the origins, scale, and attributes of the import safety issue. Following this introductory chapter, Jacques deLisle puts China under the microscope. Using his extensive knowledge of that country to shed light on the origins of many recent unsafe imports, deLisle reveals the challenges China's trade partners face in trying to ensure a flow of safe products from that global economic powerhouse. Moving from a focus on the exporters to a focus on the importers, Jonathan Baron examines the import safety issue from the perspective of the consumers in one major importing country, the United States. As well-publicized lapses in import safety sensitize consumers to the possible dangers of products they buy, Baron's survey research on consumer attitudes reveals that Americans are not terribly parochial about unsafe products—they do not like them whether they are made abroad or in the United States. However, when unsafe imports emerge, the American public has a tendency to hold U.S. government officials responsible for the failures of private actors.

The second section of the book examines international trade and its governing institutions as possible venues for—or constraints on—the improvement of import safety. Tracey Epps and Michael Trebilcock emphasize the benefits of the current rules-based system of international trade and the constraints it places on developing innovative solutions to consumer protection. The next two chapters complement the Epps-Trebilcock analysis. Tim Büthe provides a detailed, analytic account of the development of the Codex Alimentarius Commission, suggesting that international standards emerging from a majority-vote process may not preserve the best features of the scientific, economic, and political inputs to those discussions. Kevin Outterson suggests the possibility that international intellectual-property standards concerning counterfeit drugs are motivated less by a concern for safety, as often stated, and more by regulatory capture—a general concern for any international regulatory governance regime, just as with domestic regulatory institutions. In the case Outterson considers, ensuring that intellectual property rules do not prevent affordable access to needed drugs in the developing world is itself, he argues, a matter of "importing safety."

The third section of the book develops ideas for smarter government use of data-collection, standard-setting, and enforcement resources to prevent untoward harms from imported products and to respond more effectively to incipient problems that escape preventive intervention. Richard Berk explores the concept of data-driven forecasting, which can lead agencies to deploy enforcement resources where they will most likely detect nascent problems. Lorna Zach and Vicki Bier argue for greater reliance on the modern methods of quantitative risk assessment to improve priority-setting in the selection of competing targets for regulatory intervention and to help firms control their own production processes and improve the safety of their products. Writing from the perspective of the European Union, Alberto Alemanno argues that, when properly designed, a reactive system of dissemination of information about product hazards can yield several advantages over a proactive approach, especially when the comparison is appropriately sober about the limited prospects for truly preventing most problems before they emerge into commerce.

Finally, the fourth section introduces three innovative proposals for harnessing market power and incentives to drive improved product safety. Kenneth Bamberger and Andrew Guzman propose augmenting liability rules to force the domestic firms that benefit from foreign production and low-cost imports to internalize the domestic costs of their activity. Tom Baker develops the concept of bonded safety warranties, wherein importers enter into contracts with insurance companies to compensate consumers if their products fail to meet established health and safety standards, and he then explores the incentives such a system would create to avoid breaches of these warranties. Errol Meidinger evaluates the prospects for the devolution of some regulatory responsibility for product safety onto manufacturers and third-party certification, scientific, and auditing bodies.

In the conclusion, David Zaring and Cary Coglianese suggest that the complex response to the challenges of safe imports can be thought of as the difficult but rewarding task of creating a regime of delegated governance. By this they mean a global system that, in the aggregate, pursues consumer protection by combining targeted public action with private inspections, public and private standard-setting, and a degree of dependence on consumers to take some responsibility for their own safety.

Together the chapters in this book tackle the problem of unsafe imports from several directions: analyzing its sources and causes, evaluating both government and private-sector actions needed to address it, and considering the constraints under which such solutions must be implemented. Given the complexity of global systems of production, shipment, and sale of consumer goods, domestic governments and private firms will continue to be called on to prevent, interdict, and respond to hazardous imports, whether they are contaminated foodstuffs, unsafe pharmaceuticals, or consumer products with hidden dangers. Ensuring safe imports in an era of globalization will undoubtedly strain traditional domestic regulatory entities. As such, the challenges of the global society require the kind of research analysis—and new ideas about regulation, information dissemination, and policy reform—that are represented in the pages of this book.

References

Abbott, Ken and Duncan Snidal (2006) Nesting, overlap and parallelism: Governance schemes for international production standards. Paper presented at the conference "Nested and Overlapping Regimes," Princeton University, Princeton, N.J., February 2006.

Aeppel, Timothy (2007) "Accident Raises Safety Concerns on Chinese Tires: Up to 450,000 Imports May Contain a Defect; Obstacles to a Recall." *Wall Street Journal*, June 26. sec. A.

Ansell, Christopher and David Vogel (2006) *What's the Beef? The Contested Governance of European Food Safety.* Cambridge, Mass.: MIT Press.

Bamberger, Kenneth T. and Andrew T. Guzman (2008) "Keeping Imports Safe: A Proposal for Discriminatory Regulation of International Trade." 96 *California Law Review* 1405–46.

Bennear, Lori (2007) "Are Management-Based Regulations Effective?" 26 *Journal of Policy Analysis and Management* 327–48.

Bogdanich, Walt and R. M. Koster (2008) "Panama Releases Report on '06 Poisoning." *New York Times*, February 14, sec. A.

Bogdanich, Walt and Renwick McLean (2007) "Poisoned Toothpaste in Panama Is Believed to Be from China." *New York Times*, May 19, sec. A.

Bradsher, Keith (2007) "Chinese Company Says It's Sorry for Making Poisonous Toy Beads." *New York Times*, November 30, sec. C.

Coglianese, Cary and David Lazer (2003) "Management-Based Regulation: Prescribing Private Management to Achieve Public Goals." 37 *Law and Society Review* 691–730.

Das, Soma (2008) "Further Import Ban on Ranbaxy Drugs Unlikely." *Financial Express*, September 26.

DeWaal, Caroline Smith and Gonzalo R. Guerrero Brito (2005) "Safe Food International: A Blueprint for Better Global Food Safety." 60 *Food and Drug Law Journal* 393–406.

Dooren, Jennifer and Jared Favole (2009) "FDA Says Ranbaxy Falsified Data." *Wall Street Journal*, February 26, sec. B.

Douglas, Mary and Aaron Wildavsky (1982) *Risk and Culture: An Essay on the Selection of Technical and Environmental Dangers*. Berkeley and Los Angeles: University of California Press.

Esty, Daniel C. (2006) "Good Governance at the Supranational Scale: Globalizing Administrative Law." 115 *Yale Law Journal* 1490–1562.

Fan, Maureen (2008) "FDA Sending Inspectors to Other Nations." *Washington Post*, November 19, sec. A.

Hanrahan, Charles E. (2001) "U.S. European Agricultural Trade: Food Safety and Biotechnology Issues." *Congressional Research Service Report for Congress*, http://www.law.umaryland.edu/marshall/crsreports/crsdocuments/98-861_01172001.pdf.

Harris, Gardiner (2008) "The Safety Gap." *New York Times Magazine*, November 2.

Hoffmann, Sandra A. (2007) "Mending Our Food Safety Net." 166 *Resources Magazine* 11–15.

Horton, Linda (1998) "Mutual Recognition Agreements and Harmonization." 19 *Seton Hall Law Review* 692–736.

Leavitt, Michael (2008) "Import Safety: Safety at the Speed of Life." U.S. Department of Health and Human Services, http://www.importsafety.gov/importsafety_prolgoue.pdf.

Lee, Don and Alana Semuels (2009) "Corrosive, Stinking Chinese Drywall May Be Radioactive." *Los Angeles Times*, July 4, p. B-1.

Meijer, Ernestine and Richard Stewart (2004) "The GM Cold War: How Developing Countries Can Go from Being Dominoes to Being Players." 13 *Review of European Community and International Environmental Law* 247–62.

Merrill, Richard (1998) "The Importance and Challenges of 'Mutual Recognition.'" 29 *Seton Hall Law Review* 736–55.

Moore, Michael J. and W. Kip Viscusi (2001) *Product Liability Entering the Twenty-First Century: The U.S. Perspective*. Washington, D.C.: AEI-Brookings Joint Center for Regulatory Studies.

Moss, Michael and Andrew Martin (2009) "Food Problems Elude Private Inspectors." *New York Times*, March 5.

Nedzel, Nadia E. (2008) "Antidumping and Cotton Subsidies: A Market-Based Defense of Unfair Trade Remedies." 28 *Northwestern Journal of International Law and Business* 215–72.

Neef, Dale (2004) *The Supply Chain Imperative*. New York: American Management Association.

Nestle, Marion (2008) *Pet Food Politics: The Chihuahua in the Coal Mine*. Berkeley and Los Angeles: University of California Press.

Nicolaïdis, Kalypso (1996) "Mutual Recognition of Regulatory Regimes: Some Lessons and Prospects." In *Regulatory Reform and International Market Openness*. Paris: Organization for Economic Co-operation and Development.

O'Reilly, James T. (2004) "Are We Cutting the GRAS? Food Safety Perceptions Are Diminished by Dysfunctional Bureaucratic Silos," 59 *Food and Drug Law Journal* 417–26.

Oster, Shai, Loretta Chao, Jason Leow, and Jane Zhang (2008) "FDA Warns of Products in U.S. Tied to Tainted Milk; As Recalls Spread, Dairy CEO Blames China for Secrecy." *Wall Street Journal*, September 27, sec. A.

Powell, Bill (2008) "Heparin's Deadly Side Effects." *Time*, November 24.

Schmit, Julie (2009) "Drywall from China Blamed for Problems in Homes." *USA Today*, March 16, p. 6A.

Shaffer, Gregory (2002) "Reconciling Trade and Regulatory Roles: The Prospects and Limits of New Approaches to Transatlantic Governance Through Mutual Recognition and Safe Harbor Agreements." 9 *Columbia Journal of European Law* 29–78.

Slaughter, Anne-Marie (2005) *A New World Order.* Princeton, N.J.: Princeton University Press.

Story, Louise (2007) "Putting Playthings to the Test." *New York Times*, August 22, sec. C.

Sullivan, Alithea (2007) "Reforming the Food Safety System: What If Consolidation Isn't Enough?" 120 *Harvard Law Review* 1345–66.

U.S. Consumer Product Safety Commission (CPSC) (2009) *CPSC Investigation of Imported Drywall: Status Report, July 2009,* http://www.cpsc.gov/info/drywallstatus07092009.pdf.

U.S. Department of Health and Human Services (HHS) (2007a) Interagency Working Group on Import Safety. *Protecting American Consumers Every Step of the Way: A Strategic Framework for Continual Improvement in Import Safety.* Washington, D.C.: HHS.

———. (2007b) *Action Plan for Import Safety: A Roadmap for Continual Improvement.* Washington, D.C.: HHS.

U.S. Government Accountability Office (GAO) (2008a) *Federal Oversight of Food Safety: FDA's Food Protection Plan Proposes Positive First Steps, But Capacity to Carry Them Out Is Critical.* Washington, D.C.: GAO.

———. (2008b) *Food Safety: Selected Countries' Systems Can Offer Insights into Ensuring Import Safety and Responding to Foodborne Illness.* Washington, D.C.: GAO.

———. (2007) *Federal Oversight of Food Safety: High-Risk Designation Can Bring Attention to Limitations in the Government's Food Recall Programs.* Washington, D.C.: GAO.

———. (1998) *Food and Drug Administration: Improvements Needed in the Foreign Drug Inspection Program.* Washington, D.C.: GAO.

Vogel, David (2007) "The Hare and the Tortoise Revisited: The New Politics of Consumer and Environmental Regulation in Europe." In *Regulation and Regulatory Processes*, edited by Cary Coglianese and Robert Kagan. Burlington, Vt.: Ashgate.

World Health Organization (WHO) (2003) *Food and Nutrition Action Plans in the WHO European Region: Past, Present, and Future,* http://www.euro.who.int/Document/E79888.pdf.

Xin, Hao and Richard Stone (2008) "Tainted Milk Scandal: Chinese Probe Unmasks High-Tech Adulteration with Melamine." *Science*, November 28, 1310–11.

Zhang, Jane (2009) "U.S. Launches Criminal Case in Mass Recall." *Wall Street Journal*, January 31, sec. A.

Cases Cited

A.L.A. Schechter Poultry Corp. v. United States, 295 U.S. 495 (1935).

Panama Refining Co. v. Ryan, 293 U.S. 38 (1935).

World Trade Organization (WTO) (2000–2001) "Measures Affecting Asbestos and Asbestos-Containing Products." WT/DS135/R, September 18, 2000. WT/DS135/AB/R, March 12, 2001.

————. (1998) "Measures Concerning Meat and Meat Products (Hormones)." Appellate Body Report, WT/DS26/AB/R, WT/DS48/AB/R, January 16, 1998.

Agreement Cited

World Trade Organization (WTO). Agreement on the Application of Sanitary and Phytosanitary Measures (SPS). April 15, 1994, Marrakesh Agreement Establishing the World Trade Organization, Annex 1A, at Annex A, ¶ 1.

Chapter 2
The Other China Trade Deficit
Export Safety Problems and Responses

Jacques deLisle

China has an export safety problem. And given China's large and growing shares in international markets during a long era of reliably rising
trade in consumer goods and food products, the world has a Chinese
import safety problem or, more accurately, problems. The magnitude
and complexity of these problems mean that legal and policy responses
in China and abroad face daunting challenges and dim prospects. The
most promising approaches are likely those that exploit and promote
alignment among China's economic and political interests, foreign
firms' concerns about liability and reputation, and improved export
safety. Strategies with relatively good prospects also are likely those that
employ methods that have worked in other contexts.

The list of recent Chinese export safety incidents is lengthy and varied. U.S. toymakers recalled over 30 million Chinese-made units in
2007 for problems ranging from small parts to lead paint (Quittner
2007; Teagarden 2009). Nearly a quarter million Chinese-made tires
were recalled in the United States under a National Highway Traffic
Safety Administration (NHTSA) order in 2007 (AP 2007b). Diethylene glycol-tainted cold medicine traced to China disabled and killed
hundreds in Central America in 2006. The same contaminant in Chinese-made toothpaste triggered recalls and bans around the world.
Adulterated or fake ingredients in Chinese-manufactured heparin, a
blood thinner, led to dozens of deaths and injuries in 2008 (Bogdanich
2008; Harris 2008; Schweitzer 2008). Chinese fake versions of an American manufacturer's diabetes kits were found in export markets (Tang
and Zhang 2007). Pesticide-contaminated frozen dumplings sickened
ten or more in Japan in 2008 (Bloomberg News 2008). Poison pet food,
involving over 100 brands, killed hundreds of animals in the United
States in 2007. Products as varied as baby food, candy, and coffee containing milk and milk powder tainted with melamine, a chemical com-

pound often used as a fire retardant, brought unprecedented global alarms and recalls (Yardley 2008). Earlier in the decade, the European Union (EU) banned Chinese meat imports for excessive levels of veterinary medicines and Japan blocked spinach for high pesticide levels (Becker 2008; Thompson and Hu 2007).

Such singular or episodic scandals are part of a chronic pattern. The U.S. Consumer Product Safety Commission (CPSC) recalled more than 45 million units of Chinese products during 2007 (CPSC 2007; Kaplan 2007). Recently, around half of CPSC recalls have been for Chinese products (Mantell 2007; Stratfor 2007). Among Chinese foods, carcinogen-bearing or antibiotic-dosed seafood has brought numerous warnings, recalls, and import bans in the United States and East Asia, and occasionally People's Republic of China (PRC) export bans. Pork from ill pigs and dangerous seafood has faced recurrent exclusion in Hong Kong (Ahrens 2007; Lee 2005; Martin 2007; Thompson and Hu 2007). Much of the world's pharmaceutical supply that is counterfeit comes from China. International pharmaceutical companies receive reports of implausibly numerous adverse effects from a single lot, attributable to pirates having sold many fakes in packaging reproduced from one legitimate unit (Harris 2008; Hu and Gomez 2005; Looewy 2007; Wyld 2006).

China's export scandals are part of a larger domestic product quality problem. While counterfeit drugs are a significant export safety problem, their market share (perhaps 30 to 50 percent) and harmful impact are far greater inside China (Looewy 2007; Reeves 2003). The melamine milk scandal that began with the Sanlu Company and spread through the Chinese dairy industry is the most notorious example. Although it caused concern abroad, its biggest impact was in China, where tainted products killed at least four people, hospitalized 13,000, and injured perhaps 50,000. But the Sanlu-centered crisis was hardly unique. Indeed, it was only the most famous among relatively recent safety scandals in the milk products sector. Several years earlier, nutrient-deficient baby formula from domestic producers caused a dozen deaths and hundreds of injuries from malnutrition. Another baby formula, locally produced by the multinational Nestlé Company, was recalled because of high iodine levels (AFX News 2005; Wang 2004). The poisoned milk scandal was not the only melamine incident. In 2007, Chinese wheat gluten and pet food producers added melamine to boost apparent protein content and, in turn, price.

Export Safety Problems: Vast, Diverse, and Difficult

The problem of dangerous Chinese exports is so significant and intractable partly because Chinese exports are so large and quality issues are so multifaceted. China is currently the world's second leading exporter in terms of dollar value, and it will soon become the world's leading exporter. The PRC is already the largest source of manufactured imports to the United States, primarily in the form of consumer goods and components for such products (Morrison 2008; USCBC 2009). Although China's comparative advantage has been shifting, low-cost manufacturing of consumer goods for export remains a mainstay of the economy—a pattern underscored by the often-quoted anecdote that if Walmart were a country, it would be among China's top importing partners. China exports a considerable amount of food and edible ingredients, surpassing $50 billion per year. Hong Kong imports 80 percent of its food from the mainland.

China's shift toward more sophisticated exports may begin to ameliorate some familiar export safety problems. But it also introduces new ones, most notably through China's emergence as a supplier of drugs and pharmaceutical ingredients. According to one industry estimate, 70 percent of medical device and pharmaceutical companies doing business in the United States have manufacturing facilities or production agreements with manufacturers in China. Assessments remain bullish on China as a destination for investment in drug production (Harris 2008; Rhea 2007a).

Where exports flow in such quantities and make up so great a share of world totals, the danger is inevitably large. The numbers here are so big that even a small percentage of unsafe products is a significant source of potential harm. There are ample signs that the rate of substandard products is not low, perhaps reaching 15 percent or more of food products, and similar or higher rates are estimated for drugs and some manufactured goods (Becker 2008; Buckley 2007; Reeves 2003; Teagarden 2009). Sometimes Chinese export safety problems follow simply from such a high defect rate (and poor producer or state quality control or inspection). The widely acknowledged pattern in manufactured goods is a staple of foreign investors' and traders' complaints and Chinese business lore. The head of China's huge consumer appliance and electronics company Haier legendarily began his rise with an epiphany about product quality: when a customer returned a defective refrigerator, the quest for an unflawed replacement yielded many bad units, prompting the future chief to lead employees in public demolition of defective goods to symbolize a dedication to quality. More prosaically, production defect-related safety concerns have been the principal impediment to the United States and other developed countries permitting imports of Chinese cars.

The diverse nature and resulting complexity of the sources of danger make China's unsafe export problems more challenging. As the Haier example suggests, PRC-based producers of potentially harmful exports increasingly extend to the final, or near-final, and most visible-to-the-consumer link in production and sales chains. Haier nearly purchased Maytag, and Lenovo bought IBM's PC division, partly to acquire distribution channels and brand recognition abroad that could promote the Chinese acquirers' exports. Chinese automakers aspire to export self-branded products.

More often, dangerous exports from China are bought by a foreign purchaser that sells the imports under its own brands. Often, the buyer has a relatively arm's length contractual relationship with a Chinese supplier. Some cases of lead in exported toys and jewelry seem to have resulted from a choice by Chinese manufacturers—generally ones with no well-known brand or reputational interests of their own—to use unsafe inputs to cut costs or make products appear more substantial and appealing to consumers, apparently without disclosing the presence of lead to the foreign purchaser (Fairclough 2007). So, too, economically stretched, unscrupulous, or ignorant farmers, who sell to Chinese or joint-venture producers under contract or on spot markets, reportedly often resort to dangerous overuse of pesticides, fertilizers, antibiotics, and hormones to improve yields (Thompson and Hu 2007).

In other cases, foreign and Chinese parties' connections are closer. In one unusual case, Chinese contract manufacturers followed the U.S. customer's specifications, which included use of small and detachable toy parts that posed a choking risk (Story 2007). In a more common pattern, problematic exports are produced by an enterprise that is a joint venture between a foreign firm and a Chinese partner, with the latter taking the lead role in production in China (as occurred with the Sanlu dairy company, a China-New Zealand joint venture at the center of the melamine milk scandal). In many of the most serious export safety incidents, the origin of the danger lies farther from the importer or other foreign party's control or knowledge, up a supply chain or with small suppliers. While large Chinese dairy companies failed to discover (and in Sanlu's case sought to cover up) melamine contamination, the toxic ingredient generally was added by suppliers—some very small farm-level producers—who sought to fool tests that measured whether the milk met protein standards. (Protein tests often were based on a product's nitrogen content, and melamine has a high level of nitrogen.) So too, some of the lead-tainted toys appear to have come from a reputable and long-standing Chinese manufacturer for a U.S. company that was misled by its paint supplier (Barboza 2007e).

Other things being equal, such differences in legal and business relationships between Chinese and foreign parties can produce significant variation in the incentives and opportunities for foreign parties to monitor and affect practices in China. The differences in motivations and character of Chinese producers have similarly complex implications for how best to address Chinese export safety problems.

Although Chinese producers increasingly must compete on bases other than cost, and although Chinese policy seeks to accelerate movement into higher value-added industries, fierce price competition and narrow margins still characterize sectors that produce China's consumable exports. Efforts to keep down costs create pressures that lead some producers to cut corners in ways that yield dangerous goods. Sometimes this means substituting cheap and dangerous inputs for safe but more expensive ones. And sometimes this means cutting corners on inspection, quality control, or production management. While cost pressures and ignorance among initially legitimate but economically squeezed producers account for some of the dangers, deceit also accounts for an untold but large portion of the problem. Some argue that pervasive willingness to disregard legal requirements and to commit life-endangering fraud is a congenital defect in China's market-oriented reforms. In this view, the reforms began against the backdrop of disillusionment with communist ideology, a resulting moral vacuum, a new ethos of unbridled pursuit of wealth, and a recent history of market-conforming innovations that were initially illegal and later ratified in law and policy (Chi 1991; MacLeod 2009; Stratfor 2007; Yang 2008). It also may reflect the impact of many years of sudden and substantial changes in laws and policies affecting business, which can be conducive to unusually short time horizons and to steep discount rates for future costs and benefits.

Such problems may be especially prevalent where the fraud occurs outside the realm of producing, or supplying producers of, legitimate goods. Piracy of intellectual property goods is a major element in China's dangerous export problem. The most striking examples are pharmaceuticals, including completely ineffective, diluted, or contaminated drugs that are visually, but not chemically, high-quality imitations. The problem extends to other products, including counterfeit manufactured goods—and parts for them—such as computers, media devices, and other consumer electronics. By some estimates, 10 percent of electronic equipment sold globally and 30 percent of components produced in some parts of China are fakes—rates that rival those reported for drugs (Fraser 2006: 46; Quirk 2007; Spiegel 2009).

More broadly, long production chains and reliance on numerous small suppliers multiply points at which problem ingredients can be added and the actors who might introduce them. It is widely and plausibly accepted that China's consumer product export industries have, by world standards, comparatively high levels of these phenomena. China has many tens of thousands of enterprises in the export-producing manufacturing chain, many of them small, new, or newly privatized.

Many of the problems with dangerous pharmaceutical exports appear to come from chemical companies that sell relatively primary ingredients and are therefore not formally subject to regulation as drug manufacturers, and from producers located in early, remote links of long supply chains (Bogdanich 2007). China has many thousands of suppliers to its more than five thousand drug makers. The melamine milk problem appears to have started mostly at the dairy farm level. According to Chinese government reports, China has approximately 500,000 food producers, and 80 percent of them employ fewer than ten workers (Li 2009; Roberts and Tschang 2007). Many are household-level units, born of 1980s decollectivization and relatively new to commerce. Quality and safety problems are exacerbated by another common practice among Chinese manufacturers: taking on more work than a company can handle and subcontracting to less-established firms and more poorly monitored producers. Because the sources of China's dangerous export problems are so numerous and diverse, they have elicited—and surely require—a variety of legal and regulatory responses that have had mixed and generally modest records of success.

Regulatory Responses: Contents, Discontents, and Prospects

Several features of Chinese laws and institutions relevant to export safety—many characteristic of the PRC's legal and governmental system more generally—impede effective responses to unsafe consumer products. As export safety problems and their ramifications have become clearer, however, Chinese authorities have moved to address such problems, often employing—albeit with questionable zeal and promise of success—methods adapted from the regime's existing repertoire.

Laws and Regulations

Chinese laws and regulations that address product quality are variously sparse, fragmented, incomplete, and new. The most fundamental law governing tort liability—and for many years the only significant statute governing product liability—consists of a handful of articles in the 1986 General Principles of Civil Law, crafted as a prospective general part of a still-not-adopted civil code. The General Principles make "producers" liable for harms caused by "substandard" products under a rule that most Chinese interpreters regard as one of strict liability or, at least, tougher than ordinary negligence liability.

Chinese lawmakers have fleshed out product liability laws somewhat, adopting a Product Quality Law (PQL) in 1993, revised in 2000, and a Consumer Rights and Interests Protection Law (CRIPL) in 1993. The PQL holds producers and sellers liable for harms caused by products that are "defective" in the sense of being unreasonably dangerous to persons or property, or not conforming to state or industry safety-related standards, express warranties, labels, samples, or implied warranties (such as fitness for use). It also imposes testing, inspection, and labeling requirements. The CRIPL adopts broadly similar standards for consumer goods and holds "business operators" liable to purchasers harmed by their products (CRIPL 1993: arts. 11–18, 35, 41, 49; PQL 2000: arts. 40–48).

In response to recent food-quality scandals, the National People's Congress Standing Committee passed a long-pending Food Safety Law in March 2009 (Quek 2009). Building on the Food Hygiene Law from the 1990s and the Agricultural Product Quality and Safety Law from 2006 and supplemented by existing regulations, it sets forth a framework for: prohibiting some known dangers; establishing standards and procedures for approving food additives; setting quality standards; labeling and recalling food; licensing, monitoring, and inspecting products and producers; undertaking systemic risk evaluations; regulating imports and exports; and addressing food safety "emergencies" (Food Safety Law 2009; Ramzy 2009; Xinhua 2009). Other relatively basic laws also bear on export safety, including much legislation that was brought more into line with international standards in conjunction with China's accession to the World Trade Organization (WTO) in 2001. These include laws governing standard-setting and related state inspection, supervision, and certification powers; the Import and Export Commodity Inspection Law; and provisions of the criminal law that prohibit some forms of knowing production and sale of substandard products and food (Weeks and Chen 2003).

Still, this legal framework remains troublingly incomplete. A general tort law, including a chapter on product liability, remains in the drafting stage. The 2009 Food Safety Law immediately faced criticism and skepticism over its vagueness, extremely sparse treatment of export issues, and dependence on uncertain implementing rules and even more uncertain efforts to enforce them (Dickinson 2009; Li 2009; Quek 2009). Like the law, the State Council's implementing regulations were sparse (indeed, shorter than the statute) and largely assigned regulatory responsibilities to lower-ranking central agencies and local authorities (Food Safety Implementing Regulations 2009). A food and drug safety guarantee system promised by the State Council was not slated to include a new inspection system until 2010, and new dairy industry standards would not come on line until 2011 (Barboza 2007a; Jacobs 2008). Many rules adopted in response to the events of 2007–2008 inevitably remain largely untested. The state and industry standards referenced in the existing framework product and food statutes have been developing in recent years, but from a low baseline.

Whereas efforts to combat export safety problems in China thus suffer from too little law, they also suffer from too much law or, more accurately, from laws that are badly fragmented and uncoordinated. Food safety alone is the object of nearly a dozen laws, scores of State Council regulations, and myriad departmental rules and local regulations (Thompson and Hu 2007: 9). Some legal standards have unclear relationships to one another. Many are issued by organs that do not stand in clear hierarchical or coordinate relations. Some lower-level rules are not explicitly rooted in (nor do they purport to implement) the seemingly most relevant legislation or regulations. Some are grounded in amended or superseded higher-level sources of authority, leaving their meaning and sometimes their validity uncertain.

The surging concern over product, food, and export safety in the mid-2000s generated a flood of new or promised rules and procedures. These included new systems for tracking and inspecting consumer food products, certifying and recalling toys, banning lead paint in exported toys and diethylene glycol in toothpaste, and restricting the use of veterinary drugs for food fish (AP 2007a, c; Barboza 2007f, i; Lipton 2007; Xie 2007). A blizzard of quality standards for products was promised, including 10,000 new standards, nearly 10,000 revised ones, and a rise from 60 to 75 percent in the portion that track international standards (Zhu 2008).

The torrent of rules issued by Chinese authorities in response to the 2007–2008 crises, at least in the near term, contributed to legal confusion and, in turn, risks that relevant audiences at home and abroad will regard such rules as ineffective or irrelevant. Chinese authorities recognize this problem, pairing the numerous reactive legal changes with a new round of high-level framework laws (including the Food Safety Law and potentially a Tort Law), comprehensive central-level policy reports (including the 2007 White Paper on food safety and a promised one on product quality), and high-profile commitments to improved policing of quality (including statements from Prime Minister Wen Jiabao).

Adequate and clear legal standards, even when achieved, are of course not sufficient to address export safety problems. In China, the

means for enforcement and implementation remain a large and difficult part of the battle.

Civil Remedies and Public Sanctions

Some of the most high-profile and formally highest-level law in China
addressing export safety focuses on civil remedies for injured parties.
This is somewhat ironic in the Chinese context, where features that have
made product liability litigation potent in the United States are weaker.
Tort litigation generally remains in its relative infancy. Suits remain relatively few in number; those involving dangerous products are far fewer,
and product liability issues involving foreign parties fewer still.

Plaintiffs, especially foreign ones injured by exports, have comparatively weak incentives and limited opportunity to sue in China. Legal
uncertainty and ambiguity are problems, given thin, dispersed, and
complex regulatory provisions and the absence of a basic tort statute.
China has a self-consciously civil law system that does not give prior
decisions full precedential weight and that discourages the innovation
from the bench that marked the expansion of American product liability law. Chinese laws, and courts' applications of these laws, have not
aggressively reached beyond the nation's borders to cover harms occurring overseas.

Chinese damage awards are small, at least by U.S. standards. The
CRIPL is unusual among Chinese private law statutes in permitting
quasi-punitive, double damages where the defendant has committed
fraud. Chinese plaintiffs in the melamine milk cases—where high levels of publicity and outrage would have been conducive to high awards
in many systems—sought modest compensation, certainly by U.S. measures (from a few thousand dollars for physical and emotional harms to
well under $100,000 for deaths). Judgments have been difficult to col-
lect from defendants who go bankrupt (as happened with Sanlu), hide
assets, or benefit from the protection of local authorities. Central Chinese authorities have been wary of allowing class actions and expansion
of class-action-like "collective litigation." As the melamine milk scandal
illustrates, the regime's preferred response to large product safety problems, at least domestically, is state-brokered compensation, not mass
private lawsuits (Barboza 2008e; Dickinson 2009; Ford 2008; Reuters
2009; Wong 2008).

Foreign parties and potential plaintiffs worry or complain more
about court incompetence, corruption, or bias favoring the large, sometimes state-linked enterprises that produce some of China's dangerous
exports. Tellingly, the pattern in product liability suits that could be

brought in either country is for plaintiffs to file in the United States and for defendants to seek *forum non conveniens* dismissal to China.

Intellectual property law, which can address product dangers arising from violations of patent and trademark rights (especially those held by foreign firms), has had similar limitations. Here too, damage awards are small by U.S. standards, often hard to collect, and dependent on, or in practice structured as alternatives to, administrative enforcement. Injunctive relief varies in effectiveness and is vulnerable to many of the same factors that undermine administrative enforcement. Some critics assert that China's system for protecting export safety-relevant foreign intellectual property is so flawed that it fails to meet WTO/TRIPS (Trade-Related Aspects of Intellectual Property Rights) obligations (Bronshtein 2008).

Still, the trajectory has become positive. New laws and rules portend, or at least promise, more robust rights and remedies. Some of the newest laws provide higher damage awards and expanded liability, including the Food Safety Law's mandate for awards of up to ten times the value of goods (in addition to compensation for harm caused) and imposition of joint and several liability on a wider range of non-producer, nonseller actors, including typically deep-pocket celebrities who do advertisements for substandard food products (Food Safety Law 2009; Li 2009; Xinhua 2009).

Anecdotal evidence suggests a broader, growing emphasis on tort and contract remedies for food- and product-caused harms. Despite considerable resistance and delay, some melamine milk suits have been allowed to go forward, presumably reflecting perceived severity of the problem and public alarm that carries over to other product safety issues and that can undermine the opacity conducive to unlawful government and judicial practices, especially at local levels (Luo 2008; Wines 2009). Some of the official aversion to collective suits may be waning, a development seemingly pushed forward by recognition that prospects of occasional success in group litigation can help address, or at least manage, disaffected constituencies ranging from expropriated farmers to exploited minority shareholders to injured consumers (Wang 2008; Wong 2009).

Although civil remedies show signs of development, Chinese laws governing harmful products—like Chinese laws more generally—rely extensively on administrative measures and criminal sanctions (CRIPL 1993: art. 26 et seq.; PQL 2000: art. 49 et seq.). The PQL, CRIPL, and many more obviously "public" or "regulatory" laws charge relevant administrative authorities and prosecutors with responsibility for implementing product quality supervision, certification, and inspection programs, and otherwise protecting the rights of victims of harmful products. Apparently recognizing the daunting scope of enforcement tasks and the sources of many quality problems, the regime undertook a promising policy initiative—most clearly in the Food Safety Law—to encourage larger-scale enterprises and to require producers and exporters to meet minimum-size criteria. Administrative enforcement includes orders to cease offending practices and confiscation of products and profits. Relevant laws also provide for fines for substantive violations, interference with regulators, and noncompliance with oversight obligations. These have been modest, typically a small multiple of the value of nonconforming goods or fixed fines of no more than several thousand dollars. But recent laws, including the Food Safety Law and the proposed Recall Law, have sought to increase fines substantially, sometimes several fold. Even modest levies, if fully enforced, can be substantial relative to the scale and profit margins of some violators.

Laws governing recalls have become an area of focus and development. A draft of a national Defective Product Recall Law is under consideration by the National People's Congress. The Food Safety Law adopted enhanced provisions for food product recalls. Earlier administrative regulations—many responding to export and product safety concerns of the mid-2000s—targeted key sectors, including food, toys, drugs, and auto parts. These laws generally establish obligations for voluntary or state-mandated recall of products defined as defective.

More significantly, violating firms risk losing export privileges or their business licenses. Company officers, and government officials charged with overseeing companies, can face heavy sanctions, including severe criminal punishments (Food Safety Law 2009; PQL 2000: arts. 49–64). Beyond the ordinarily capacious sanctioning powers of state officials, extraordinary state powers are arguably authorized by the Emergency Response Law, and the Food Safety Law, to address threats to public health from unsafe food (and potentially other product quality threats) (deLisle 2009; Weeks and Chen 2003).

As product and, in turn, export safety issues have reached near-crisis levels, Chinese authorities have turned to more aggressive, high-profile enforcement measures, relying on the deterrent effect such sanctions offer when employed against prominent targets or with great fanfare. Authorities stepped up inspections and testing at export-oriented toy factories, rescinded the export rights of producers of lead paint-bearing toys and tainted pet food, and imposed new export certificate requirements on categories of toys that included the lead-laced ones (Tschang 2007). Officials claimed one third of nearly 2,000 toy factories inspected in the Guangdong heartland of Chinese toy manufacturing in 2007 lost licenses required for export and another nearly one third were ordered to take remedial measures (Barboza 2007h). Regulators also reportedly increased inspections and imposed new requirements on milk producers after the Sanlu episode. Authorities reportedly seized tons of counterfeit versions of U.S.-based multinationals' pharmaceuticals, stripped more than 150 drug manufacturers of certificates of good manufacturing practices, shut down more than 300 drug firms in 2007, and ordered increased oversight of heparin production in 2008 (Barboza 2007b, d; 2008a). Such moves followed an earlier crackdown on unlicensed pharmaceutical manufacturers, more than 400 of which were reported closed by authorities in 2005. One government agency claimed to have closed over 100,000 unlicensed food manufacturers and sellers dealing in counterfeit or substandard products in 2006 (Becker 2008). Officials also claimed to have seized tons of tainted food products and food-tainting chemicals amid stepped-up enforcement efforts in 2008 (Barboza 2008c). Company officials have faced severe sanctions. Officers of Sanlu and their suppliers, for example, received lengthy prison terms or were executed (Barboza 2008d). Authorities claimed to have filed several hundred to more than one thousand criminal cases involving substandard food, drugs, and other products during a 2007 campaign (Barboza 2007g). The head of the firm that produced Mattel's lead-tainted toys committed suicide, surely fearing in part the legal consequences he faced (*Economist* 2007).

So, too, quality control and inspection officials who perform their duties badly or take bribes face potentially severe consequences. Most famously, the former head of the State Food and Drug Administration (SFDA), Zheng Xiaoyou, was executed for taking $800,000 in bribes to approve drug production licenses improperly, based partly on false safety data. The chief of the division of the Administration of Quality Supervision, Inspection, and Quarantine (AQSIQ) responsible for food safety, Wu Jianping, killed himself while under investigation for corruption and amid the melamine-tainted milk scandal. Observers saw both cases as also reflecting general concerns about their institutions' poor performance in ensuring consumer safety (Barboza 2008b; Kahn 2007). Several officials were ousted and others disciplined for their roles in the melamine incident.

Although such measures are dramatic, they fall far short of showing that China has put, or is putting, in place an effective system for addressing export or broader product safety problems. Official claims of crackdowns, and their enduring efficacy, have faced skeptical reviews. To the extent that enhanced enforcement revealed tens of thousands of food safety violations and well over one hundred thousand cases of illegal medicine and medical equipment production, it suggests the great magnitude of underlying problems that lead to unsafe exports (Barboza 2007b, c).

Administrative Weakness and Fragmentation and Regime Responses

Several persistent and often-problematic features of the Chinese state apparatus extend to regulation of export safety (and product safety more broadly). And they have presented obstacles to—or problematic foundations for—effective responses (Huang 2008; Yang 2008; see also Lieberthal 2004: ch. 6; Lieberthal and Lampton 1992; Mertha 2005). As the foregoing suggests, responses continue to rely heavily on top-down administrative and policing measures that strain the state's limited capacity. The state organs that have been primarily and immediately responsible for handling food and product safety—especially SFDA and AQSIQ—have had comparatively modest resources to tackle large, complex, and growing safety issues. In terms of formal bureaucratic stature, SFDA, AQSIQ, and other export and product-quality control organs rank relatively low and share powers within their core domains with other actors, such as the Ministry of Agriculture and state standard-setting and certification organs. In China's informal bureaucratic politics as well, they have had significantly less clout than numerous other ministries and commissions whose agendas—including short-term economic growth, tax revenue extraction, and so on—put them frequently at odds with product and export safety goals.

Much of the responsibility and necessary authority for regulating export quality lies scattered across numerous government bodies, some much more formidable than SFDA or AQSIQ. More than a dozen departments are responsible for food safety alone (Li 2009; MacLeod 2009). The gigantic Ministry of Commerce, for example, regulates a vast swath of the Chinese economy, including enterprises that manufacture goods for export. It also regulates, and seeks to attract, foreign investors in joint ventures or wholly foreign-owned firms that produce for export. The State Administration for Industry and Commerce (SAIC) also has a portfolio that includes registration and oversight functions for most enterprises (and thus a role in monitoring and punishing a wide range of enterprise misbehavior). The SAIC includes a trademark division that is the principal administrative enforcer of trademark rights in China, a function that includes policing the types of violations that lead to dangerous exports, particularly counterfeit goods. The State Intellectual Property Office has a major, but incomplete, role in addressing patent registration and infringement, which also have been implicated in some export safety problems. Ensuring export safety and product quality have not historically topped the long and complicated agendas of these bureaucracies and sometimes have been in tension with higher priorities or more central missions.

Similarly, the Health Ministry has a significant role in the food safety regime, but it too has not been among China's more formidable bureaucratic actors. Much of its energy has been focused elsewhere as China has sought to rebuild public health systems, extend care to the underserved, and handle possible pandemics such as SARS and the avian and swine flus. The Ministry of Agriculture has partial responsibility for food product safety, but it is another notoriously weak department and has daunting responsibilities for dealing with economic crises facing China's 900 million peasants. The Customs Ministry has some responsibility for policing dangerous exports, primarily counterfeit or unauthorized goods. It is, however, another fairly small and marginal department, and much of its attention focuses on imports into China. Although bureaucratic rivalry and interagency noncooperation are a universal problem, the problem—called "departmentalism" in Chinese political parlance—has been particularly intense and dysfunctional in China, where the state apparatus is vast, the functional units within the bureaucracy have endured for decades (despite several reshufflings into different ministries and commissions), and all but the highest officials serve entire careers in, and fiercely identify with, their "unit."

Criminal actions contributing to unsafe exports are a tiny and traditionally low priority part of the workload for public security officials and procurators. While this pattern is hardly unique to China, Chinese police and prosecutors arguably face especially strong pressures to focus elsewhere, including a generally rising crime rate, tens of thousands of "incidents" of mass unrest annually, and imperatives to suppress political dissent, unauthorized civil organizations, and so on.

A sprawling, multilayered bureaucracy in a huge, poor country inevitably brings implementation challenges, all the more so given China's relatively thin—and, amid opportunities for entering commerce or extracting rents, thinning—supply of competence and honesty at local levels. Monitoring costs are inevitably high. They are higher still because of central authorities' proclivity for uniform, centralized policy responses—a pattern rooted in Leninist habits and reflecting more recent frustrations with recalcitrant local officials. Such factors underpin distinctive and problematic phenomena: "local protectionism" and de facto local autonomy. These pose formidable obstacles to effective regulatory responses to product and export safety challenges. Provincial and local arms of functionally defined central organs responsible for export safety and related matters do not answer only to their bureaucratic superiors in Beijing. They also are integral parts of provincial and lower-level governments. Considerable tension is inherent in this long-standing PRC system of "dual rule"; however, the tilt toward local interests has been ascendant for much of the time since the radical decentralization of political authority (particularly over economic issues) that launched the reform era in the early 1980s.

Local political authorities are widely acknowledged to emphasize near-term growth and the immediate health of local businesses more than is consistent with central authorities' interests and agendas. Provincial and lower-level cadres are evaluated—and their careers affected —largely based on the near-term economic performance of their localities. This encourages systematic slighting of other regime goals, even where doing so can exact significant economic costs in the long run. Environmental protection policies and intellectual property rights are two much-noted examples, but the same logic and practice extends to product safety, especially where dangerous products are not primarily consumed locally.

While unsafe products from one locality can injure China's reputation and export markets, the locality often will bear only a small part of that cost. But the locality likely would bear much more of the cost if it zealously enforced product safety-related standards locally, shutting down local enterprises that generate employment and revenue (in the form of taxes, profit distributions, or fines for product quality and other violations), or driving up such enterprises' costs (and damaging their competitiveness), or incurring the direct costs of tougher inspections that can strain cash-strapped local governments. Moreover, through personal connections, corruption, and other avenues, enterprises sometimes can induce local authorities to condone or acquiesce in violations of legal restrictions affecting product quality and export safety. Such problems are generally more pronounced in rural areas than in cities; in the rural areas, the quality of government and respect for law are generally lower, local economic dependence on a handful of enterprises higher, and resources and personnel for enforcing central directives fewer (deLisle 2007; Lubman 2002: 263–80; Peerenboom 2002: 280–342, 394–430).

Facing these institutional and structural problems and rising concerns about export and product safety, the regime has resorted to venerable PRC methods of reform and crisis management. First, it has committed greater resources to product and export safety. In 2007, China announced that it would increase spending on food and industrial product monitoring and inspection by $1.2 to $1.6 billion (U.S.), with some of the resources going to drug and medical device testing and to extending the much-publicized, beefed-up oversight and shutdowns of substandard factories (D'Amico 2007). Foreign technical assistance and collaboration, including with the United States, have been pursued to strengthen the SFDA and AQSIQ.

Second, reforms have sought to enhance the stature of relevant bureaucratic actors. The SFDA was a relatively recent creation, a product of the 2003 promotion of the former State Pharmaceutical Administration to the status of an entity directly under the State Council and the expansion of its mandate to include food safety. More recently, the SFDA was folded into an augmented Health Ministry, for which public safety has become an increasingly important concern in the wake of the SARS and melamine milk crises. Official Chinese sources described the restructuring as an effort to consolidate responsibility over product safety and other public health matters and to strengthen product safety work (Xinhua 2008). More recently still, the Food Safety Law mandated a central-level Food Safety Commission, charging it with overseeing the much-criticized food inspection system, assigning a central coordinating role to the Ministry of Health and allocating expanded mandates to develop and enforce higher safety standards.

Third, the Food Safety Law and other major laws and policy documents perform important "signaling functions." Whatever their shortcomings in content and implementation, they tell lower-level bureaucrats, perpetrators, and society that the leadership has made the issues a higher political priority. This was all the clearer with the Food Safety Law's provisions specifically addressing a list of problems at the center of the scandals that preceded its adoption.

Fourth, the leadership launched an intense drive against scandalous product-quality problems, and, fifth, it established a top-level task force to lead the state's product safety work. These are time-honored PRC tactics for managing crises—coordinating across fragmented functional bureaucracies and local governments and steering the far-flung and fractious reaches of China's party-state. The increased inspections, the self-congratulatory reports of large-scale exposure and correction of wrongdoing, the imposition of harsh sanctions against the worst apostates, and the rhetorical insistence on the supreme importance of the work that marked the product and food safety drives of 2007 and 2008 evoked the hallmarks of a Chinese Communist Party-led "campaign."

The elite task force to deal with the product safety crisis was headed, tellingly, by the formidable Wu Yi, who had played similar roles in responding to the SARS crisis, leading crucial and difficult phases of negotiating China's entry into the WTO, and addressing mounting foreign complaints about counterfeit products (Roberts and Tschang 2007; Tang and Zhang 2007). Wu pledged that the regime would "strengthen the system of supervision and control over product quality, especially relating to exports" and that China would meet "its responsibilities and obligations" concerning "product quality and food safety." This would be pursued across several product sectors and through twenty specific goals. According to Wu, this required improved "accountability" by imposing responsibility on "each department" and every level, down to the most local governments and individual enterprises (Stratfor 2007; Wu 2007).

Finally, as Wu's comments reflect, leaders at the highest level pledged progress on product and export safety. President Hu Jintao and Prime Minister Wen both declared food safety a top priority in mid-2007. Wen reiterated the point and asserted a stronger commitment to meeting international standards amid the melamine milk scandal the following year.

To be sure, these moves do not guarantee success. Rhetoric touting greater commitment, coordination, and efficacy does not always bring promised change, especially where foreign audiences are a key focus and the costs of implementation are high. Skeptics and critics were quick to point out that some proclaimed improvements in product and export quality oversight were merely prospective, recent accomplishments likely inflated, and foreign cooperation meager. They argued that the Food Safety Law had little operative content, apparently perpetuated a structure of multiple regulators, and relied on an overburdened and still-weak Ministry of Health to coordinate. The regulatory system was so weak that lawmakers had to prohibit explicitly the conflict-of-interest-creating roles AQSIQ had undertaken as quality regulator and owner of a major certification company (Lee 2008; Li 2009; MacLeod 2009; Ramzy 2009; Xinhua 2009). Insiders and close observers despaired that measures that had been announced, or might conceivably be pursued, could not overcome the formidable obstacles to dealing effectively with product safety problems.

Still, such highly public, elite-level commitments do matter in China. They have something of a mast-binding quality with the Chinese public and foreign audiences, implicitly accepting (or even asserting) that failure to make progress counts as a failure by the regime and perhaps a reason to distrust its earnestly, if not always successfully, cultivated commitment to ruling the country by law and assimilating to international standards. These commitments are more plausible, of course, where they coincide with the leadership's genuine priorities.

Regime Motivations

As this account suggests, prospects for effective policy and legal responses to export safety problems depend on regime motivations,

which, in turn, depend on perceived self-interest. The regime can deploy considerable resources and skills to address challenges and emergencies when it identifies them as priorities. Especially by standards
of countries at its level of development, China has a strong and capable state and, at times, the will to pursue ambitious bureaucratic reforms seeking to enhance state capacity and discipline (deLisle 2005;
Yang 2004).

There are ample indications that the leadership's and broader regime's perceived self-interest favors stronger and more effective approaches to product and export safety. The legal, bureaucratic, and
political measures that have followed recent scandals are far from cost-
less and thus should not be lightly dismissed, even if they have not yet
achieved significant results.

As long as exports of manufactured consumer goods, components,
processed food, and the like remain key contributors to China's growth
and employment, anything that threatens the demand for such products abroad will be a matter of grave concern. According to a leading
2007 survey, 78 percent of U.S. consumers are "worried" or "very worried" about the safety of Chinese goods (Blanchard 2007). With scandals over tainted foodstuffs from the mainland, demand in Hong Kong
fell sharply and consumption of pricier imported substitutes rose (Tang
and Leung 2008). Chinese authorities have complained, and economic
studies shown, that heightened food safety standards imposed by importers in response to concerns about Chinese exports weaken demand
significantly (Chen et al. 2008). Such phenomena are danger signs requiring a response, as Wu Yi recognized in her commitment to wage a
"special battle" to "reestablish the positive image" of Chinese products'
safety (*People's Daily* 2007).

Unresolved export safety problems could imperil other items on the
regime's core agenda of economic development. Such problems can
make it more difficult to attract foreign investment, much of which still
flows to export-oriented manufacturing. They also undermine initiatives to move China's economy into more sophisticated sectors. China's
drug export quality and piracy problems are recognized as inimical
to ambitious plans to develop, including through foreign investment,
research-intensive industries (Jia 2006).

Addressing product safety problems dovetails with key regime goals
beyond economic development. The Hu-Wen leadership is often described as "populist"—concerned about the less well off members of
society, and committed to "human," "overall," or "scientific" (rather
than purely "economic") development or "GDP fundamentalism." They
proffer an image of a government that takes care of citizens' welfare
and seeks a "harmonious society." Hu and especially Wen have empha-

sized and publicized on-the-front-lines solidarity with ordinary people in recent crises, including the 2003 SARS outbreak and the 2008 Sichuan earthquake. The melamine milk incident brought parallels on an issue of product safety. While the crucial urban well-off classes have responded by buying imported goods and thus have not become politicized over the issue, there has been growing public alarm over dangerous goods—and ensuing anger at authorities for not preventing or redressing such problems—which underscores that issues of product safety (and therefore export safety) could begin to harm the regime's fundamental interest in political stability and legitimacy.

In this context, efforts to improve export safety without also tackling broader product safety could be politically costly. They could imply that the regime worries more about foreigners than Chinese (Barboza 2007g). That is a mixed blessing for addressing export safety concerns —on one hand linking their resolution to other regime priorities but on the other dimming hopes for a seemingly less ambitious and more feasible solution that targets exports.

The leadership's foreign policy agenda also supports efforts to improve at least the image, and therefore potentially the reality, of Chinese exports' safety. Moving beyond earlier reform-era efforts simply to join—or rejoin—the international system, an increasingly prosperous, powerful, and confident China seeks acceptance as a fully "normal" nation and a "responsible stakeholder" in the international system. The appearance that the regime cannot, or will not, stem a tide of harmful exports would damage this pursuit.

To Change China? Strategies for the United States and Other Foreign Actors

Although key impetuses and means to address China's export safety problems are domestic, opportunities for influence from abroad exist but have varying, and limited, prospects for success. One approach relies primarily on unilateral efforts by the United States (or other importing states). Concern about the safety of imports, primarily from China, has brought a surge in agency action plans, congressional criticism of the U.S. government entities responsible for import safety, and calls for greater resources and improved bureaucracies to enforce existing rules. Legislation proposing tougher standards, increased inspection, and mandated certification for imports has been proposed (Becker 2008: 14–17, 19–21; King and Blumenstein 2007; Morgan 2007; Spiegel 2009).

These approaches, however, have significant limitations. Given the volume of Chinese exports to the United States and other markets, any strategy that relies on importers' stricter standards and increased enforcement risks being either insufficient or unsustainably expensive. Congressional rhetoric and U.S. agency commitments are unlikely to yield resources adequate to address the problems, given starting points that include, for example, the tiny fraction of imports that the U.S. government inspects. Other priorities compete for limited funds. Substantial mutually independent federal agencies are not easily overhauled or made to coordinate.

International legal rules can stand in the way. WTO-conforming trade restrictions to protect public health and safety require adequate substantive foundations and permit only limited trade-restricting means. WTO rules on sanitary and phytosanitary measures allow importing countries to set substantive safety levels but require adequate risk assessments and scientific bases and permit exporters to adopt implementation methods that satisfy a standard of "equivalence." China can challenge such measures in the WTO dispute resolution process and has signaled its willingness to do so (TBT 1994: arts. 13–14; Mantell 2007; WTO 1994: arts. 4–5, 11).

Unilateral import restrictions could escalate trade frictions. The U.S. media's focus on dangerous Chinese toy exports was followed by indignant statements in the PRC press when it became known that some goods were produced according to U.S. purchasers' designs. Broadbrush U.S. complaints about unsafe Chinese exports sometimes elicit Chinese tit-for-tat reactions, including allegations that U.S. exports to China are unsafe and measures that delay or prevent U.S. products' entry into China (Zamiska 2007; D'Amico 2007; Weisman 2007). China's Ministry of Commerce answered American criticisms with an implausible claim that 99 percent of China's exports to developed markets were "safe and up to the standard" applicable to such goods. The head of China's bureau for food export and import safety dismissed reports of tainted goods as sensational, arguing that U.S. inspectors had approved almost all Chinese shipments (Cody 2007; Harris 2008; King and Blumenstein 2007).

Although such responses cannot be taken at face value, they cannot be dismissed either. They can impede bilateral cooperation and stifle more accommodating views within the Chinese system. They may exacerbate conflicts over dumping, currency manipulation, non-market-conforming trade practices, and other neuralgic issues in bilateral relations (Calmes 2009; Morgan 2007; Stakelbeck 2006).

A second approach is more accommodating or collaborative. It presses and sometimes assists Chinese authorities to enforce their own export safety laws and commitments. Whereas foreign states have limited capacity to set Chinese priorities, the PRC has formally endorsed an export and product safety agenda. Foreign pressure here is less susceptible to the pushback that has faced, for example, U.S. demands for greater efforts to protect intellectual property.

Cooperation and capacity-building—long features of U.S. and other states' policies toward Chinese legal development (deLisle 1999)—have become more prominent in the export safety arena. Amid fallout from quality scandals and recalls of Chinese exports, the United States and China adopted two memoranda of agreement (MOA) in December 2007, one governing food and feed, and the other drugs and medical devices. China committed to requiring manufacturers of exports to register and receive certification from Chinese government organs; to increase regulatory transparency, information-sharing, and harmonization with international standards; and to allow greater inspections and strengthen quality regulation of early-stage inputs to ensure compliance with U.S. import quality standards. Washington undertook to provide technical assistance and training (AP 2007c; HHS 2007). Similar efforts have been pursued at lower levels, including a 2007 deal between the CPSC and AQSIQ to support compliance with U.S. safety standards and especially to address lead paint in toys (Schmidt 2008). China also agreed to station U.S. inspectors in China (Becker 2008; Jacobs and McDonald 2008; Yang 2008).

As critical observers have noted, however, concrete cooperation has been small in scale (e.g., stationing of a mere eight to ten U.S. Food and Drug Administration [FDA] inspectors in China and inspecting 2 percent of relevant Chinese pharmaceutical plants). The MOAs and similar agreements contain little detail (Fan 2008; Harris 2008; Rhea 2007b). As other aspects of U.S.-China economic relations (including intellectual property) illustrate, bilateral agreements can fail and increase conflict.

A third approach may hold more potential. It relies on U.S. (and potentially other foreign) law to affect behavior of importers of potentially dangerous Chinese goods and their Chinese suppliers. The robust U.S. legal regime for defective products—imposing strict liability, extending liability to sellers and those farther up production and distribution chains, and awarding high damages, sometimes to large plaintiff classes—can give U.S. importers and purchasers, and U.S. owners or co-venturers in China-based manufacturing operations, strong incentives to improve their monitoring of Chinese suppliers and partners. Given the obstacles foreign parties can face in suing or enforcing judgments in China, U.S. defendants cannot count on Chinese parties to indemnify them. Class action and consolidated multidistrict litigation has gone forward in U.S. courts, principally against U.S. defendants, over Chinese-produced pet food, toys, drywall, and heparin.

With U.S. (or other non-Chinese) parties thus facing the principal risks of liability, they have powerful incentives to demand and implement improvement of quality control (Gottlieb 2007; Huang 2008: 132–34; Stratfor 2007).

Such defensive moves appear to have relatively good prospects for success. At least one U.S. industry group has sought stronger control over Chinese providers' manufacturing processes to reduce its exposure to liability (D'Amico 2007). U.S. and other foreign companies that buy components for or manufacture high-value and potentially high liability-creating durable goods in China have developed elaborate and proven means for reducing defect rates to world-class levels. Executives at such firms, Chinese experts, and China industry watchers agree that many foreign firms with China joint ventures or production contracts in lower-end sectors have been lax or willfully blind to the risky behavior of their partners and suppliers.

U.S. (or other foreign) public or regulatory law can reinforce these incentives. Hospitals and drug and medical device companies in the United States have faced increasing pressures to ensure that the imports they use meet FDA standards—in part by going beyond the suspect documentation of quality control and inspection provided by Chinese manufacturers (Rhea 2007a). Recalls of dangerous toys by U.S. manufacturers in response to CPSC threats or actions, congressional consideration of tougher legislation, and California authorities' lawsuit to enforce quality standards against companies have spurred pledges of more aggressive efforts to address Chinese import quality problems by Mattel and other U.S. toy firms (Lifsher and Goldman 2007; Teagarden 2009). Federal prosecutors also secured an indictment of U.S. and Chinese companies and their executives in connection with tainted pet food imports (CNN 2008).

In the end, the most powerful forces for improving export safety may lie beyond the direct influence of law and policy. Rising perceptions in importing markets that Chinese exports are disproportionately unsafe may overwhelm the cost advantage-based demand that Chinese producers have enjoyed. Tellingly, U.S. and other foreign producers of internationally traded higher-margin goods that are acutely vulnerable to loss of reputation for safety have found ways to manage quality assurance in their China operations. At least in the United States, weakening demand might be compounded by a resurgence of negative popular images of China, as outrage over export safety interacts with long-running concerns about human rights, trade imbalances, job losses, and wariness of China's rise as a potential strategic rival and exploiter of leverage gained through financing American deficits. Long-term shifts in China's comparative advantage, with rising labor and other factor costs, currency appreciation, and a push for more sophisticated exports may leave Chinese producers and officials with no economic alternative to improving quality and safety.

Finally, some assessments suggest that solutions to China's export safety—and underlying product safety—problems will come only from the emergence of a more developed economy and a much more robust rule of law, government accountability, business ethics, and civil society (including industry and consumer groups) (Cody 2004; Johnson 2008; Kaplan 2007; Thompson and Hu 2007). Changes such as these are not yet, however, sufficiently imminent to rely on to the exclusion of pursuing second (or third) best approaches to the serious and urgent problem of dangerous exports from China.

References

AFX News Limited (2005) "Nestle China JV Ordered to Recall Second Type of Baby Milk Powder." *Forbes*, June 23.

Ahrens, Frank (2007) "FDA Halts Imports of Some Chinese Seafood." *Washington Post*, June 29, sec. D.

Associated Press (AP) (2007a) "China Bans Diethylene Glycol in Toothpaste." *Fox News*, July 11. http://www.foxnews.com/story/0,2933,288979,00.html.

———. (2007b) "Importer Recalls 255,000 Chinese-Made Tires." *USA Today*, August 9.

———. (2007c) "China Signs Pact to Ban Lead Paint in Export Toys." *New York Times*, September 12, sec. C.

Barboza, David (2008a) "China Orders New Oversight of Heparin." *New York Times*, March 22, sec. A.

———. (2008b) "Questions Swirl After Death of China's Food Safety Chief." *New York Times*, August 14, sec. C.

———. (2008c) "Chinese Regulators Destroy Tons of Tainted Animal Feed." *New York Times*, November 2, sec. A.

———. (2008d) "Former Head of Chinese Dairy Pleads Guilty." *New York Times*, December 21.

———. (2008e) "Chinese Dairies Agree to Pay $160 Million to Tainted Milk Victims." *New York Times*, December 30.

———. (2007a) "China to Revise Rules on Food and Drug Safety." *New York Times*, June 7.

———. (2007b) "Food Safety Crackdown in China." *New York Times*, June 28, sec. C.

———. (2007c) "For Two Children, Ban of a Drug Came Too Late." *New York Times*, July 13, sec. A.

———. (2007d) "China Moves to Change Damaged Global Image." *New York Times*, July 29.

———. (2007e) "China Suspends Exports by Two Firms over Lead Paint." *New York Times*, August 10.

———. (2007f) "China Steps Up Efforts to Cleanse Reputation." *New York Times*, September 5.

———. (2007g) "774 Arrests in China over Safety." *New York Times*, October 31.

————. (2007h) "China Bars Exports by 750 Toy Makers." *New York Times*, November 2.

————. (2007i) "China Moves to Improve Quality of Its Seafood." *New York Times*, December 28, sec. C.

Becker, Geoffrey S. (2008) "Food and Agricultural Imports from China." *Congressional Research Service Report for Congress* 2-5, September 26, Washington, D.C.

Blanchard, Ben (2007) "China Tries Charm to Convince World Its Goods Safe." Reuters, September 19.

Bloomberg News (2008) "China Says Poisoning Was Isolated." *New York Times*, February 28, sec. C.

Bogdanich, Walt (2008) "Heparin Find May Point to Chinese Counterfeiting." *New York Times*, March 20.

————. (2007) "Chinese Chemicals Flow Unchecked onto World Drug Market." *New York Times*, October 31.

Bronshtein, Dina M. (2008) "Counterfeit Pharmaceuticals in China." 17 *Pacific Rim Law and Policy Journal* 439–66.

Buckley, Chris (2007) "China Finds 15 Percent of Foods Fail Quality Check." Reuters, August 17.

Calmes, Jackie (2009) "Geithner Hints at Harder Line on China Trade." *New York Times*, January 23, sec. A.

Chen, Chunlai, Jun Yang, and Christopher Findlay (2008) "Measuring the Effect of Food Safety Standards on China's Agricultural Exports." 144 *Review of World Economics* 83–106.

Chi, Hsi-sheng (1991) *Politics of Disillusionment: The Chinese Communist Party Under Deng Xiaoping*. Armonk, N.Y.: M.E. Sharpe.

CNN (2008) "China: Tainted Milk Suppliers Charged." September 16. http://www.cnn.com/2008/WORLD/asiapcf/09/16/china.formula/.

Cody, Edward (2007) "China Says Food Export Inspections Are Effective." *Washington Post*, June 1.

————. (2004) "Chinese Whistleblower Punished." *Washington Post*, November 12.

D'Amico, Esther (2007) "Flagging Up Quality Concerns." *Chemical Week*, September 5.

deLisle, Jacques (2009) "Exceptional Powers in an Exceptional State: Emergency Powers Law in China." In *Emergency Powers in Asia: Exploring the Limits of Legality*, edited by Victor V. Ramraj and Arun K. Thiruvengadam. Cambridge: Cambridge University Press.

————. (2007) "Traps, Gaps and Law in China's Transition." *Policy Brief*. Oxford: Foundation for Law, Justice and Society.

————. (2005) "Chasing the God of Wealth While Evading the Goddess of Democracy." In *Democracy and Development: New Perspectives on an Old Debate*, edited by Sunder Ramaswamy and Jeffrey W. Casson. Hanover, N.H.: Middlebury College Press.

————. (1999) "Lex Americana?" 20 *University of Pennsylvania Journal of International Economic Law* 179–308.

Dickinson, Steven M. (2009) "Food Fumble." *Wall Street Journal*, March 3.

Economist (2007). "China's Toxic Toymaker," August 18.

Fairclough, Gordon (2007) "Lead Toxins Take a Global Roundtrip." *Wall Street Journal*, July 12, sec. B.

Fan, Maureen (2008) "FDA Sending Inspectors to Other Nations." *Washington Post*, November 19, sec. A.

Ford, Peter (2008) "What China's Tainted Milk May Not Bring: Lawsuits." *Christian Science Monitor*, September 22.

Fraser, David (2006) "On the Trail of Counterfeit Chips." *Electronic Engineering Times*, May 22.

Gottlieb, Scott (2007) "How Safe Is Our Food?" *USA Today*, May 21, sec. A.

Harris, Gardiner (2008) "The Safety Gap." *New York Times Magazine*, November 2.

Hu, Peggy B. and Bertha Gomez (2005) "Public Safety Jeopardized by Chinese Counterfeiters, Experts Say." Washington File (May 20). http://usinfo.org/wf-archive/2005/050520/epf508.htm.

Huang, Hao (2008) "Maximizing Chinese Imports' Compliance with United States Safety and Quality Standards." 18 *Southern California Interdisciplinary Law Journal* 131–60.

Jacobs, Andrew (2008) "China Pledges New Measures to Safeguard Dairy Industry." *New York Times*, November 20, sec. A.

Jacobs, Andrew and Mark McDonald (2008) "F.D.A. Opens Office in Beijing to Screen Food and Drug Exports." *New York Times*, November 19, sec. A.

Jia, Hepeng (2006) "Poor Enforcement Could Jeopardize China's Drug Innovation Policy." *Nature Biotechnology*, 20: 1182–83.

Johnson, Toni (2008) "China's Troubled Food and Drug Trade." Council on Foreign Relations. http://www.cfr.org/publication/17545/.

Kahn, Joseph (2007) "China Quick to Execute Drug Official." *New York Times*, June 11, sec. C.

Kaplan, Nicole J. (2007) "Analyzing the Recent Recall of Chinese-Made Products." 4 *American University Business Law Brief* 39–43.

King, Neil, Jr., and Rebecca Blumenstein (2007) "China Launches Public Response to Safety Outcry." *Wall Street Journal*, June 30, sec. A.

Lee, Don (2008) "Chinese Firms Sue Product Safety Agency." *Los Angeles Times*, September 1, sec. C.

Lee, Matthew (2005) "Freshwater Fish Banned." *The Standard*, August 22.

Li, Li (2009) "In Food We Trust." *Beijing Review*, March 19.

Lieberthal, Kenneth G. (2004) *Governing China: From Revolution to Reform*. New York: W.W. Norton.

Lieberthal, Kenneth G. and David M. Lampton, eds. (1992) *Bureaucracy, Politics and Decision Making in Post-Mao China*. Berkeley and Los Angeles: University of California Press.

Lifsher, Marc and Abigail Goldman (2007) "Lead in Toys Sparks Lawsuit." *Los Angeles Times*, November 18, sec. C.

Lipton, Eric (2007) "China Plans to Inspect More Food." *New York Times*, August 16, sec. C.

Looewy, Matias (2007) "Deadly Imitations." *Perspectives in Health*, 11, 3.

Lubman, Stanley B. (2002) *Bird in a Cage: Legal Reform in China After Mao*. Stanford, Calif.: Stanford University Press.

Luo, Jun (2008) "China Milk Scandal Sees First Lawsuit: Beijing Youth Daily Says." Bloomberg News, September 30.

MacLeod, Calum (2009) "Some Skeptical of China's New Food Safety Law." *USA Today*, March 1.

Mantell, Ruth (2007) "Our Slipshod Product Safety." *Marketwatch*, December 7.

Martin, Andrew (2007) "FDA Curbs Sale of 5 Seafoods Farmed in China." *New York Times*, June 29, sec. A.

Mertha, Andrew C. (2005) "China's 'Soft' Centralization: Shifting *Tiao Kuai* Authority Relations." *China Quarterly*, 791–810.

Morgan, David (2007) "U.S. Senator Wants 'Czar' to Ensure Import Safety." Reuters, July 1.

Morrison, Wayne M. (2008) "Health and Safety Concerns over U.S. Imports of Chinese Products." *Congressional Research Service Report for Congress*, January 24. Washington, D.C.

Peerenboom, Randall P. (2002) *China's Long March Toward the Rule of Law.* Cambridge: Cambridge University Press.

People's Daily (2007) "China Takes Measures to Enhance Product Quality, Food Safety," September 12.

Quek, Tracy (2009) "Food Safety Situation Still Grim, Says China." *Straits Times*, June 2.

Quirk, Gregory A. (2007) "Under the Hood Special Report: Counterfeit Parts, Legitimate Woes." *Electronic Engineering Times*, August 6.

Quittner, Jeremy (2007) "The China Code." *Business Week on Line*, August 17.

Ramzy, Austin (2009) "Will China's New Food Safety Laws Work?" *Time*, March 3.

Reeves, Amy (2003) "Clamping Down on Counterfeit Drugs." *Investors Business Daily*, October 20, sec. A.

Reuters (2009) "China Melamine Victim's Parents Paid $29,000." *MSNBC.com*, January 16.

Rhea, Shawn (2007a) "This Problem Made in China." *Modern Healthcare*, October 22.

———. (2007b) "U.S.-Sino Safety Pact Called 'Modest Start'." *Modern Healthcare*, December 17.

Roberts, Dexter and Chi-Chu Tschang (2007) "Wu Yi: China's Enforcer of Last Resort." *Business Week*, September 24.

Schmidt, Charles W. (2008) "Face to Face with Toy Safety." *Environmental Health Perspectives*, February.

Schweitzer, Stuart O. (2008) "Trying Times at the FDA." *New England Journal of Medicine*, 358, 1773–77.

Spiegel, Rob (2009) "Counterfeit Components Remains a Huge Electronics Supply Chain Problem." *Electrical Design News*, March 3.

Stakelbeck, Frederick W., Jr. (2006) "Schumer-Graham 'Nuke' Holstered." *Asia Times Online*, March 31.

Story, Louise (2007) "Mattel Official Apologizes in China." *New York Times*, September 21.

Stratfor: Global Intelligence (2007) "China: Product Quality, Reform and the Rule of Law." Stratfor: Global Intelligence, August 27.

Tang, Eugene and Zhang Dingmin (2007) "China Defends Its Food Safety Record After Scares." Bloomberg News, August 17.

Tang, Theresa and Weny Leung (2008) "Hong Kong Avoids China Food as Milk Scandal Drives Up Costs." Bloomberg News, September 25.

Teagarden, Mary B. (2009) "Learning from Toys: Reflections on the 2007 Recall Crisis." *Thunderbird International Business Review*, 51, 5–17.

Thompson, Drew and Hu Ying (2007) "Food Safety in China: New Strategies." 1 *Global Health Governance*, 1–19.

Tschang, Chi-Chu (2007) "Bottlenecks in Toyland." *Business Week*, October 5.

U.S. China Business Council (USCBC) (2009) "U.S.-China Trade Statistics and China's World Trade Statistics." http://www.uschina.org/statistics/tradetable.html.

U.S. Consumer Product Safety Commission (CPSC) (2007) *2007 Performance and Accountability Report.* http://www.cpsc.gov/cpscpub/pubs/reports/2007par.pdf.

U.S. Department of Health and Human Services (HHS) (2007) *New Agreement Will Enhance the Safety of Drugs and Medical Devices Imported from the People's Republic of China.* December 11. Washington, D.C.: HHS.

Wang, Bingqiang (2008) "Lawyers Rally Victims Against Milk Producer Sanlu." *Economic Observer Online*, November 24.

Wang, Ying (2004) "Severe Punishment Vowed for Fake Milk Powder Producers." *China Daily*, April 21.

Weeks, Ann and Dennis Chen (2003) "Navigating China's Standards Regime." *China Business Review*, May–June.

Weisman, Steven R. (2007) "China-U.S. Talks Continue amid Legal Volleys." *New York Times*, July 30, sec. C.

Wines, Michael (2009) "Local Court Is China's First to Accept a Tainted-Milk Suit." *New York Times*, March 26, sec. A.

Wong, Edward (2009) "Families File Suit in Chinese Tainted Milk Scandal." *New York Times*, January 21.

———. (2008) "More Families in China File Lawsuits over Tainted Milk." *New York Times*, October 31, sec. A.

Wu Yi (2007) "Address to the National Political Meeting on Product Quality and Food Safety Rectification." http://www.gov.cn.ldhd/2007-08/24/content_726932.htm.

Wyld, David C. (2006) "Genuine Medicine?" 18 *Competitiveness Review* 206–16.

Xie, Chuanjiao (2007) "Food Safety Drive Stepped Up." *China Daily*, September 19.

Xinhua (2009) "China Adopts Food Safety Law." *China Daily*, February 28.

———. (2008) "China to Upgrade Health Ministry to Better Monitor Food and Drug Safety," March 11. http://news.xinhuanet.com/english/2008-03/11/content_7766320.htm.

Yang, Dali L. (2008) "Total Recall." *National Interest*, March-April.

———. (2004) *Remaking the Chinese Leviathan: Market Transition and the Politics of Governance in China.* Stanford, Calif.: Stanford University Press.

Yardley, Jim (2008) "More Candy from China, Tainted, Is in the U.S." *New York Times*, October 2, sec. A.

Zamiska, Nicholas (2007) "China Takes Aim at U.S. on Quality Control." *Wall Street Journal*, October 10, sec. B.

Zhu, Zhe (2008) "More Legislation to Help Combat Shoddy Products." *China Daily*, January 5.

Laws and Agreements Cited

Consumer Rights and Interests Protection Law of the People's Republic of China (CRIPL) (adopted 1993).

Final Act Embodying the Results of the Uruguay Round of Multilateral Trade Negotiations, April 15, 1994, Agreement on Technical Barriers to Trade (TBT), Annex 1A, Legal Instruments—Results of the Uruguay Round, 33 I.L.M. 1125.

Food Safety Law of the People's Republic of China (adopted 2009).

Implementing Regulations for the Food Safety Law of the People's Republic of China (adopted 2009).

Product Quality Law of the People's Republic of China (PQL) (adopted 1993, amendments 2000).

World Trade Organization (WTO). Agreement on the Application of Sanitary and Phytosanitary Measures (SPS). April 15, 1994, Marrakesh Agreement Establishing the World Trade Organization, Annex 1A, pmbl., Legal Instruments—Results of the Uruguay Round, 1867 U.N.T.S. 493.

Chapter 3
Parochialism About the Safety of Imports

Jonathan Baron

If we were all rational, our concern about risks would be in proportion to how much we can reduce their harm. We would take protective action, and ask government to take protective action to the extent to which the outcome is bad, the probability is high, the cost of protection is low, and the effectiveness of protection is high.

A number of studies of risk perception make the point that risk perceptions are influenced by ideology, politics, and general anxiety levels of individuals, which, in turn, are affected by various demographic variables, such as sex (Slovic 1998). My own collaborative research has shown that worry, which is on a continuum with clinically significant anxiety, has an independent influence on preferences for protective action by both government and individuals (Baron et al. 2000). We have also found differences among various groups in specific biases that lead people to oppose rational efficiency of the sort I have just sketched. For example, environmentalists are more inclined to say that people or companies should "clean up their own waste" even when some other solution has better outcomes in terms of cost or risk (Baron et al. 1993).

One way in which ideology or political views can affect risk perception is through what Jervis (1976) called "belief overkill" (Baron 2008: ch. 9). Once people adopt a position on what should be done, they tend to adjust their beliefs to be congruent with the position. For example, if people favor protection of domestic jobs, they might be more inclined to believe that imported products are risky.

Parochialism

The desire to protect domestic jobs may arise from a bias called *parochialism*. This is a technical term referring to the tendency of people to favor a group that includes them while underweighing or ignoring harm to outsiders (Schwartz-Shea and Simmons 1991) to such an extent that they can favor policies that harm outsiders more than they benefit insiders. A prime example is nationalism, a value that goes almost unquestioned in many circles, just as racism and sexism went unquestioned in the past. Nationalists are concerned with their fellow citizens, regardless of the effect on outsiders. Nationalists are willing to sacrifice their own self-interest to harm outsiders—in war, for example—for the benefit of co-nationals.

Parochialism has been demonstrated in laboratory experiments and in questionnaire studies, some involving real money, some involving hypothetical situations based on national loyalty (see, e.g., Baron 2001; Bornstein and Ben-Yossef 1994). Such studies might be models for cases of real-world conflict, in which people sacrifice their own self-interest to help their group at the expense of some other group. We can look at such behavior from three points of view: the individual, the group, and everyone else (the world). Political action in favor of one's group is beneficial for the group but (in these cases) costly to both the individual and the world.

In the case of trade policy, parochialism is one justification (among others) for protectionist policies. People care more about the workers in their own country than they do about foreign workers (Baron and Kemp 2004). Typically, this is not a matter of personal knowledge of the affected individuals.

In defining parochialism as neglect of the interests of outsiders, I do not mean to imply that group loyalty entails such neglect or that group loyalty itself has no benefits. People have many good reasons to cooperate with in-group members, reasons that do not apply to out-group members. Group loyalty provides emotional benefits, but these do not need to come at the expense of others to such an extent that the harms exceed them. And it is not necessarily parochial when we refuse to do something to improve things for out-group members. Many groups (including nations) operate within a scheme of local responsibility, in which, for efficiency reasons, they are given local control. In such cases, interference with a group by outsiders, even for what appears to be the greater good, would have the negative effect of undermining local control and setting a precedent for outsiders coming in and making things worse (Baron 1996).

Parochialism may be in part an inevitable side effect of group loyalty that exists for good reasons combined with thoughtlessness about outsiders. But some of it may result from fallacious or "biased" thinking, or particular ways of framing the situation. Fallacies can be corrected, and people can be encouraged to use other frames. Thus, the study of cognitive biases and framing effects can give us a way of correcting a small piece of a large problem. The problem is so large that even a small piece is worthy of our attention.

The study of people's conscious reasons can help us understand the phenomenon, even if these reasons are not the only determinant of behavior. In part, parochialism results from an illusion in which people see self-sacrifice for their group as really not sacrifice at all, an "illusion of morality as self-interest" (Baron 2001). Parochialism is more evident in omission than in acts; we are less reluctant to hurt foreigners through omissions than through actions. And it is more evident when we think about foreigners as abstractions rather than as real individuals (Baron forthcoming). People often think of themselves as having a duty to act to favor their nation, even when they admit that harm to outsiders is greater than the benefit to co-nationals (Baron forthcoming). Parochialism can be reduced by the use of approval voting, at least if everyone votes. That is, given a choice between three proposals—one favoring their group, one favoring the other group, and one a compromise that is better on the whole but best for neither group—people tend to approve the compromise (as well as the proposal favoring their own group), so that, if both groups vote, the compromise wins (Baron et al. 2005).

Import Safety

In recent years, government and the press have paid considerable attention to food risks, perhaps especially to the risks of imported food (Brewer and Prestat 2002; USDA and Calvin 2004). In general, consumers are not well informed about food risks (Wilcock et al. 2004), and it is not clear whether imports come in for special attention. On the one hand, it is clear that imports are treated differently because various laws and regulations that apply to domestic food cannot be applied so easily to imports, as other chapters in this book demonstrate. On the other hand, enforcement of even domestic regulations often suffers from lack of funding and incompetence.

Of interest in this chapter is whether people are parochial about risks. Are they more concerned about risks of imported products than domestic ones, even when the difference lacks justification in evidence? If so, how does this concern arise? Is it, for example, the result of favoring domestic over foreign workers? If people have some reason to favor domestic products, they are likely to find justifications for their preference by distorting beliefs, such as beliefs about riskiness.

To look for such distortions, I conducted several studies using questionnaires presented on the Internet. The subjects were from a panel of about 1,400 people who had joined over a period of 10 years. The members of the panel are typical of Americans in median income and education (i.e., approximately $50,000 per year with some college education), but they are mostly women. They were paid between $3 and $6 for each study through PayPal (a Web-based service for transferring money), depending on its length, with a goal of about $3 for 10 to 15 minutes. Subjects knew that they would not get paid if they did not "take the study seriously," which, in practice, usually meant that they did not rush through it so quickly that they could not read the items: they were timed, without their knowledge, on each page. I aimed for 80 subjects in each study. Each study consisted of a short introduction followed by several experimental conditions, one to a page. The pages/conditions were presented in a random order chosen for each subject.[1] The subject had to answer all questions before proceeding to the next page and, once on the next page, could not go back. There was a space for an optional comment on each page, as well as at the end. Usually the responses involved clicking radio buttons (designed so that clicking the text next to a button would also work).

The items on the different pages were usually different consumer products made in different countries. Each page then presented a series of questions about the product.

Experiment 1: Product Safety

Experiment 1 was an initial test for parochialism. I examined twelve products and asked about willingness to sacrifice overall availability of the product to reduce a risk based on where the product came from: the United States, Canada, or Mexico.

Method

Each of the twelve items was presented three times, once from each of the three possible origins (United States, Canada, Mexico). The order of the thirty-six items was randomized for each subject. An example of the presentation of one item is the following:

> Product: meat
> Made in: Mexico
> Risk: bacterial contamination
> Outcome: acute illness

• Suppose the Risk could be eliminated completely, but the price of the Product would have to increase to cover the cost of inspections and monitoring. (Suppose there is no other way to reduce this risk.) What is the greatest increase in price that you would find acceptable to eliminate this Risk?

- ○ I would rather accept the current risk than any increase in price.
- ○ 10%   20%   30%   40%   50% or more

- How often does the Outcome happen now?
  - ○ "almost never"   "rarely"   "fairly often"   "too often"

- How bad is the Outcome, typically, when it happens?
  - ○ "not bad at all"   "bad but tolerable"   "very bad"   "intolerable"

- Suppose that inspections and monitoring would not cause the price to increase, but they would cause some producers of the Product to stop selling it in the United States. What is the greatest reduction in availability of this product—from *all* sources—that you would find acceptable to eliminate this Risk?
  - ○ I would rather accept the current risk than any reduction in availability.
  - ○ I would accept a 10% reduction in availability to eliminate the risk, but no more.
  - ○ 20%   30%   40%   50% or more

Table 1 shows the products with the risk and outcome associated with each. I used data from 77 subjects (60 females and 17 males). Ages ranged from 24 to 72, with the median age 44. Seven subjects lived out-

Table 1. Items Used in Experiment 1

Product	Risk	Outcome
Prescription drugs	incorrect formulation	ineffectiveness
Nonprescription drugs	additional ingredients not labeled	allergic reactions
Vegetables	bacterial contamination	acute illness
Fruit	bacterial contamination	acute illness
Meat	bacterial contamination	acute illness
Seafood	bacterial contamination	acute illness
Automobiles	faulty brakes or steering	crashes
Toys	dangerous design	serious injuries of children
Tires	weak spots	blowouts
Laptop batteries	overheating	fires
Children's pajamas	flammable	severe burns of children
Peanut butter	bacterial contamination	acute illness

side the United States (6 in Canada, 1 in Scotland), but they did not differ from the others in their characteristics and responses, so I used their data. Four others (not included in the 77) were omitted for giving identical answers to all questions about risk, and one was omitted for going much faster than everyone else.

Results

For data analysis, I used the approach described by Baayen et al. (2008). I fit a model to predict each dependent variable, such as Price (the answer to the first question), from other relevant variables, such as Origin (country of origin). Note that each subject answered twelve Price questions for each of the three Origins. Very likely, subjects differ in their overall tendency; products differ as well, regardless of Origin. These consistent differences would introduce dependencies among the items, which would make it invalid to carry out statistical tests as if each of the 12×82 observations for each Origin were independent of each other. To take these dependencies into account, the model included two additional terms, each a vector (list of numbers). One was an estimate of the deviation of each subject from the mean of all subjects and the other was an estimate of the deviation of each item from the mean of all items. These are called "random effects"; the software described by Baayen et al. (2008) can handle random effects from both subjects and items simultaneously. This approach has many other advantages. In particular, it does not require balanced designs, so it can handle missing data, and it considers the effects of item and subject variation simultaneously.[2]

In this experiment, the main question was whether the various questions depended on Origin. I compared Canada and Mexico to the United States. Figure 1 shows the results. To do a more sensitive test, I added the two response measures, Price and Supply, into one number, which I called *Control*. Control was significantly higher when the product was from Mexico ($p = .0210$), but nonsignificantly lower when it was from Canada. (The subjects' geographic location had no effect.) Similarly, I combined Frequency and Badness into one measure of Risk.[3] Risk was significantly lower in Canada than in the United States ($p = .0084$), but Mexico and the United States did not differ.

It would appear that the willingness to take action against Mexican products is not, then, a function of their additional perceived risk. I tested directly the different attitudes toward Canada and Mexico by computing the difference between Control and Risk (after standardizing both). This difference was greater for Mexico than for Canada

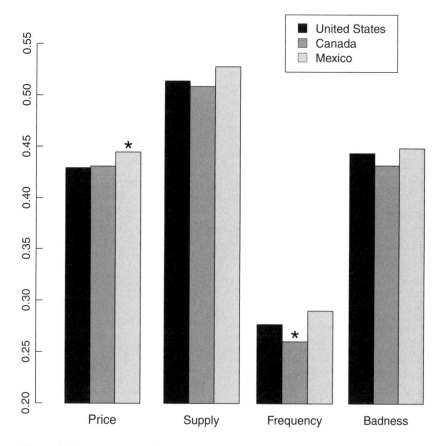

Figure 1. Mean responses for experiment 1. Note: 0 is the bottom and 1 is the top of each scale. Asterisks indicate significant ($p < .05$) differences from the United States. The supply difference between Mexico and the United States was $p = .0662$.

(mean difference of .065, in z scores, $p = .0262$). In sum, the increased willingness to sacrifice to control imports from Mexico cannot be accounted for by their additional risk. It may be a manifestation of parochial bias—in this case, a kind of protectionism.

Subjects seemed quite happy with Canadian imports—they saw them as having less risk than U.S. products—but were no less willing to regulate them. Perhaps Canada is not the ideal example, though, of a "foreign" nation. Canadians often complain that Americans see Canada as the 51st state; this perception, if present, may have advantages as well as disadvantages. (Note that the U.S. political movement against the

North American Free Trade Agreement was generally inspired by concerns about Mexico, not Canada.)

Experiment 2: Purchases

Experiment 2 approached the same questions about bias against foreign products using a more sensitive method. Specifically, this experiment compared foreign and domestic products explicitly on the same page (rather than separate pages as in Experiment 1), referred to products as "foreign" or "domestic," left open the type of harm that the product might cause, asked whether subjects had any experience with the item in question, and asked about their actual preference as the main dependent variable. In addition, it asked about a second reason, aside from perceived risk, that could lead people to favor domestic products, namely, greater sympathy for the workers who make them. The application of parochialism to workers has been a major topic of other studies of parochialism (Baron forthcoming; Baron et al. 2005).

Method

The study used thirty-two products: prescription drugs, nonprescription drugs, vegetables, fruit, eggs, meat, seafood, automobiles, toys, candy, pesticides, airplane flights, tires, computers, power tools, cell phones, chairs, wine, beer, bicycles, cheese, pet food, portable audio devices, personal digital assistants, children's pajamas, peanut butter, televisions, shoes, home audio equipment, cameras, everyday clothes, and sports equipment. Each page began with a product name and asked six questions about the product. The order of the products was randomized for each subject. An example of a page with the six questions is the following:

Consider purchasing fruit.

- Do you buy fruit?
  - "no and do not plan to"   "not yet but plan to"   "yes"
- When you buy it, do you (or would you) look to see where it came from?
  - "never" "sometimes" "usually" "always" "will never buy it"[4]
- When you have a choice of imported or domestic fruit, what do you choose most often?
  - "imported"   "domestic"   "ignore the source"
    "never make this choice"

- How would you compare the probabilities that domestic and imported fruit would cause some sort of harm?
  - ○ Domestic is at least twice as likely to cause harm.
  - ○ Domestic is more likely to cause harm, but not twice.
  - ○ The two are equally likely to cause harm.
  - ○ Imported is more likely to cause harm, but not twice.
  - ○ Imported is at least twice as likely to cause harm.
- In buying fruit, how do you think about the workers who produce it?
  - ○ It is better to try to help foreign workers.
  - ○ Foreign and domestic workers are equally worthy.
  - ○ It is better to try to help domestic workers.
  - ○ This issue is irrelevant to my decisions.
- How would you compare the quality of domestic and foreign fruit for a given price?
  - ○ "domestic usually better"   "no consistent difference"
    "imported usually better"   "don't know"

I used data from 80 subjects: 61 females and 19 males. Ages ranged from 24 to 75, with the median age 46.5. Eleven subjects lived outside the United States (all Canadian), but as before they did not differ from the others in their responses and characteristics, so I used their data. Five other subjects were omitted: four had too many missing data; one went much faster than everyone else.

Results

Responses to the main questions—those about Choice, probability of Harm, Workers, and Quality—were coded so that "neutral" was zero and positive numbers favored domestic products. "Never choose" responses to Choose and "Don't know" responses to Quality were counted as missing data. I reported unstandardized regression coefficients (β): a coefficient of 1 means that one step on the scale of the dependent variable is associated with one step on a predictor. (Note that Choice and Harm had 5-point scales, while Workers and Quality had 3-point scales.)

Choice was affected by all three predictors in a mixed-model regression on all three: Harm ($\beta = .048$, $p = .0040$); Workers ($\beta = .224$, $p = .0001$); and Quality ($\beta = .581$, $p = .0001$). The intercept was also significant ($.082$; $p = .0014$), indicating that these three predictors did not fully account for the preference for domestic goods, since the preference was found when the predictors were all (in theory) neutral (i.e., zero, but note that the intercept without predictors was .384, so these predictors accounted for most of the preference).

Of interest, Harm was also affected by Workers (β = .081, p = .0260) and Quality (β = .205, p = .0001). When subjects were more concerned about workers, they tended to think that the risk was greater. It is difficult to know what is cause and what is effect here because of the possibility of belief overkill in both directions. But it seems reasonable to think that a general parochial attitude will express itself as a bias toward workers in one's nation, which, in turn, would lead to a preference for domestic products, and this can be rationalized further by thinking that foreign products are less safe.

Experiment 3: Food Risks

Experiment 3 again asked for explicit comparisons of risks of domestic and foreign products, but it was limited to food. It asked about priority for risk reduction, and which methods of risk reduction were appropriate: the government should ban the product; the government should fine the distributor for violations; the government should require the seller to provide information; the government should require the distributor to carry out inspections; the government should do the inspections; or consumers should avoid the product on their own. It also asked about worry (following Baron et al. 2000) and about the prevalence and badness of the risk.

Method

The introduction to the survey read: "This is about how government should deal with risks from food products. Each page presents an example of a risk of a food product from a foreign country (F, for foreign) and one from your country (D, for domestic). If the risk happens, the bad effect is identical for D and F. (It may or may not be equally likely to happen, however.)" The risks were as follows, each contrasted with the risk from the same product "grown in [or 'raised in,' or 'produced in,' or 'from'] your country":

- bread made from genetically modified wheat, grown in Brazil;
- grapes with residue of pesticides, grown in Chile;
- beef from animals given antibiotics against bacteria that infect humans (thus causing antibiotic-resistant bacteria to develop), raised in Argentina;
- beef from herds in which mad cow disease has been found, raised in Argentina;
- beef from animals given growth hormones, raised in Argentina;

- frozen dinners that fail to list ingredients to which some people have allergies, imported from Mexico;
- lettuce contaminated with *E. coli* bacteria, from Mexico;
- strawberries contaminated with hepatitis, from Mexico;
- yogurt with a "use by" date that expired a month ago, from Greece;
- tomatoes that have been irradiated with radioactive rays to prevent spoilage, from Morocco;
- grapes that have been poisoned with cyanide, from Chile.

An example of a survey page is as follows:

F: beef from animals given antibiotics against bacteria that infect humans (thus causing antibiotic-resistant bacteria to develop), raised in Argentina
D: the same identical risk but raised in your country

- What priority should government give to the control of these risks?
  - "F should get higher priority"   "the same"
    "D should get higher priority"

- How much do you worry about these risks? (Choose the closest.)
  - "not at all"   "more about F"
    "more about D"   "equally about both"

- About how many people in your country are ever affected by this?
  - "none"   "more by F"   "more by D"   "equally by both"

- How bad is it for the average person who is affected? (Remember, the two effects are identical, so they do not differ here.)
  - "not bad at all"   "somewhat"   "moderately"
    "very bad"   "as bad as death"

- How appropriate is each of the following ways of dealing with this risk?
  - Ban the sale of D. [Response options for this and the following items: "inappropriate," "OK," "good," "excellent."]
  - Ban the sale of F.
  - The distributor of D should be fined for violations.
  - The distributor of F should be fined for violations.
  - The seller should be required to inform the consumer of the risk from D.
  - The seller should be required to inform the consumer of the risk from F.
  - The distributor should be required to carry out inspections and monitoring of D to avoid this (thus increasing the cost).

    ○ The distributor should be required to carry out inspections and monitoring of F to avoid this (thus increasing the cost).

    ○ The government should carry out inspections and monitoring of D to avoid this (thus requiring money from taxes or cuts in other programs).

    ○ The government should carry out inspections and monitoring of F to avoid this (thus requiring money from taxes or cuts in other programs).

    ○ Consumers should avoid D.

    ○ Consumers should avoid F.

The order of D and F within each pair of questions was counterbalanced across subjects. I used data from 83 subjects: 65 females and 18 males. Ages ranged from 24 to 70, with the median age 43. No subjects were omitted.

Data from questions about Priority, Worry, Number of people affected, and the ways of dealing with the risk—Ban, Fine, Provide information, Inspect, Government inspect, or Self-protect—were transformed so that 0 represented "equal" or "none," 1 represented preference for domestic, and –1 represented preference for foreign. Thus, a positive mean indicates a domestic preference.

Results

I used the mixed-model approach to test the hypothesis that each mean was 0. (The model had only an intercept and the two usual random effects.) Table 2 shows the results for all variables of primary interest.

Again, subjects wanted to give priority to foreign risks, even when the instructions emphasized (and repeated on every page) that the outcomes were equally bad, and even when they thought that, on the average, the foreign risk affected no more people. (Note the nonsignificant but negative value for people affected in Table 2.)

Two protective methods were favored more for foreign than domestic risks: banning the product and self-protection. Perhaps these two are distinguished from others because they seem not to involve government expenditures or forced expenditures of domestic businesses. It may seem wrong to force spending "our" money on protection against foreign risks. Of course, enforcing a ban is also costly, and so is foregoing foreign products if they are otherwise preferable; however, these costs may be less obvious.

Regardless of the origin of the product, subjects favored information provision over more paternalistic approaches in which the consumer was unable to choose.

Table 2. Mean Responses (F-D Difference) in Terms of Bias Toward Domestic

Variable	Mean F-D Difference	MCMC p-level	Mean Sum
Priority	.072	.0098	
Worry	.054	n.s.	
Number of people affected	−.048	n.s.	
Ban	.128	.0001	1.78
Fine	.023	n.s.	2.15
Provide information	.010	n.s.	2.44
Inspect	.015	n.s.	2.06
Government inspect	−.022	n.s.	1.77
Self-protect	.116	.0001	1.92

Abbreviations: F-D: foreign-domestic; MCMC: Markov chain Monte Carlo sampling; n.s.: not significant.

Note: The F-D scale used runs from 0, as neutrality, to 1, as complete bias. The rightmost column shows the mean endorsement of each type of protective measure, ignoring foreign or domestic, on a 0–3 scale.

Experiment 4: Product Risks

Experiment 4 further explored subjects' attitudes about who should pay for needed inspections. It used the same items as Experiment 3, plus "toys painted with lead-based paint," which were either from China or domestic.

Method and Results

The study was completed by 79 subjects, ranging in age from 26 to 72, with the median age 44, of whom 19 percent were male.

The first question about priority was the same as in Experiment 3. The rest were as follows, with the options "Inappropriate, OK, Good, Excellent" used for questions about payment, scaled as 0–3, and "Unfair, Somewhat fair, Very fair" for fairness, scaled as 0–2. The means on the 0–3 or 0–2 scales are shown after each item.

- Suppose that someone had to pay for inspection of these products. The inspection would largely eliminate the risk. How appropriate is each of the following as a source of funds for the inspection of F?
  ○ The foreign government of the country that produced the product (1.10)
  ○ The government of your country, the importer (2.15)
  ○ The foreign producer of the product (1.60)

- ○ The domestic importer of the product (2.41)
- ○ The domestic seller of the product (1.70)
- How appropriate is each of the following as a source of funds for the inspection of D?
  - ○ The government of your country (1.35)
  - ○ The producer of the product (1.95)
  - ○ The seller of the product (2.38)
- How fair is it for each of the following groups to pay for inspection of F?
  - ○ The citizens of the producing country (through taxes) (1.43)
  - ○ The producers (owners and workers) in the producing country (through lower pay or reduced investment income) (1.06)
  - ○ The citizens of your country (through taxes) (1.63)
  - ○ The people in your country who buy the product (through higher prices) (0.59)
- How fair is it for each of the following groups to pay for inspection of D?
  - ○ The citizens of your country (through taxes) (0.95)
  - ○ The producers (owners and workers) in your country (through lower pay or reduced investment income) (0.85)
  - ○ The people in your country who buy the product (through higher prices) (1.55)

Of interest is the difference between the fairness ratings for the buyers of domestic products (1.55) and foreign products (0.59; p = .001 for the difference). The same result was found for the sellers paying for domestic products versus foreign products (1.70; p = .001).

Alternately, subjects thought it was fair for their own citizens to pay through taxes for inspections of foreign products (1.63), but not for inspections of domestic products (0.95; p = .001). The same result was found for willingness to have their own government pay for foreign inspections (2.15 vs. 1.35, p = .001).

These results are inconsistent if we think that the role of government is mainly to provide goods that serve the public interest, even for those who do not purchase them. That should not depend on where the good is made. Other factors seem to be involved. Possibly people think that the inspections will be done better if their own government pays for them.

Public Policy and Parochialism

The studies discussed in this chapter have found that Americans (and a few Canadians putting themselves in the position of Americans) are more concerned about the safety of imports than about the safety of domestic goods. This is so even when the risks are specifically equated, or are not judged to be different. Part of the reason for the concern is apparently a desire to help American workers.

Yet, foreign workers are people too, typically with jobs that are no less precarious than the jobs of Americans. Moreover, it is not as if the workers who produce the goods we consume are known to us individually, at least for the kinds of goods used in these experiments. Thus, the preference for Americans cannot be explained in terms of basic human attachments. Rather, as I have argued elsewhere, it is based in a cognitive abstraction of nationhood, an abstraction that is if anything opposed by more fundamental human feelings of empathy that arise from seeing people as individuals.

The third study suggested that parochialism expresses itself in part through a desire to ban foreign products, although other subjects favor self-protection. The last study, which limited itself to who should pay for inspections (and did not have an option of banning the import), suggested that people are willing to tax themselves and their fellow citizens to pay for inspections, even for goods that cannot reasonably be seen as serving the public good rather than the good of those who buy them. Although I did not look at trust, it is possible that people think their own government would do the best job of this, hence justifying the expense on grounds of efficiency, even though the benefits accrue only to buyers.

Finally, it is worth pointing out that the parochialism effects in these studies are not large. Many subjects, in comments, explicitly said that it did not matter to them where goods came from. In Experiment 4, for example, although the mean priority response (to the first question) was significantly positive (p = .0006, favoring domestic products), the mean was only 0.10 on a scale of –1 to 1, and 22 percent of the subjects favored foreign products, 48 percent were neutral, and 30 percent favored domestic products (usually to a greater degree than those who favored foreign, thus accounting for the mean effect). It is possible that parochial concerns rise and fall with the latest news, or with other determinants that are more like fads than rational responses to events (Loewenstein and Mather 1990).

An implication of this last possibility is that public policy should not react to public concerns of the moment, as these may change. Policies are, however, very slow to change. It may even be true that the greater trust Americans have in the U.S. government to inspect imports might yield to experience, if producers or importers proved to be trustworthy, perhaps with the help of a U.S. government certification program. Such a solution might be more economically efficient as it would put the costs of inspection on the consumers of the products in question. I am happy that so many fine grapes from Chile come into Philadelphia during our winter months. I am willing to pay more so that they are safe, and I do not see why my fellow citizens who do not share my love of grapes should pay through taxes so that I can have them all year round.

Acknowledgments

The work for this chapter was supported by a grant from the United States-Israel Binational Science Foundation to Jonathan Baron and Ilana Ritov.

Notes

1. This allowed for a test for order effects. Of primary interest, in the first two experiments, order (position in the session) did not affect any of the reported results significantly. In the third experiment, the measure of parochialism declined over the session, but it was still significant overall.

2. A possibly troublesome feature of this approach is that ordinary significance testing is problematic because the concept of "degrees of freedom" is not well defined. As recommended by Baayen et al. (2008), I estimated reliability of results using Markov chain Monte Carlo (MCMC) sampling. This samples the parameters 10,000 times using selections from their Bayesian posterior distributions (as described clearly by Kuss et al. 2005). The proportion of the 10,000 on the wrong side of 0 is taken as the p-level.

3. In theory, these should multiply to yield expected disutility, but the interaction between them was nonsignificant. The additivity of Frequency and Badness is consistent with other evidence (Gurmankin et al. 2005).

4. I mistakenly gave "usually" the same code as "never," so I collapsed the first three responses. Only "always" provided any information. Perhaps as a result, the results of this item were not worthy of reporting.

References

Baayen, R. Harald, D. J. Davidson, and D. M. Bates (2008) "Mixed-Effect Modeling with Crossed Random Effects for Subjects and Items." 59 *Journal of Memory and Language* 390–412.

Baron, Jonathan (forthcoming) "Parochialism as a Result of Cognitive Biases." In *Understanding Social Action, Promoting Human Rights*, edited by Andrew K. Woods, Ryan Goodman, and Derek Jinks. Oxford: Oxford University Press.

———. (2008) *Thinking and Deciding*, 4th ed. New York: Cambridge University Press.

———. (2001) "Confusion of Group-Interest and Self-Interest in Parochial Cooperation on Behalf of a Group." 45 *Journal of Conflict Resolution* 283–96.

———. (1996) "Do No Harm." In *Codes of Conduct: Behavioral Research into Business Ethics*, edited by David M. Messick and Ann E. Tenbrunsel. New York: Russell Sage.

Baron, Jonathan, Nicole Y. Altman, and Stephan Kroll (2005) "Parochialism and Approval Voting." 49 *Journal of Conflict Resolution* 895–907.

Baron, Jonathan, Rajeev Gowda, and Howard Kunreuther (1993) "Attitudes Toward Managing Hazardous Waste: What Should Be Cleaned Up and Who Should Pay for It?" 13 *Risk Analysis* 183–92.

Baron, Jonathan, John C. Hershey, and Howard Kunreuther (2000) "Determinants of Priority for Risk Reduction: The Role of Worry." 20 *Risk Analysis* 413–28.

Baron, Jonathan and Simon Kemp (2004) "Support for Trade Restrictions, Attitudes, and Understanding of Comparative Advantage." 25 *Journal of Economic Psychology* 565–80.

Bornstein, Gary and Meyrav Ben-Yossef (1994) "Cooperation in Intergroup and Single-Group Social Dilemmas." 30 *Journal of Experimental Social Psychology* 52–67.

Brewer, M. Susan and Charlotte J. Prestat (2002) "Consumer Attitudes Toward Food Safety Issues." 22 *Journal of Food Safety* 67–83.

Gurmankin, Levy Andrea and Jonathan Baron (2005) "How Bad Is a 10% Chance of Losing a Toe? Judgments of Probabilistic Conditions by Doctors and Laypeople." 33 *Memory and Cognition* 1399–1406.

Jervis, Robert (1976) *Perception and Misperception in International Politics.* Princeton, N.J.: Princeton University Press.

Kuss, Malte, Frank Jäkel, and Felix A. Wichmann (2005) "Bayesian Inference for Psychometric Functions." 5 *Journal of Vision* 478–92.

Loewenstein, George F. and Jane Mather (1990) "Dynamic Processes in Risk Perception." 3 *Journal of Risk and Uncertainty* 155–75.

Schwartz-Shea, Peregrine and Randy T. Simmons (1991) "Egoism, Parochialism, and Universalism." 3 *Rationality and Society* 106–32.

Slovic, Paul (1998) "Trust, Emotion, Sex, Politics, and Science: Surveying the Risk-Assessment Battlefield." In *Environment, Ethics and Behavior: The Psychology of Environmental Valuation and Degradation,* edited by Max H. Bazerman, David M. Messick, Ann E. Tenbrunsel, and Kimberly A. Wade-Benzoni. San Francisco: New Lexington Press.

U.S. Department of Agriculture (USDA) and Linda Calvin (2004) *Responses to U.S. Foodborne Illness Outbreaks Associated with Imported Produce.* Agriculture Information Bulletin 789-5. Washington, D.C.: Economic Research Service, USDA.

Wilcock, Anne, Maria Pun, Joseph Khanona, and May Aung (2004) "Consumer Attitudes, Knowledge and Behaviour: A Review of Food Safety Issues." 15 *Trends in Food Science and Technology* 55–56.

Part II
International Trade Institutions

Chapter 4
Import Safety Regulation and International Trade

Tracey Epps and Michael J. Trebilcock

In making regulatory decisions concerning import safety, governments not only have to take into consideration domestic costs and benefits, but must also consider whether their chosen measures are consistent with World Trade Organization (WTO) obligations. The risks of failing to comply with WTO rules are not trivial, due to procedures that allow member nations to request a panel to hear a complaint that another member nation (or any of its subgovernments) has violated obligations under international trade law. Nations found to have violated trade rules may ultimately be subject to significant tariffs imposed on their exports. Countries have proven willing to bring complaints about other countries' health and safety measures: at least 10 cases have been heard by a dispute panel since 1994, and over 270 trade concerns have been discussed by delegates in the WTO's committees (WTO Secretariat 2009). The prospect of WTO dispute proceedings highlights how important it is that countries ensure that any new innovations in their import safety systems are WTO compliant. WTO rules do not prevent innovation, but call for careful design and implementation to ensure that free trade is not compromised any more than necessary.

The purpose of this chapter is to explain the international trade implications of proposed reforms to improve the safety of imported products in the United States and, in doing so, to highlight issues that will also be relevant to other countries with the same or similar objectives. We begin by outlining the international trade rules against which any country's import safety measures will be evaluated in the event another country files a formal complaint. Having introduced the relevant trade rules, we turn to an analysis of several major proposals for reform of the U.S. import safety regime, highlighting those aspects that have the most potential to create barriers to imports. We pay particular attention to issues of food safety, simply to focus the discussion; however, most of the same trade issues are also relevant to other types of products.

WTO Rules Applicable to Import Safety

Overview

A central theme of international trade law is the tension between liberalizing trade and the interests of individual countries in maintaining domestic regulatory autonomy. This tension is particularly evident in the case of import safety due to a state's interest in protecting the health and safety of its citizens (Trebilcock and Soloway 2002).

Three key WTO agreements are applicable to import safety. The first, the General Agreement on Tariffs and Trade (GATT), sets out the basic legal framework for international trade in goods. The second, the Agreement on the Application of Sanitary and Phytosanitary Measures (WTO 1994a), places procedural and substantive constraints on the manner in which countries enact and maintain sanitary and phytosanitary (SPS) measures. Such measures include those designed to protect human life or health from risks arising from "additives, contaminants, toxins or disease-causing organisms in foods, beverages or feedstuffs," or from diseases carried by animals, plants, or products thereof (WTO 1994a: Annex A). Finally, the Technical Barriers to Trade (TBT) Agreement places procedural constraints on the creation of mandatory technical regulations and voluntary standards other than SPS measures.

GATT

The cornerstone of the GATT is the prevention of discrimination in trade. Article I, the most-favored-nation provision, prohibits member states from discriminating against products from one member in favor of like products from another. Article III.4, the national treatment provision, is concerned with preventing discrimination by governments against foreign importers in favor of domestic producers of like products. Countries may justify violation of these rules under Article XX(b), which allows measures "necessary" to protect human health, so long as they do not constitute a means of arbitrary or unjustifiable discrimination, or a disguised restriction on international trade (GATT 1947). Interpretation of Article XX requires dispute panels established under the WTO's Dispute Settlement Understanding (DSU) to balance the GATT's trade liberalizing objectives with members' interest in regulating to protect health. Such panels are composed of three individuals nominated by the parties or the WTO Secretariat, and their decisions may be appealed to the WTO's Appellate Body, which is a standing body of trade law experts. In seeking a balance between trade liberalization and health protection, the critical task facing dispute panels is to make a determination of "necessity," which is assessed by weighing and balancing the importance of the objective or common interest that is the target of the measure; the effectiveness of the measure at meeting the target; and the impact of the measure on international trade (WTO 2007: para. 178).

The SPS Agreement

The SPS Agreement addresses the problem that countries might enact protectionist measures under the guise of health protection. It aims to achieve a balance between maintaining a free flow of goods while ensuring that countries have the right to protect health. The agreement encourages countries to harmonize their SPS measures, and provides that measures that conform to relevant international standards are presumed to be in compliance with the agreement (WTO 1994a: art. 3.2). Relevant international standards are those developed by international organizations, such as the sanitary standards issued by the Codex Alimentarius Commission (as discussed by Büthe in chapter 5). If countries wish to introduce or maintain more stringent measures than those provided for by the relevant international standards, they must ensure that they are supported by a scientific justification (WTO 1994a: art. 3.3). Members must ensure that any such measure is "applied only to the extent necessary to protect human, animal or plant life or health, is based on scientific principles and is not maintained without sufficient scientific evidence" (WTO 1994a: art. 2.2). These provisions allow countries the freedom to choose their own substantive standards, while imposing some constraints designed to prevent the use of standards for protectionist purposes.

Scientific justification is subject to Article 5.1, which states that members must show that their SPS measures are "based on an assessment, as appropriate to the circumstances, of the risks to human, animal or plant life or health, taking into account the risk assessment techniques developed by the relevant international organizations" (WTO 1994a). Further, Article 5.2 requires the risk assessment to take into account "available scientific evidence," along with relevant processes and production methods; relevant inspection, sampling and testing methods; prevalence of specific diseases or pests; existence of pest- or disease-free areas; relevant ecological and environmental conditions; and quarantine or other treatment. Once scientific evidence has established the presence of a risk, Article 5.3 recognizes the right of members to set their appropriate level of protection.

Under Article 4, members are required to accept other members' SPS measures as equivalent, even if these measures differ from their own or from other members trading in the same product, if the exporting member "objectively demonstrates" to the importing member that its measures achieve the importing member's appropriate level of SPS protection.

Several general obligations should also be noted. The SPS Agreement recognizes that discrimination may be necessary where goods from one source pose a greater risk than those from others. Article 2.3 nevertheless requires member states to ensure that any discrimination is not arbitrary or unjustifiable and that measures are not "applied in a manner which would constitute a disguised restriction on international trade." This provision is linked to Article 5.5, which requires members to avoid arbitrary or unjustifiable distinctions in the levels of SPS protection considered appropriate in different situations, if such distinctions result in discrimination or a disguised restriction on international trade. A violation of Article 5.5 is likely, by implication, to constitute a violation of Article 2.2 (WTO 1998a: para. 246). The object of these provisions is to detect regulatory inconsistencies at the national level that may indicate unnecessarily maintained SPS regulations and possible disguised trade protection (Quick and Bluthner 1999: 620).

Article 5.4 provides that members should, when determining the appropriate level of SPS protection, take into account the objective of minimizing negative trade effects. This is a "best efforts" clause that does not impose an actual obligation. However, Article 5.6 obliges members to ensure that SPS measures are "not more trade-restrictive than required to achieve their appropriate level of sanitary or phytosanitary protection, taking into account technical and economic feasibility" (WTO 1994a). The footnote to Article 5.6 provides further that there must be no other SPS measure that is reasonably available, taking into account technical and economic feasibility, that achieves the member's appropriate level of protection, and is significantly less restrictive to trade than the SPS measure contested. WTO dispute panels are required to assess the impacts of alternative policies on trade, administrative difficulties, and resource costs associated with alternative policies, and the regulatory efficacy of those policies (Sykes 2003: 419).

The same measure may give rise to a claim that it violates both the SPS Agreement and the GATT. In such a case, a panel is required to examine the measure first against the more specific rules of the SPS Agreement and then consider the more general provisions of the GATT

(Trebilcock and Howse 2005: 207). A measure that relates to health and safety but does not qualify as an SPS measure may nevertheless fall afoul of the GATT or the TBT Agreement if it violates the relevant obligations.

The TBT Agreement

Mandatory technical regulations and voluntary standards covered by the TBT Agreement include matters such as specifications for products or related process and production methods (e.g., ingredients, labeling, marketing, packaging, size, dimension, weight, design, or function). Such matters are often considered to relate to issues of quality. However, as suggested by Lorna Zach and Vicki Bier in chapter 8, safety issues are a subcategory of quality issues, and it is therefore relevant to consider the TBT Agreement here.

The TBT Agreement requires that, with respect to technical regulations, imported products be accorded treatment "no less favorable" than that accorded to like domestic products (WTO 1994b: art. 2.1). Article 2.2 requires members to ensure that technical regulations "are not prepared, adopted or applied with a view to or with the effect of creating unnecessary obstacles to international trade." The agreement also encourages harmonization, stating that technical regulations should be based on international standards where they exist unless to do so would be an ineffective or inappropriate means of fulfilling the legitimate objective pursued. With respect to voluntary standards, governments must ensure that their central standardizing bodies accept and comply with the Code of Good Practice set out in Annex 3 of the agreement.

Import Safety Reform Proposals Under International Trade Rules

Overview

Chapter 1 of this book highlighted some of the recent, highly publicized scandals in the United States arising from imported products. It is worth noting trends relating to food imports in particular. Safety problems with imported food are expected to grow as U.S. food imports increase (GAO 2008: 6). Currently, approximately 15 percent of the overall U.S. food supply is imported, with the figure significantly higher for some foodstuffs—approximately 60 percent of fruit and vegetables are imported, as is 75 percent of seafood (FDA 2007: 8). Further, the type of foods that are imported is changing. In the past, a greater percentage of imported foodstuffs consisted of unprocessed ingredients that were processed in the United States, where they were subject to FDA regulations. Today, however, a larger percentage of imported foods are ready-to-eat products, fresh produce, or seafood (FDA 2007: 8). These products tend to present a greater risk of food-borne illness (GAO 2008: 1).

In response to the challenges facing the U.S. import safety system, President George W. Bush established the Interagency Working Group on Import Safety (IWGIS) in July 2007. The IWGIS produced an action plan and strategic framework for import safety later that year (IWGIS 2007a, 2007b). In addition, the FDA released its Food Protection Plan, which was integrated with the IWGIS's action plan and addresses domestic and imported food products. More recently, President Barack Obama has called for more stringent regulation of import food safety, announcing the formation of a Cabinet-level food safety working group (Reuters 2009). Also, at least two bills dealing with food safety (including imports) were introduced in Congress in early 2009 (FDA/FSMA 2009; FSMA 2009).

A review of these proposals reveals four broad trends in proposals for addressing import safety problems: a move toward a risk-based preventative approach; greater involvement of the private sector through corporate responsibility for import safety; use of third-party certification of facilities in foreign countries; and implementation of good importer practices.

Risk-Based Prevention

Proposals for a risk-based preventative approach would ensure that products are monitored at high-risk phases throughout their life cycle. The IWGIS's Strategic Framework, for example, refers to a "paradigm shift" from "viewing a 'snapshot' of the product at the border to achieving a real-time 'video' across the product's import life cycle at the most appropriate points of production and distribution" (IWGIS 2007b: 11). This approach is also reflected in legislation introduced in the U.S. Congress by Senator Richard J. Durbin (D-IL), which would require preventative planning by all food processing facilities (FDA/FSMA 2009: sec. 103). Advantages of a risk-based preventative approach are highlighted by Lorna Zach and Vicki Bier in chapter 8, although the enormous variety of consumer products may make it difficult to apply risk-based regulation in all contexts.

Focusing on risk prevention involves identifying and managing risk at critical points along the import life cycle (IWGIS 2007b: 14). Various quality management systems may be used, the most well known of which is Hazard Analysis and Critical Control Points (HACCP), which the U.S. government currently mandates for fish and seafood products, juice processing and packaging, and meat and poultry plants. HACCP systems address safety hazards that can be introduced at different points in the production process, identifying risks at the points they are most likely to occur—such as time and temperature requirements for cooking—and targeting application of controls at those critical points (IWGIS 2007b: 15; Unnevehr 2000: 469).

As suggested by Richard Berk in chapter 7, border inspections may also be targeted and risk-based. Inspections and testing could focus on those imports that are forecasted to pose the greatest risk to public health, which can mean that imports arriving from firms located in certain countries could be singled out for greater scrutiny, or even refused entry, if those countries had safety problems in the past (FDA 2007: 12–15).

As attractive as a risk-based system may be, it presents opportunities for discriminatory measures that may violate the GATT's national treatment principle. A violation of Article III.4 may occur when foreign products are treated less favorably than like domestic products (or a violation of Article I, if some foreign producers are treated less favorably than others). Such discrimination may occur on a de facto basis—that is, while on its face the same requirement may apply to both foreign and domestic products, if its effect is to treat the foreign product less favorably, then GATT principles can be violated. This might occur, for example, when producers are required to follow HACCP guidelines that would in reality impose greater costs on the foreign producers. This would be particularly likely when HACCP is applied to smaller producers with less ability to absorb increased costs. In a recent study of the implications of U.S. HACCP requirements for seafood products, Anders and Caswell (2007: 1) found that processors in exporting countries were often unfamiliar with many elements of HACCP. They also found that imposing HACCP requirements can have a negative effect, particularly on developing country exporters, who may deflect export flows to other countries because of the increased compliance costs in the United States, which then deprives them of their comparative advantage. From the U.S. perspective, importers may choose not to buy from developing countries if their safety levels are lower overall and harder to verify (Anders and Caswell 2007: 1).

Violations of GATT Article III.4 may also occur if foreign producers are explicitly subjected to stricter risk-based requirements than those applied to domestic producers. Such violations may occur when foreign producers must comply with certain HACCP guidelines even though domestic producers have a choice of following those guidelines or complying with domestic law, or when stricter penalties are applied to importers than to domestic producers.

Until proposals are finalized and laws and regulations passed, it is not clear how implementation of an HACCP requirement might work—whether, for example, it would be a performance standard under which regulators would require producers to develop and implement an HACCP plan but without specifying its elements in detail, or whether it would be a process standard whereby regulators specify particular elements for given products, such as chilling temperatures in meat processing plants (Caswell and Hooker 1996: 776). HACCP may be more likely to create a trade barrier if it were based on practices common within the United States and required foreign producers to meet the same standards regardless of their circumstances or context.

Of course, even if a measure violates the GATT's national treatment principle, it may be justified under Article XX(b), provided the regulating country can show that the measure is necessary. For example, a U.S. regulation that subjected imported goods to a special procedure whereby allegedly patent-infringing imports were banned from entry into the United States was found to violate Article III.4, but the GATT panel also considered whether the ban was necessary (GATT Panel Report 1989). In asking whether this measure was necessary under Article XX(d), the panel looked to practices in other countries and found that the U.S. ban was not necessary because many other countries granted to their civil courts jurisdiction over patent claims involving imported products manufactured abroad—just as the United States provided for patent claims involving domestic products.

In the current context, an argument might be made that mandating HACCP or other quality management systems is not necessary because the proposed systems are ineffective when used domestically in the United States and therefore cannot be considered necessary under Article XX. While supportive of the concept of risk-based regulation, Lorna Zach and Vicki Bier also acknowledge in chapter 8 that knowledge gaps may negatively impact the effectiveness of risk-based regulation and that it is best used where the science is mature, and cause and effect relationships are well understood. Their analysis supports the use of risk-based prevention but also suggests that it may not be equally effective in all cases. Yet, even if the effectiveness of risk-based approaches to regulation is uncertain, a dispute panel adjudicating a complaint would have to weigh this uncertainty against the importance of the objective and level of trade restrictiveness. The United States could argue in response that any alternatives to risk targeting, such as inspecting all imports, would be enormously expensive and nearly impossible to implement in any effective manner, as the editors of this book suggested in their introduction. In the end, the general concept of a risk-based preventative import safety system may be defensible under GATT

Article XX—but the devil will be in the details. The possibility of various different methods of implementing HACCP requirements or other risk-based approaches makes it difficult to reach a general conclusion about their permissibility under trade rules (Orriss and Whitehead 2000: 347).

A country seeking to justify trade-restrictive measures under Article XX(b) must also show that its measures do not constitute arbitrary or unjustifiable discrimination, or a disguised restriction on international trade. An HACCP system that imposed detailed requirements and actual risk levels to be achieved would give countries little flexibility in terms of actions required for compliance. Such absence of flexibility may lead to an argument that the measures constitute arbitrary or unjustifiable discrimination. In the *United States-Shrimp* case, for example, U.S. measures aimed at protecting turtles required exporters of shrimp to use "turtle excluder devices" (WTO 1998b). These measures failed to pass the Article XX test because the panel found it arbitrary and unjustifiable to require other countries to implement exactly the same regulatory measures as the United States did, even though their circumstances may be unique and not require such measures to protect turtles. In the import safety and HACCP context, much would depend on the conditions in question. Arguably, the nature of food pathogens would justify certain standardized rules such as those relating to clean surfaces and refrigeration. However, where farming and manufacturing processes vary, so may the appropriate standards. Likewise, different environmental factors may augur for different standards in different countries. For this reason, HACCP requirements that provide flexibility, allowing importers to design systems that are appropriate for their particular circumstances, may lead both to better public policy outcomes as well as to a reduced risk of trade violations.

Similar issues may arise under Article 2.1 of the TBT Agreement, which, as was noted earlier, applies the national treatment rule to technical regulations and voluntary standards. Types of risk-based preventative regulations that may be covered by the TBT Agreement include design specifications for toys, labeling of genetically modified ingredients in food products, or requirements for a particular method of vacuum packaging.

The establishment of a risk-based preventative system may also raise questions under the SPS Agreement (Unnevehr 2000: 236). Where requirements impede trade, importing countries may argue under Article 5.6 that they are more trade restrictive than necessary and that the United States has failed under Article 5.4 to "minimize negative trade effects." Countries may also challenge an HACCP requirement on the grounds that it is not "necessary" as required by Article 2.2, relying on similar arguments as might be developed pursuant to GATT Article XX(b).

Detailed requirements under management systems such as HACCP might also be challenged under the SPS Agreement's Article 2.2 requirement that SPS measures must be based on scientific principles and must not be maintained without sufficient scientific evidence. Any such challenge will be dependent on the nature of the requirements and will not always be straightforward. Orriss and Whitehead (2000: 348) note many uncertainties in the HACCP system, such as the fact that there is often inadequate information about the levels of microbiological contamination at different segments of any given food chain and controversy as to what constitutes a hazard. The SPS Agreement does not specify what is meant by "scientific principles" and this term has not been elucidated in the jurisprudence. However, it is likely that the United States would be challenged if a trading partner believed that it had failed to obtain its scientific evidence by way of methods generally accepted as being scientifically credible (Epps 2008: ch. 11).

Where an HACCP system sets process standards, the SPS Agreement requires that the risks that are being controlled first be identified through a risk assessment that evaluates the potential for adverse effects on human health arising from the presence of additional contaminants, toxins, or disease-causing organisms in food, beverages, or feedstuffs (WTO 1994a: Annex A[4]). Such risks must be real; for example, public fears of products cannot alone justify SPS measures aimed at those products—there must be some credible basis in science. However, the WTO Appellate Body will accept a risk assessment even if its conclusions reflect a minority scientific opinion, so long as that opinion is credible. Once a risk assessment has been conducted, the resulting policy measure (such as HACCP) must be "based on" that assessment. In other words, there must be a rational or objective relationship observable between the measure and the risk assessment (WTO 1998c).

The WTO Appellate Body has not fully defined what its rational or objective relationship requirement demands; it will be determined on a case-by-case basis depending on the particular circumstances of the case (WTO 1999). This is a fairly flexible standard. The SPS Agreement does not specify what level of risk is required, and thus a fairly minor risk might be addressed (whether low probability of harm, or not very serious harm). However, the less likely the risk or the less serious the probable harm identified, the more likely that less-trade-restrictive alternatives may be reasonably available. It would be prudent to assume that: (1) any measure must be appropriate to the particular product and processing environment in question; and (2) the relationship must be rational from the perspective of a reputable scientist who may be more or less risk-averse. Thus, if there is, for example, a mandated requirement for certain temperature and humidity controls in storing fruit, there must be scientific evidence of the risk caused by failing to implement such controls. In the *Japan-Apples* dispute, the WTO Appellate Body held that Japan failed to adduce sufficient scientific evidence for the imposition of various requirements for orchard inspections and a postharvest chlorine treatment (WTO 2003).

An important question in any SPS dispute is what standard of review a panel should apply when reviewing a country's scientific evidence. Should it have freedom to substitute its own scientific view for that of the risk assessor in the regulating country, or should it take a deferential approach that only seeks to determine whether the risk assessment is supported by coherent reasoning and respectable scientific evidence and is, in that sense, objectively justifiable? The Appellate Body has recently adopted the latter view (WTO 2008), but it remains to be seen exactly how panels will approach future reviews in the light of this decision. Regulating authorities can likely expect panels at least to examine the methods used in their risk assessments to determine whether the evidence available justifies the conclusions reached.

The question of equivalence will also be important. How would the United States determine equivalence among HACCP or other quality management systems in different countries? The uncertainties and inconsistencies associated with such systems—such as how to identify critical control points—will likely make it difficult to determine equivalence (Oriss and Whitehead 2000: 348). Indeed, past experience under the SPS Agreement has shown that even when countries have similar levels of technical capacity, there are significant administrative burdens in evaluating equivalence (Orden and Roberts 2007: 111). Further, practice has shown that developing countries may not have the technical capacity to demonstrate that their SPS measures meet the importing member's standards. Article 4 of the SPS Agreement may thus have more validity between equal (developed) countries than for the developing world (Swinbank 1999: 330).

Private Sector Involvement

The IWGIS (2007b: 11, 22) suggests that the public and private sectors should work together to identify risks and that the private sector must take a lead role in strengthening import safety. The Strategic Framework and the FDA's Food Protection Plan would require producers and importers to implement preventative approaches and promote corporate responsibility by requiring the same from their suppliers, while the Durbin bill would require importers to perform various risk-based foreign supplier verification activities (FDA/FSMA 2009: sec. 805). This emphasis on corporate responsibility could lead to increased use of standards designed and promulgated by private parties such as supermarkets or trade associations (GMA 2007), as discussed in chapter 12 by Errol Meidinger.

The prospect of increased private sector involvement in import safety raises the question of whether the standards are subject to WTO rules. The GATT and the SPS Agreement are arguably not applicable to private standards, while the TBT Agreement is only applicable insofar as regulations are enacted by nongovernmental bodies with legal power to enforce a technical regulation. The definition of SPS measures in Annex A(1) refers to "all relevant laws, decrees, regulations, requirements and procedures." These words are not defined in the agreement, but cases considering similar phrasing in the GATT suggest that the phrase is to be read narrowly, and that many private standards would not meet the definition because there is not a sufficient nexus between the standards and any government action such that the government can be held responsible for the standards (WTO 1997: paras. 5.33–5.36; WTO 1998d: paras. 10.373–10.377; WTO 2000: para. 10.107; WTO 2001: para. 7.184; see also Epps 2009).

Nevertheless, much would depend on the actual measures implemented. If government could be seen as having deliberately "outsourced" the task of standard-setting to the private sector, a WTO dispute panel may be more willing to find the requisite "nexus" between the standards and government action. A strong legislative mandate for the private sector to undertake certain tasks, for example, would likely create such a nexus.

There are potential dangers in private standards. If unregulated by the WTO, standard-setting entities may be captured by domestic producer groups that would like to establish standards that would give them a competitive advantage. However, their inclusion under the WTO's jurisdiction would upset the balance of interests achieved by the SPS Agreement's negotiators, namely, the balance between liberal trade values and domestic regulatory autonomy. Application of the rules to privately developed standards would impose more restrictions on domestic activities than the negotiators intended (Stewart 2003: 707; Trebilcock and Howse 2005).

Third-Party Certification

Third-party certification would facilitate the verification of foreign producers or products for compliance with U.S. standards and is a feature of the legislation introduced by Senator Durbin as well as similar food safety reform legislation introduced in the U.S. House of Representatives by Congresswoman Rosa L. DeLauro (D-CT). The IWGIS's action plan would identify high-risk products and subject them to mandatory certification, while other products would be subject to voluntary certification programs. It would use incentives to motivate voluntary participation, such as expedited processing at U.S. ports of entry.

Identification of high-risk products must be in accordance with the SPS Agreement and will require a risk assessment based on a sound scientific methodology. The SPS Agreement does not set any quantitative threshold as to the level of risk, but the more severe the risk, either in terms of probability or harm caused, the more readily measures will satisfy the Article 5.6 test of not being more trade restrictive than necessary (Sykes 2003: 419).

In 2009, the FDA released a guidance document with respect to voluntary third-party certification programs for food and feeds (FDA 2009) that supports the use of voluntary certification programs as one means to ensure products meet U.S. standards. The document is not binding but "represents the current thinking" of the U.S. Department of Agriculture, FDA, and other relevant agencies (FDA 2009). The document sets out the attributes that the FDA believes a certification program should have in order to provide quality verification of product safety. These include matters such as qualifications and training for auditors, elements of an effective audit program, and quality assurance programs. If the FDA has confidence in a certification program, it may choose to recognize the program, thus acknowledging that certification is a reliable reflection that the foods from an establishment certified under that program meet applicable FDA requirements (FDA 2009: sec. I). The document highlights potential advantages for producers participating in a certification program, including that the FDA may take into consideration an establishment's product-specific certification when determining its establishment inspection priorities, as well as entry admissibility decisions. The FDA may also take into consideration certification when determining "may proceed" rates for imported products, which may expedite entry for certain product types from particular establishments.

The concept of third-party certification has provoked trade concerns. In comments submitted on the draft FDA guidance document in October 2008, the European Commission (EC) argued that the FDA's proposed guidance may violate the GATT's national treatment rule by treating foreign suppliers less favorably than domestic U.S. suppliers. This argument is based on several key factors. First, the Commission argued that the guidance would de facto apply to businesses in foreign countries rather than U.S. domestic facilities, and therefore would be discriminatory (Maier 2008: 1–2). U.S. domestic businesses already have to comply with domestic U.S. food laws and thus would have little incentive to seek third-party certification. Foreign producers and importers, on the other hand, would have to choose between obtaining third-party certification (with all its attendant costs) or facing delays and detentions in entry clearance. Put simply, market access would cost foreign producers more than domestic producers.

Second, the Commission submitted that the scope of the proposed voluntary measures (e.g., HACCP systems, crisis management plans, and traceability systems) would go far beyond levels of protection required by U.S. domestic laws (Maier 2008: 2). In doing so, the draft guidance would discriminate against foreign producers that may have little choice but to comply with those voluntary measures. Not only would the requirements exceed those in place domestically, they would require businesses to have "available documentation for all ingredients 'all the way back'—basically to the very plot of production," causing organizational difficulties disproportionate to the safety gains (Maier 2008: 2).

Third, with respect to European products, the Commission argued that it appears from the guidance document that the FDA would not take account of European inspection systems and regulatory control. Instead, it would require European businesses to subject themselves to "an additional, essentially redundant, layer of third party inspection in order to qualify for expedited entry into the United States" (Maier 2008: 3).

The EC's concerns are as yet untested, but they provide an indication of the types of issues that may arise with reliance on third-party certification. This does not mean that the concept is fatally flawed; the key will be in ensuring that foreign producers are not treated less favorably than domestic producers (GATT 1947: art. III). This will require a close comparison of U.S. rules that are applicable to domestic producers and the rules that are proposed for foreign producers.

Good Importer Practices

Good Importer Practices (GIP) are related to the concept of third-party certification, as they would be verified through private sector-based programs. In 2008, the FDA released a guidance document with respect to GIP that provides recommendations to importers on "possible practices and procedures they may like to follow to increase the likelihood the products they import comply with applicable U.S. safety and security requirements" (FDA 2008). The guidance document anticipates an advantage for importers that follow the recommendations. As these importers "may be less likely to import products that may be harmful to U.S. consumers," the government "may, in some cases, facilitate admissibility determinations, and, therefore, expedite the entry of their products into the United States" (FDA 2008: 4).

The GIP recommendations or similar guidelines would impact directly on the way in which foreign businesses operate and the likelihood of their gaining access to the U.S. market. Some practices may impose costs on foreign producers that are higher than costs faced by domestic producers (e.g., costs of certification or licensing). They may impose process and production methods on foreign producers that they may not have otherwise adopted (e.g., implementing HACCP, record-keeping, sampling, and testing). They may also cause some producers to be favored over others (the recommendation to consider purchasing from certified firms). Where foreign producers are treated less favorably than domestic U.S. producers, there may be a violation of GATT Article III.4, subject to justification under Article XX. Whenever producers from some countries are favored over others, concerns will also arise in relation to the most-favored-nation principle in GATT Article I.

Labeling

Other options for consumer protection include labeling and other right-to-know measures that let consumers assess risk through purchasing decisions. These could include country-of-origin labeling, or labeling to indicate that a product has been refused entry into the United States. As benign as these requirements may seem, labeling laws do carry burdens on producers, such as the cost of preparation. Conformity of any labeling regime with the GATT and TBT Agreements will depend on whether it imposes a burden on foreign producers compared to domestic producers of like products, or otherwise treats them less favorably. Problems may arise, for example, if a scheme implementing country of origin (or other) labels is implemented in such a way as to give consumers the impression that the foreign products must be riskier than domestic products or else they would not be labeled as such. Labeling may also play into people's biases and fears, such as the tendency noted by Jonathan Baron in chapter 3 for people to want to protect parochial interests, such as their own nation's workers.

Making the Rules Work

The safety of imported food is arguably subject to greater scrutiny by the WTO than other types of products. This is because of the SPS Agreement's requirements that not only must measures be the least trade restrictive available, but also that they be based on scientific evidence and a risk assessment. Regulation of other, nonfood consumer products where SPS measures are not involved must only comply with the GATT and the TBT Agreement. The cornerstone of the GATT is the principle of nondiscrimination, requiring that member states not discriminate among foreign producers of like products or treat foreign producers less favorably than domestic producers of like products. The TBT Agreement also prohibits discrimination and otherwise imposes slightly less stringent requirements than the SPS Agreement. Recent U.S. proposals offer innovative approaches to the problem of import safety and, in principle, they could be made compatible with these trade agreements. However, there are a number of areas to which careful attention must be paid to ensure compliance, including efforts to demonstrate the necessity of new regulations and to ensure that they do not operate with discriminatory effect.

With respect to each of the proposals discussed, the details and manner of application will require close scrutiny to ensure compliance with the various obligations to which nations are bound under trade law. In almost every case, regardless of whether the subject of regulation is a food or another type of product, it will be important for the United States—or any other country contemplating similar measures—to ensure that there is no other reasonably available measure that achieves its appropriate level of protection and is significantly less restrictive of trade than the measure contested.

With respect to a risk-based preventative system, any requirements imposed on foreign producers must be flexible enough to allow those producers to implement systems appropriate to their specific circumstances. The blanket imposition of a system used in the United States without consideration for those circumstances is likely to be problematic.

With respect to third-party certification and good importer practices, it will be critical to scrutinize the effect of the requirements put in place to ensure that foreign producers are not disadvantaged. Simply because a scheme is voluntary does not mean that it does not have the potential to discriminate.

Increasing the role of the private sector raises fundamental issues for the international trading system. To avoid undermining the liberal trading system by private standards that are vulnerable to capture by protectionist interests, it is preferable that governments act to regulate import safety standards themselves so that they can be judged pursuant to WTO rules. Alternatively, governments should set clear guidelines for the private sector to ensure that their standards do not undermine trade.

Compliance with WTO rules is desirable on various levels. First, and most obviously, it avoids potential claims of violation by trading partners, and the attendant costs of defending such claims. Second, compliance benefits exporters who seek access to foreign markets. In theory unilateral trade liberalization is beneficial, but political realities diverge from theory. If a country is perceived to be raising barriers to entry to its market, this increases the likelihood that other countries will respond by imposing (possibly protectionist) barriers to their markets. In the United States, agricultural product exporters already complain of the extensive nontariff barriers they face in foreign markets (U.S. Trade Representative 2009). Unilateral action by the United States that restricts imports may lead to an increase in these kinds of measures; it is therefore in the interests of U.S. exporters to ensure compliance with the rules. Finally, compliance with WTO rules is desirable from a systemic perspective. The field of import safety regulation presents multiple opportunities for countries to disguise trade barriers as health or safety measures. This is not in the interests of the multilateral trading system. Any major participant in this system—particularly the United States—bears a responsibility for ensuring continuing commitment to a rules-based system of international trade.

References

Anders, Sven M. and Julie Caswell (2007) "Standards-as-Barriers Versus Standards-as-Catalysts: Assessing the Impact of HACCP Implementation on U.S. Seafood Imports." Working Paper, Department of Resource Economics, University of Massachusetts, Amherst, July.

Caswell, Julie A. and Neal H. Hooker (1996) "HACCP as an International Trade Standard." 78 *American Journal of Agricultural Economics* 775–79.

Epps, Tracey (2009) "Demanding Perfection: Private Food Standards and the SPS Agreement." In *International Economic Law and National Autonomy,* edited by Meredith Lewis and Susy Frankel. Cambridge: Cambridge University Press.

———. (2008) *International Trade and Health Protection: A Critical Assessment of the WTO's SPS Agreement.* Cheltenham, UK: Edward Elgar.

Grocery Manufacturers Association (GMA) (2007) "A Commitment to Consumers to Ensure the Safety of Imported Foods: Four Pillars of Public-Private Partnership." http://bipac.net/gma/Four_Pillars_Combined_FINAL.pdf.

Interagency Working Group on Import Safety (IWGIS) (2007a) *Action Plan for Import Safety.* Washington, D.C.: IWGIS.

———. (2007b) *Protecting American Consumers Every Step of the Way: A Strategic Framework for Continual Improvement in Import Safety: A Report to the President.* Washington, D.C.: IWGIS.

Maier, Wolf (2008) *Comments of the EU Commission on the FDA Draft Guidance Document on Voluntary Third Party Certification Programs for Foods and Feeds.* Docket FDA-2008-D-0381, October 13. http://www.regulations.gov/fdmspublic/ContentViewer?objectId=090000648076356b&disposition=attachment&contentType=msw8.

Orden, David and Donna Roberts (2007) "Food Regulation and Trade Under the WTO: Ten Years in Perspective." 37 *Agricultural Economics* 103–18.

Orriss, Gregory D. and Anthony J. Whitehead (2000) "Hazard Analysis and Critical Control Point (HACCP) as a Part of an Overall Quality Assurance System in International Food Trade." 11 *Food Control* 345–51.

Quick, Reinhard and Andreas Bluthner (1999) "Has the Appellate Body Erred? An Appraisal and Criticism of the Ruling in the WTO Hormones Case." 2 *Journal of International Economic Law* 603–40.

Reuters (2009) "Obama Picks Food and Drug Chief." *Financial Times. FT.com*, March 14.

Stewart, Terence P. (1993) *GATT Uruguay Round: A Negotiating History (1986–1992)*, vol. 1, *Commentary*. Boston: Kluwer Law International.

Swinbank, Alan (1999) "The Role of the WTO and the International Agencies in SPS Standard Setting." 15 *Agribusiness* 323–33.

Sykes, Alan O. (2003) "The Least Restrictive Means." 70 *University of Chicago Law Review* 403–20.

Trebilcock, Michael J. and Robert Howse (2005) *The Regulation of International Trade*, 3rd ed. London: Routledge.

Trebilcock, Michael J. and Julie Soloway (2002) "International Policy and Domestic Food Safety Regulation: The Case for Substantial Deference by the WTO Dispute Settlement Body Under the SPS Agreement." In *The Political Economy of International Trade: Essays in Honor of Robert E. Hudec*, edited by Daniel L. M. Kennedy and James D. Southwick. Cambridge: Cambridge University Press.

Unnevehr, Laurian J. (2000) "Food Safety Issues and Fresh Food Product Exports from LDCs." 23 *Agricultural Economics* 231–40.

U.S. Food and Drug Administration (FDA) (2009) *Guidance for Industry: Voluntary Third-Party Certification Programs for Foods and Feeds, Draft Guidance*. Washington, D.C.: FDA.

———. (2008) *Guidance for Industry: Good Importer Practices, Draft Guidance*. Washington, D.C.: FDA.

———. (2007) *Food Protection Plan: An Integrated Strategy for Protecting the Nation's Food Supply*. Washington, D.C.: FDA.

U.S. Government Accountability Office (GAO) (2008) *Federal Oversight of Food Safety: FDA's Food Protection Plan Proposes Positive First Steps, But Capacity to Carry Them Out Is Critical*. GAO-07-785T. Washington, D.C.: GAO.

U.S. Trade Representative (2009) *2009 National Trade Estimate Report on Trade Barriers*. Washington, D.C.: Office of the U.S. Trade Representative.

World Trade Organization Secretariat (WTO Secretariat), Committee on Sanitary and Phytosanitary Measures (2009) *Specific Trade Concerns*. G/SPS/GEN/204/Rev9. February 5. Geneva: WTO.

Cases Cited

GATT Panel Report, *United States Section 337 of the Tariff Act of 1930* (1989), L/6439, BISD 36S/345 (November).

World Trade Organization (WTO). *Canada—Measures Concerning Periodicals (Canada-Periodicals)* (1997). WT/DS31/R (Panel Report).

———. *Australia—Measures Affecting Importation of Salmon (Australia-Salmon)* (1998a). WT/DS18/AB/R (Appellate Body Report).

———. *United States—Import Prohibition of Shrimp and Certain Shrimp Products (United States-Shrimp)* (1998b) WT/DS58/AB/R (Appellate Body Report).

———. *European Communities—Measures Concerning Meat and Meat Products (Hormones)* (1998c). WT/DS48/R (Appellate Body Report).

———. *Japan—Measures Affecting Consumer Photographic Film and Paper (Japan-Consumer Photographic Film and Paper)* (1998d). WT/DS44/R (Panel Report).

———. *Japan—Measures Affecting Agricultural Products* (1999). WT/DS76/AB/R (Appellate Body Report).

———. *Canada—Certain Measures Affecting the Automotive Industry (Canada-Automotive Industry)* (2000). WT/DS139/R, WT/DS142/R (Panel Report).

———. *India—Measures Affecting the Automotive Industry (India-Automotive Industry)* (2001). WT/DS146/R, WT/DS175/R (Panel Report).

———. *Japan—Measures Affecting the Importation of Apples (Japan-Apples)* (2003). WT/DS245/AB/R (Appellate Body Report).

———. *Brazil—Measures Affecting Imports of Retreaded Tires (Brazil-Retreaded Tires)* (2007). WT/DS322/R (Panel Report).

———. *United States—Continued Suspension of Obligations in the EC-Hormones Dispute (United States-Hormones Dispute)* (2008). WT/DS320/AB/R (Appellate Body Report).

Legislation and Agreements Cited

FDA Food Safety Modernization Act (FDA/FSMA) (2009) S. 510, 111th Cong. (Bill introduced by Sen. Richard Durbin, March 3, 2009).

Food Safety Modernization Act of 2009 (FSMA) (2009) H.R. 875, 111th Cong. (Bill introduced by Rep. Rosa DeLauro, April 2, 2009).

General Agreement on Tariffs and Trade (GATT) (1947) October. 30, 61 Stat. A-11, 55 U.N.T.S. 194.

World Trade Organization (WTO), Agreement on the Application of Sanitary and Phytosanitary Measures (SPS) (1994a) April. 15, Marrakesh Agreement Establishing the World Trade Organization, Annex 1A, pmbl., Legal Instruments, Results of the Uruguay Round, 1867 U.N.T.S. 493.

———. Agreement on Technical Barriers to Trade (TBT) (1994b). April. 15, Final Act Embodying the Results of the Uruguay Round of Multilateral Trade Negotiations, Annex 1A, Legal Instruments, Results of the Uruguay Round, 33 I.L.M. 1125.

Chapter 5

The Politics of Food Safety in the Age of Global Trade
The Codex Alimentarius Commission in the SPS Agreement of the WTO

Tim Büthe

International trade in food increases real and imagined risks to food safety. These risks primarily arise either from noncompliance with existing food safety standards or from substantive differences in sanitary and related standards for agriculture or food processing industries, which may differ across countries in stringency or due to differences in the fundamental principles embodied in the standards (Ansell and Balsiger 2009; Ansell and Vogel 2006; Echols 2001; Levi et al. 2009; Pollack and Shaffer 2009).

As noted in chapter 1, one way to deal with the governance issues that arise from cross-national differences in food safety standards is for governments to cooperate in developing international standards for common use. Where using common international standards is feasible, it has many benefits, which have been discussed at least since the Tokyo Round negotiations of the General Agreement on Tariffs and Trade (GATT) in the 1970s (Bhagwati and Hudec 1996; Trebilcock and Howse 2005). Common standards, for instance, make the detection of compliance problems easier. In addition, policy proposals such as the one outlined in chapter 10 by Kenneth Bamberger and Andrew Guzman, under which importers assume legal responsibility for imported products being "safe," may require common international standards for their practical implementation. Moreover, many food safety standards are embedded or referenced in government regulations. Common international standards reduce the likelihood that these regulatory measures create unnecessary nontariff barriers to trade—an important consideration for food-exporting countries such as the United States (Büthe 2008; Epps 2008: 12ff; Josling et al. 2004).

During the Uruguay Round of the GATT (1986–1993), which led to the creation of the World Trade Organization (WTO), the member states of the GATT addressed the issue of cross-national differences in food safety standards by negotiating the Agreement on the Application of Sanitary and Phytosanitary (SPS) Measures. Discussed further in chapter 4, the SPS Agreement is an integral part of the treaty establishing the WTO, binding on all member states, and enforceable via the Dispute Settlement Mechanism (see also Alemanno 2007). Through the SPS Agreement, member states committed themselves, among other things, to using "international standards" whenever international standards exist that can achieve the desired (explicitly specified) level of consumer protection. If a country's regulations mandate compliance with standards that differ from international standards, they may be challenged as nontariff barriers to trade. The regulating country must then provide scientific evidence, using "risk assessment techniques developed by the relevant international organizations" (WTO 1994: Art. 5[1]), to show that the risks against which the regulatory measure is supposed to protect indeed exist and that international standards could not achieve the desired level of consumer protection against these health or food safety risks. By contrast, domestic regulations that effectively "convert" an "international standard" into a domestic one are categorically presumed to be compliant with WTO law.[1]

Where do these international standards come from? As I have shown in previous work (Büthe 2008), the Uruguay Round negotiators recognized quickly that setting technical or scientific standards for food safety during the Uruguay Round trade negotiations would be impractical. Setting or selecting such standards required specialized expertise that the GATT negotiators generally did not have, and having diplomats or trade experts set standards through international negotiations was likely to be excruciatingly slow and therefore not suitable as a method for developing international food safety standards, given the heterogeneity and changing nature of food products traded in global markets. GATT negotiators therefore agreed early on to delegate the task of setting standards to outside bodies of technical experts (Büthe 2008). Specifically, Annex A(3) of the SPS Agreement defines international standards "for food safety" as the standards "established by the Codex Alimentarius Commission" (Codex)[2] (WTO 1994). But how did Codex get written into the treaty? What explains its selection as *the* international food safety standard-setter under the SPS Agreement?

The selection of Codex might seem like a foregone conclusion. There are hundreds of Codex standards for agricultural trade and food safety that are concerned not only with matters such as pesticide residues, but also quality, labeling, safe handling, transport, and storage of fruits, vegetables, milk products, and many processed foods. An international organization (IO) with 180 countries as members, Codex now is the clear focal point for international food standard-setting. Codex's centrality today, however, is unsuitable as an explanation for why Codex was selected as the international standard-setter, as causation runs the other way. Codex is in many ways a function of the prominence that it acquired by being selected as the designated food safety standard-setter in the SPS Agreement (Tarullo 2000; Veggeland and Borgen 2005). At the launch of the Uruguay Round negotiations in 1986, Codex had a twenty-three-year history of rather modest achievements and faced an uncertain future; some characterized it as "moribund."

Taking Charles Tilly's (1975) warning against teleology seriously (see also Spruyt 1994), I study this case of institutional choice prospectively. I start by analyzing food standard-setting at the beginning of the Uruguay Round and explore the options at that time, rather than starting from the end result, assuming that it was the only possible outcome. Doing so, I find that there were, by the mid-1980s, at least four organizations that developed widely used international standards for food and food safety. Each was viable and credible as an international food standard-setter, and all were discussed repeatedly during the negotiations of the SPS Agreement. At the same time, the four organizations differed in their decision-making rules, with the level of support required for standards adoption ranging from simple majority to unanimity. Moreover, many individuals and diverse groups have a stake in food safety standards—and the four organizations differed in which stakeholders were represented. The choice was therefore likely to be consequential. What explains the choice in favor of Codex?

Because the material and political stakes are high, any government negotiator should want to delegate standard-setting to a body that is likely to set standards that will be favorable to the politically powerful interests from his country. But informational constraints may impede a negotiator's ability to accurately anticipate the distributional consequences of delegating to one organization rather than another. In the absence of good information, I argue, negotiators will form their preferences over multiple available standard-setting bodies based on the perceived legitimacy of those bodies. Extracting a key element of a more comprehensive theoretical discussion of IO legitimacy that I have developed elsewhere (Büthe 2009), I hypothesize that countries oppose delegation of standard-setting authority to organizations that exclude them, provided that more inclusive alternatives exist. Finally, I conceptualize international standard-setting organizations not just as passive institutional structures but as actors, with interests of their own and the potential for genuine agency. The more central the setting of food safety standards is to an organization's mission and independent existence, the greater should be the organization's incentive to proactively foster its perceived legitimacy, increasing the chance that it will be selected as the standard-setter.

I develop these hypotheses more fully in the next section, then examine them empirically. For the empirical analysis (only summarized here due to space constraints), I was able to draw on a large number of original documents from the Uruguay Round negotiations, released well ahead of the normal schedule for diplomatic documents, through the GATT Digital Library (2006). I supplement information from those documents with insights gained through extensive not-for-attribution interviews with almost all of the surviving core SPS Agreement negotiators and background information provided by other participants. In the conclusion, I discuss some of the policy implications for food safety in a world of global trade.

Explaining the International Delegation of Regulatory Authority

The regulation of domestic economic activities has long been one of the hallmarks of sovereignty. Preserving this prerogative of the modern state (at least for advanced capitalist democracies) was part of the compromise of embedded liberalism that characterized the post-World War II international economic order (Goldstein 1993; Ruggie 1983). The economic integration that was enabled by this postwar order, however, meant that, by the 1970s, cross-national differences in standards and regulations had become important nontariff barriers to trade (Ray 1987). At the same time, poor sanitary standards for food handling and processing in one country could affect consumers in another. Continued national regulatory prerogatives in an age of international interdependence thus not only carried increasing economic costs but became increasingly politically risky for governments since, in the event of trade-related food scares or health crises, they would be blamed for "failing" to protect their citizens from differing standards (or poor regulatory enforcement) abroad.

The international harmonization of standards through the delegation of standard-setting to international or transnational expert bodies became the means through which governments sought to achieve both high-quality standards and the benefits of reduced cross-national variation in regulatory environments. Yet, while economic globalization increased the demand for international food safety standards, multiple suppliers of such standards already existed. Negotiating a formal agreement that recognized the standards from a particular source as "international standards"—not just retroactively but also prospectively for yet-to-be-developed standards—therefore entailed a choice from among several existing bodies, none of which was technically superior to the others, nor clearly socially or economically "optimal" for the task at hand (Büthe 2009). What explains the selection of the Codex Alimentarius Commission?[3]

I start from the observation that the GATT Uruguay Round negotiating framework combined formal rule-based, egalitarian consensus decision-making with informal, power-based bargaining procedures (Steinberg 2002). Specifically, the SPS Agreement was negotiated in the Working Group on Sanitary and Phytosanitary Regulations and Barriers (WGSP), a subcommittee of Negotiating Group 5 (Agriculture). WGSP held formal meetings every few months, which were open to every member state. These official negotiating sessions, however, were interspersed by meetings in various informal settings among the SPS negotiators from an "inner core" group of countries, consisting of Australia (informally representing the Cairns Group of agricultural exporters),[4] Canada, Finland (representing the Nordic countries), the European Union (EU), and the United States. Representatives of Argentina, Japan, and New Zealand were part of a larger core group of eight but less involved in the negotiations.

This kind of arrangement leads me to expect that advanced industrialized countries set the agenda for the formal negotiations. At the same time, they needed to foster the perception that the SPS Agreement would benefit least developed countries (LDCs) through agricultural trade liberalization, since LDC support or at least acquiescence was crucial for a successful conclusion of a negotiating round in which LDCs were asked to reduce their protectionist barriers for manufactured goods and agree to bring intellectual property rights protection into the GATT/WTO. This leads me to expect that developing countries were able to veto the selection of standard-setters that they found clearly objectionable. At the same time, the informal institutions should make it unlikely that developing countries would have succeeded in setting the agenda, that is, in successfully proposing a standard-setter not also desired by developed countries.

Among developed countries, the United States and the EU are usually the most prominent actors (Drezner 2007; Mattli and Büthe 2003). Although I explicitly recognize that others may play an important role (Helfer 2004), U.S. and EU consensus (where or when it can be reached) usually is the blueprint for the final agreement.[5] The key analytical task is therefore to explain government negotiators' preferences, especially the preferences of the United States, the EU, and developing countries as a group.

A Theory of Preference Formation in International Regulatory Delegation

Institutional choices have distributional consequences (Knight 1992; Krasner 1991), and the material stakes are high when selecting an international organization to set standards that affect market access. Moreover, writing the delegation of standard-setting authority into a treaty creates a new status quo, which may be hard to change subsequently. Government negotiators thus have strong incentives to "get it right." I therefore assume that each government is strategic when forming its preferences in that it will seek to shift governance to an institutional setting in which it expects to do well or to a body whom it expects to set standards that will be favorable to the interests of the country's domestically powerful groups.

I am interested not just in the outcome but in the decision-making process that leads to the delegation of regulatory governance. I therefore assume that governments have incentives to behave strategically, but I do not assume that negotiators can fully anticipate the consequences of their choices. Instead, I recognize that it is materially and/or politically costly for a negotiator to acquire the kind of information that would allow him or her to make the optimal choice among the possible regulators through backward induction based on an accurate anticipation of the distributional consequences. Prospective analysis, which takes the informational constraints of the negotiators seriously and examines them empirically instead of assuming them away, is warranted because there are strong theoretical reasons to expect that negotiators *could* not fully anticipate the consequences of their choice between the possible standard-setters, as well as strong empirical evidence that they *did* not.

Theoretically, there are at least three reasons to be cautious when making strong assumptions about negotiators' ability to anticipate the consequences of institutional choices.[6] First, the specific actors involved in the standard-setting organizations often differ from those involved in the international or transgovernmental negotiations that lead to the delegation of the standard-setting task (Büthe 2006). Negotiators may therefore be expected to have incomplete information. Second, changing the legal status of the technical standards developed by a particular international organization, for instance, by making compliance with previously optional standards a prerequisite for market access, changes the stakes. Actors who previously did not bother to participate in international institutionalized rule-making now have incentives to seek a voice in the standard-setting process. Such changes in the cast of characters who want to influence the regulatory outcomes are likely to undermine informal norms against political-strategic behavior because new actors have not been socialized to act in norm-compliant ways. Even without a change in the set of actors, the delegation of authority will change the incentives to use the organization's decision-making rules and procedures strategically to influence specific outcomes—for instance, by building minimum winning coalitions rather than complying with consensus norms. The precise nature of these changes and the shape of the likely coalition, however, is often very difficult to predict, especially in the long run. Third, delegation itself may lead to changes in the standards-developing organization's formal or informal institutions.

Empirically, many of the countries whose government representatives negotiated the SPS Agreement have expressed their regrets, and they often explicitly ascribe blame to not having correctly anticipated the consequences of delegating standard-setting to Codex. The EU's efforts to have Codex standards reflect the principles underlying its approach to food safety, for example, have had "mixed success" (Poli 2004), prompting attempts to shift standard-setting for genetically modified organisms out of the Codex to other institutional settings that are more congenial to EU concerns (Pollack and Shaffer 2009). Developing countries have been increasingly frustrated by their relative marginalization in Codex and the costliness of the obligations that they undertook by committing to Codex standardization (Dubey 1996; Singh 2006; Wilson and Abiola 2003). Even in the United States, where agricultural exporters and food industry multinationals have generally been quite happy with the delegation to Codex, consumer groups and others have expressed concerns about industry domination of the nominally intergovernmental Codex (Post 2005; Rosman 1993; Victor 2004).[7]

While governments may seek to anticipate the consequences of delegation, the difficulties in actually forming such expectations suggest that governments' preferences are largely based on their past experience with the organizations that they are considering as international standard-setters. Here, countries may differ not only in how well their stakeholders have objectively done in the alternative institutional settings in the past, but also in how much past experience a country's stakeholders have. Expectations based on only a small number of past experiences, for instance, are more likely to be erroneous than expectations based on extensive experience. This is likely to be a serious issue for developing countries, many of which had little prior experience with the actual standard-setting in each standards-developing organization.

When governments or other representatives of a country's stakeholders lack information about an international organization, they can generally obtain it, but may differ in how costly it is to do so. Domestic institutional structures in particular can raise or lower the economic or political costs of information for a given issue. For example, when a country has no domestic regulatory agency, it is unlikely to have public officials with the requisite expertise to assess the consequences of delegating standard-setting in that issue area to one particular international body or another. This disadvantage is likely to be common among developing countries. At the same time, advanced capitalist countries may also differ significantly from each other in this regard, as the existence of well-informed individuals or groups within a country does not make that information automatically available to those who represent the country's interests at the international level (Mattli and Büthe 2003).

In sum, the better the information that a country's representative in international negotiations has at his disposal, the more closely will the preferences that he pursues resemble those that can be predicted by assuming complete information. To the extent that some or all countries have informational limitations, explaining institutional selection requires also taking other factors into account.

For reasons examined more fully elsewhere (Büthe 2009), institutional selection should also be a function of the perceived legitimacy of the institutions to which standard-setting authority may be delegated. A full analysis of the legitimacy of international organizations is beyond the scope of this chapter; I focus on what Buchanan and Keohane call "sociological legitimacy," that is, the extent to which it is widely *believed* that the organization has the authority to rule (2006: 405). Existing analyses of the perceived legitimacy of IOs suggest that it is to a large extent a function of an organization's inclusiveness (Coicaud and Heiskanen 2001). I therefore argue that organizations with limited geographical scope—especially IOs that formally restrict membership or participation—have little global legitimacy. This is not to say that such bodies do not sometimes play a prominent role in global governance, but I argue that when there is an alternative international body with at least the appearance of universal scope, then the universal alternative will have greater legitimacy than the organization with limited geographical scope.

Finally, an organization's perceived legitimacy and technical capacity are not fixed but can be influenced by the organization itself. I view IOs as actors with organizational interests of their own, as suggested by the principal-agent literature, in which the "agent" (to whom authority is delegated) is an actor pursuing a distinct set of interests. This allows me to specify conditions under which I would expect IO attempts to influence their own selection. In situations where multiple bodies have previously been involved in setting international standards for a product or service, *not* being selected is likely to reduce a body's importance. The political and economic costs of not being officially recognized as the international standard-setter may, however, have to be weighed against the costs of increased scrutiny and politicization that result from the delegation of regulatory authority. Concretely, if an international or transnational body is first and foremost an issue-specific standards-developing organization, not being designated an international standard-setter may call into question the viability of the organization, giving it strong incentives to seek selection as *the* standard-setter. By contrast, an organization for which developing a particular kind of international standards is only one activity among many is more likely to view a fight to gain recognition as *the* international standard-setter for the issue area in question as an unwelcome distraction and therefore should not seek selection particularly forcefully. In sum, I would expect pure issue-specific standard-setters to be more likely to actively seek delegation and even fight against the selection of other, competing standards-developing organizations.

The Institutional Status Quo Ante

Four international organizations had been engaged in setting a broad range of food (safety) standards during the decades prior to the Uruguay Round negotiations in 1986: the United Nations/Economic Commission for Europe (UN/ECE), the International Organization for Standardization (ISO), the Organization for Economic Cooperation and Development (OECD), and the Codex Alimentarius Commission (Codex).

UN/ECE

The UN/ECE—one of five regional suborganizations of the UN Economic and Social Council (ECOSOC)—was founded in 1947 to facilitate the reconstruction of Europe after the Second World War. Its mission is to advance economic integration and cooperation among its member states and promote sustainable development and economic prosperity in Europe and beyond, through policy dialogue and other means. As part of this mission, it started early on to set standards for perishable foods—most important, quality standards for fresh and dried fruits and vegetables. These standards were by the 1980s used by agricultural producers as well as import/food safety regulators in many parts of the world, including the United States and many developing countries. But there were few developing countries among its members, and none from outside Europe. And although the UN/ECE explicitly allows participation of all UN member states in its standardization activities, it was clearly perceived as a European regional organization.[8]

ISO

The ISO, an international nongovernmental body headquartered in Geneva, was founded in 1947 to develop international standards for a broad range of economic activities; it adopted its first standards in 1951 (Latimer 1997; Murphy and Yates 2008: 11–20). Whereas most of ISO's early work was focused on standards for manufactured goods, one of its 67 original Technical Committees (TC)—specifically TC34 for "Agriculture and Food Products"—sets standards, for instance, for the safe storage and transport of fruits and vegetables. Several other ISO TCs also develop standards relevant for food safety: TC54 (essential oils), TC93 (starch), TC134 (fertilizers and soil conditioners), TC147 (water quality), and TC234 (fisheries and aquaculture). Membership in the ISO is open to the body "most representative of standardization" in each country; most of these member bodies are also nongovernmental or hybrid public-private entities. By the beginning of the Uruguay Round negotiations, ISO membership had grown to 74 "full" and 16 "correspondent" member bodies from around the world (ISO 2005; Latimer 1997).[9]

Actual standard-setting in the ISO is the task of highly specialized technical committees, subcommittees, and working groups of technical experts appointed by the member bodies, coordinated by a small Central Secretariat in Geneva. Each committee has a secretariat from a national member body that pays for the TC's administrative costs, as well as a chairman from a different member body.[10] ISO standard-setting takes place in six stages (Büthe and Mattli forthcoming 2010a). ISO decision-making rules require consensus (defined as the absence of opposition for which technical reasons are provided) for the committee work to move forward, and standards adoption requires large supermajorities in formal votes on the two final drafts. At the same time, effective interest representation in the ISO requires involvement during the standards-development process because the draft standard becomes successively more specific as it moves through the stages, which in turn requires good information dissemination and effective preference aggregation at the domestic level. Büthe and Mattli's work shows that domestic institutions differ in how well they are suited to these tasks—even among advanced industrialized countries, with domestic institutional fragmentation in the United States often impeding effective participation.

OECD

The OECD, an intergovernmental organization independent of the UN, compiles statistics, provides economic analyses, and develops policy recommendations on behalf of its now thirty industrialized member states. Developing countries sometimes welcome the OECD's analyses and its role in coordinating development aid, but often describe the OECD as an "exclusive club" of rich countries (Büthe 2009; Woodward 2009: 85). Founded in 1961, it soon afterward became involved in setting standards for agricultural and forest tree seeds and seedlings, as well as for fruits and vegetables. These standards have long been used in the certification of agricultural commodities for domestic and international commerce in OECD countries and beyond. Standard-setting takes place in some 200 separate, specialized working groups, which are officially subcommittees of the OECD's Committee on Agriculture. Participation is also open to non-OECD countries, though it is limited in practice, except for the working group on agricultural seeds, which has long had participants from several countries from every continent. However, OECD member states are assured a gatekeeping function in that the standards, once agreed on by the standards-developing working group, must be unanimously approved by the OECD Council to become OECD standards.

Codex

Codex is the central institution of the Food and Agriculture Organization (FAO) and World Health Organization (WHO) Joint Food Standards Program, set up in 1963. The members of Codex (which numbered 130 in 1986) are states, represented usually by national governments' ministries or departments of agriculture and/or food regulatory agencies, though many representatives from food industry multinationals and business associations, as well as an occasional representative of a consumer group, serve as appointees on national delegations (Braithwaite and Drahos 2000: 401; Rosman 1993). Codex develops standards for food commodities, for labeling and hygienic handling of food, as well as for the assessment of food-related safety risks. Actual developing country participation in standard-setting, and even such countries' attendance at the plenary sessions of Codex, was very low at the time of the Uruguay Round negotiations, but many of them had nominally been members of Codex for years, and there were virtually no restrictions on their membership. Membership is open to all countries that are members or associate members of both FAO and WHO.

Actual standard-setting is the task of specialized Codex committees, such as the Committee on Food Additives, the Committee on Pesticide Residues, or the Committee on Milk and Milk Products. These committees follow an eight-step procedure to develop the standard through various draft stages (Codex 2008; Victor 1997). The committees' standards become proposals to the commission's plenary session, which may formally adopt or reject it. Codex's norms call for reaching consensus in the committees that develop the standard and for passing the standard by consensus in the plenary meeting, but Codex rules allow for adoption of a standard by simple majority, where each country has one vote.

Institutional Selection in International Regulatory Delegation

For decades, the international food standards of the UN/ECE, ISO, OECD, and Codex coexisted as voluntary standards. None of the four organizations became the clear focal point for food safety standard-setting. Until the 1990s, domestic regulatory measures that controlled agricultural production or imports (i.e., market access) drew only occasionally on international standards, and the international standards as such were not binding on anyone. The stakes in international standardization were consequently low. There was little cost to letting any subset of countries proceed with developing any "international standard" they desired. Abstentions from a large number of countries were common in the international SPS standard-setting bodies, and anyone who felt that a proposed standard was too lax or too stringent focused his or her energies on getting a different standard adopted domestically.[11] Moreover, Codex was no more prominent than the other organizations. Quite to the contrary: Having gained prominence as an international food standard-setter in the early 1970s (Kay 1976: 33f), it was characterized by the mid-1980s by "apathy and inaction" (Victor 1997: 188), and it was described to me in an interview with a long-term observer as "largely moribund" by the time the Uruguay Round was launched in 1986.[12]

Economic globalization, however, raised the costs of continued divergence of standards and increased the potential benefit of having a common set of international standards. Specifically, the reduction of tariff levels had rendered existing cross-national differences in standards a significant nontariff barrier to trade (NTB), and in many cases countries had raised standards with the intent of creating NTBs (Baldwin 2000; Bhagwati and Hudec 1996; Mansfield and Busch 1995). For trade in agriculture, SPS measures were by the 1980s the most important NTB, and agricultural exporters were concerned that any liberalization of agriculture negotiated during the Uruguay Round would be undone by protectionist importing countries raising SPS standards to compensate for lower tariffs and quantitative restrictions.

Governments that approached the Uruguay Round primarily as agricultural exporters (especially the United States, Canada, and the Cairns group, led by Australia) therefore sought a binding agreement on SPS measures. Given that an agreement on agriculture was from the start a prerequisite for successfully concluding the Uruguay Round, agricultural importing countries also realized the need to address this issue. But they emphasized that SPS standards are at the heart of often politically sensitive health and food safety regulations, and that an international agreement must not fundamentally impede their ability to protect their populations against diseases and pests.

The resulting SPS Agreement is an ambitious compromise between the objectives of liberalizing agricultural trade and safeguarding regulatory flexibility. With the exceptions noted in the introduction, the Agreement commits all member states of the WTO to use international standards in their SPS measures. The negotiators, however, rejected as impractical the suggestion that they write a specific list of international standards into the treaty. Maintaining the flexibility to develop new standards as new health and food safety issues might warrant, required delegating the ongoing task of setting SPS standards to more specialized bodies (Büthe 2008). But which international standard-setting bodies (from the set depicted in Figure 1) should be recognized under the SPS Agreement? This question was the source of discussion and contention for a long time, as the consequences of the other provisions hinged to a large extent on whose standards would be recognized as "international standards" (/WGSP/2, /WGSP/3, and /WGSP/W/22).[13]

The EU in particular sought to get the UN/ECE and the OECD written into the Agreement (/W/56, /W/103: 4, /W/146). The other members of the inner-core group were largely indifferent vis-à-vis UN/ECE and OECD, but the official recognition of these two standard-setters in the SPS Agreement was strongly opposed by developing countries. While few developing countries regularly sent a representative to attend the SPS negotiations (and almost never SPS specialists), their views carried some weight because the conclusion of the Uruguay Round required their support, especially for the agriculture negotiations. And they clearly saw the UN/ECE and OECD as geographically limited bodies that lacked legitimacy for global governance, and in-

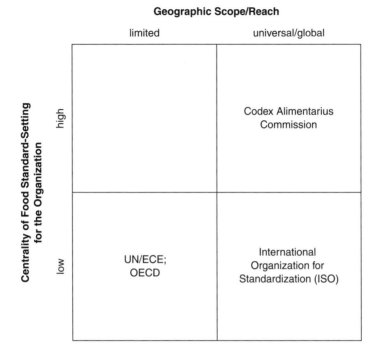

Figure 1. Competing international food safety standard-setters.

sisted that the recognized standard-setters would have to be open to participation from all GATT/WTO member states *and* have actual participation from countries from all regions of the world (/W/130).[14] Lacking legitimacy, the bodies with limited scope thus had no chance to be written into the SPS Agreement, as suggested by the theoretical argument above.

The decision in favor of Codex and against the ISO was more complex. The ISO had support from the EU and the Nordic countries but also from some Cairns Group countries and many developing countries, as it enjoyed special legitimacy from having already been noted as an international standard-setter in the Tokyo Round Technical Barriers to Trade (TBT) Agreement. Codex meanwhile also had broad support and had been noted in numerous discussions prior to the launch of the Uruguay Round. Both organizations had access to substantial technical expertise, though neither was intimately familiar even to the core negotiators. Particularly important, the small EU SPS-negotiating team had no member with any expertise in Codex. The EU lead negotiator noted in interviews that he had simply assumed—with regret in retrospect—that Codex worked like the World Animal Health Organization, with its strong consensus norms, where he had represented the EU for years. Only the U.S. negotiators had a very good understanding of how Codex worked, thanks to the presence of multiple experts with experience in Codex in the U.S. domestic "interagency" committee charged with developing the U.S. negotiating position. On that basis, the United States strongly supported Codex strategically.

Given most negotiators' incomplete information, it was important that Codex actively sought delegation as an actor in its own right, something ISO did not do. Codex and FAO (as Codex's primary "parent" organization) made frequent submissions to the WGSP, praising the unique scientific expertise of Codex committees and emphasizing Codex's norm of setting standards by consensus—usually with no mention of the fact that at any stage of the Codex standard-setting process, a simple majority is sufficient to advance and adopt a standards proposal. In addition, FAO built a constituency for Codex among developing countries by linking Codex to FAO development and technical assistance (/WGSP/W/15; /WGSP/W/20). Representatives of Codex even sought to delegitimate the ISO as an alternative source of international SPS standards by arguing that, as a nongovernmental organization, the ISO was dominated by private, particularistic interests (GATT-TBT 1989)—hardly a credible claim for those with complete information given the dominant role of private industry in Codex, but effective in that it diminished the legitimacy of the ISO in the eyes of some developing country governments, for which relinquishing regulatory authority to nongovernmental bodies was anathema.[15]

By contrast, and consistent with the argument presented above, the ISO, for which setting food safety standards was only one concern among many, far less actively sought recognition through a mention in the SPS Agreement. When invited to give a presentation about the organization and its standard-setting procedures to the SPS Working Group at its June 1990 meeting, the ISO obliged and certainly emphasized its technical expertise and history of consensual, scientific standard-setting (/WGSP/W/24), but its representatives never lobbied the negotiators to delegate to the ISO.

Policy Implications

Concerns about food safety make international trade in food products a public policy issue that goes well beyond trade policy. Conversely, food safety is an issue that can no longer be studied as a purely domestic policy issue. Many of the key food safety standards are today developed by the Codex Alimentarius Commission, which seeks to adopt standards by consensus but, if conflicts of interest cannot be resolved, adopts standards by a simple majority of its now 180 member countries (as of April 2009). Codex attained its current prominence by being designated the international standard-setter in the SPS Agreement.

This chapter has analyzed why the authority to set international food safety standards was delegated to Codex in the SPS Agreement. This prominent delegation of regulatory authority is puzzling not only because food safety issues are politically sensitive but also because there were at least four international bodies that had for decades set food and food safety standards when the Uruguay Round negotiations were launched, but only one of them was written into the treaty.

I have argued that, to explain the selection of Codex as the designated source of "international standards" for food safety under the SPS Agreement, we must examine and take seriously the informational constraints of GATT negotiators' strategic calculations, as well as their perceptions of the available standard-setting bodies' legitimacy—perceptions that could be influenced by those international bodies, understood as actors rather than mere institutional structures. I have found that the SPS standard-setting organizations with geographically limited scope (the UN/ECE and the OECD) lacked legitimacy in the face of universal/global alternatives and were therefore opposed by developing countries. They stood little chance of being designated international standard-setters for purposes of the SPS Agreement, although their inclusion was repeatedly suggested. Among the two global bodies, Codex had a much stronger organizational imperative to seek designation as the official international standard-setting organization, and it sought this designation forcefully, shaping perceptions of its technical capacity and legitimacy while building on strategic support from the United States. As a consequence, Appendix A of the SPS Agreement defines "international standards . . . for food safety" as "the standards, guidelines and recommendations established by the Codex Alimentarius Commission relating to food additives, veterinary drug and pesticide residues, contaminants, methods of analysis and sampling, and codes and guidelines of hygienic practice" (WTO 1994). It is one of the most robust and near-exclusive cases of international delegation of regulatory authority.

Two sets of questions remain to be addressed, which are particularly important from a policy perspective. First, did it matter that Codex rather than the ISO was selected? Would the actual standards, developed by Codex since the SPS Agreement came into force, have differed if they had been developed by the ISO instead? And second: in light of the now-common criticisms of Codex as a standard-setter, how might international food safety standard-setting be improved?

How standards might have differed had they been developed in one institutional setting rather than another is very difficult to predict, because the formal-legal delegation of standard-setting authority (and the publicity that goes with it) often changes the politics of standard-setting (Büthe and Mattli 2009). That said, there are several reasons to think that the choice mattered: Codex allows for adopting international standards by simple majority vote, whereas the ISO requires much broader supermajorities. The most controversial Codex standards, adopted with a bare majority, would therefore probably not have been adopted in the ISO. More generally, the power resources of states are far less usable in international nongovernmental organizations than in traditional international (intergovernmental) organizations (Büthe and Mattli forthcoming 2010a; forthcoming 2010b). This suggests that delegation to Codex rather than the ISO was detrimental to the interests of the small highly developed countries, who often play a prominent role in the ISO, but quite beneficial to large developed countries, such as the United States, whose government has a wealth of power resources at its disposal.

Whose interests, however, are represented by the U.S. government? One of the key concerns about Codex in recent years has been the over-representation of industry and the underrepresentation of consumer interests. My research suggests that this skewed representation of stakeholders contributed to the attractiveness of Codex to U.S. government negotiators because it largely replicated the domestic political power structure within the United States (see also Vogel 1995: 211f). In part, the imbalance in favor of commercial interests (especially food industry multinationals) is simply a function of the uneven distribution of technical expertise—a general constraint on any policies or procedures to make standard-setting more inclusive (Mattli and Büthe 2005). The underrepresentation of noncommercial stakeholders in U.S. delegations to Codex technical committees, however, is also a function of the long-standing U.S. policy to treat willingness to pay as the "true" measure of the seriousness of any stakeholder's interest. Nongovernmental appointees to Codex committees therefore pay their own way. Since Codex standard-setting stretches over multiple years and involves attending meetings in various countries around the globe, the lack of any public support for noncommercial participants is bound to reinforce the underrepresentation of consumer safety advocates and other noncommercial stakeholders. Subsidies for noncommercial participants thus hold greater promise for a better balance of interest representation than shifting standard-setting to another organization or boosting the transparency of the Codex process through increased use of administrative law procedures.

Acknowledgments

For helpful discussions and comments, I am grateful to Marsha Echols, Judith Goldstein, Robert Keohane, Walter Mattli, Michael Munger, Ted Ruger, David Singer, Neil Smelser, Richard Steinberg, Alan Swinbank, David Vogel, David Zaring, and John Zysman, as well as my colleagues in the Robert Wood Johnson Foundation Scholars in Health Policy Research Program at the University of California Berkeley and the University of California at San Francisco. I also have benefited from questions and comments at meetings of the International Political Economy Society and Midwest Political Science Association, and workshops at the Graduate Institute of International and Development Studies, Geneva, and the University of Pennsylvania Law School. The research for this chapter was made possible in part by a research grant from the Center for International Studies, Duke University, and a Robert Wood Johnson Foundation research fellowship. The opinions expressed in this chapter are those of the author and do not necessarily reflect the opinions of the Robert Wood Johnson Foundation.

Notes

1. See the Appellate Body's interpretation of "conform to international standards" in EC-Hormones, para. 170ff. Several WTO disputes have been brought against, and lost by, powerful member states based on the provisions of the SPS Agreement (e.g., Pauwelyn 1999).

2. The SPS Agreement deals not only with the safety of human food but also with animal and plant health and safety.

3. Delegation to Codex is nonexclusive insofar as Annex A, Article 3(d) allows for the possibility that "for matters not covered by [Codex], standards promulgated by other relevant international organizations open for membership to all Members" might be recognized explicitly as "international standards" for the purposes of the SPS Agreement, though no such additions have ever even been proposed (WTO 1994).

4. The Cairns Group is a coalition of nineteen agricultural exporting countries focused on reform of agricultural trade policy. Its members consist of Argentina, Australia, Bolivia, Brazil, Canada, Chile, Colombia, Costa Rica, Guatemala, Indonesia, Malaysia, New Zealand, Pakistan, Paraguay, Peru, Philippines, South Africa, Thailand, and Uruguay.

5. This analytical position does not require the assumption that "great power politics" is all that matters. The international coalition required to achieve agreement may be much broader, but I focus analytically on the United States and the European Union because, on many issues, they exhibit the great-

est divergence in initial preferences, so any compromise agreeable to them is likely to be also agreeable to many others.

6. Jupille and Snidal (2006) offer an alternative theoretical rationale for not assuming complete information, based on Herbert Simon's notion of bounded rationality. Their reasoning is complementary to, rather than competing with, mine.

7. In the late 1980s and early 1990s, the multinational Nestlé alone had thirty-eight representatives on various national delegations; Coca Cola, Unilever, and Monsanto were not far behind (Avery et al. 1993).

8. More information can be found at the UN/ECE website, including current use (UN/ECE 2009). The actual standard-setting takes place in "specialized sections" of the Working Party on Agricultural Quality Standards, part of the Committee on Trade (UN/ECE 2006).

9. "Correspondent" membership was created in 1968 to bring developing countries into the ISO even if their shortage of technical experts or lack of a national standards-developing organization did not (yet) allow for full membership (Frontard 1997: 46). Correspondent members pay greatly reduced membership fees but have no voting rights.

10. Consequently, most secretariats are held by member bodies from developed countries.

11. This limited role of international food standards organizations prior to the SPS Agreement was corroborated by not-for-attribution interviews conducted on July 18, 2007, and November 9, 2008.

12. The quoted language is from a not-for-attribution interview conducted on June 19, 2007.

13. Unless otherwise noted, all citations listed for the Uruguay Round negotiations documents under the SPS Agreement start with MTN.GNG/NG5/. Only the unique document numbers for the documents from the negotiations (available from the GATT Digital Library, GATT 2006) are shown in the parenthetical citations in the text.

14. Developing countries' emphasis on these characteristics of IOs as important to their perceived legitimacy was also noted in not-for-attribution interviews conducted on June 19, July 30, and August 2, 2007.

15. This diminished legitimacy of ISO was corroborated in not-for-attribution interviews conducted on June 19 and July 17, 2007.

References

Alemanno, Alberto (2007) *Trade in Food*. London: Cameron May.
Ansell, Christopher and Jörg Balsiger (2009) The circuits of regulation. Manuscript, University of California, Berkeley, and Swiss Federal Institute of Technology, Zurich.
Ansell, Christopher and David Vogel, eds. (2006) *What's the Beef? The Contested Governance of European Food Safety*. Cambridge, Mass.: MIT Press.
Avery, Natalie, Martine Drake, and Tim Lang (1993) *Cracking the Codex: An Analysis of Who Sets World Food Standards*. London: National Food Alliance.
Baldwin, Richard E. (2000) "Regulatory Protectionism, Developing Nations, and a Two-Tier World Trade System." 3 *Brookings Trade Forum* 237–93.
Bhagwati, Jagdish and Robert Hudec, eds. (1996) *Fair Trade and Harmonization*. Cambridge, Mass.: MIT Press.

Braithwaite, John and Peter Drahos (2000) *Global Business Regulation*. New York: Cambridge University Press.

Buchanan, Allen and Robert Keohane (2006) "The Legitimacy of Global Governance Institutions." 20 *Ethics and International Affairs* 405–37.

Büthe, Tim (2009) Agent selection in the international delegation of regulatory authority. Manuscript, University of California, Berkeley.

————. (2008) "The Globalization of Health and Safety Standards: Delegation of Regulatory Authority in the SPS Agreement of 1994 Agreement Establishing the World Trade Organization." 71 *Law and Contemporary Problems* 219–55.

————. (2006) The dynamics of principals and agents. Manuscript, Duke University.

Büthe, Tim and Walter Mattli (forthcoming 2010a) *Global Private Governance: The Politics of Rule-Making for Product and Financial Markets*. Princeton, N.J.: Princeton University Press.

————. (forthcoming 2010b) "Standards for Global Markets: Domestic and International Institutions for Setting International Product Standards." In *Handbook on Multi-Level Governance*, edited by Henrik Enderlein, Sonja Wälti, and Michael Zürn. Cheltenham, UK: Edward Elgar.

————. (2009) Politics after institutional choice. Manuscript, University of California, Berkeley, and Oxford University.

Codex Alimentarius (2009) "Current Official Standards." FAO/WHO. http://www.codexalimentarius.net/web/standard_list.jsp.

————. (2008) *Procedural Manual*, 18th ed. FAO/WHO. http://www.codexalimentarius.net/web/procedural_manual.jsp.

Coicaud, Jean-Marc and Veijo Heiskanen, eds. (2001) *The Legitimacy of International Organizations*. New York: United Nations Press.

Drezner, Daniel (2007) *All Politics Is Global*. Princeton, N.J.: Princeton University Press.

Dubey, Muchkund (1996) *An Unequal Treaty: World Trading Order After GATT*. New Delhi: New Age International.

Echols, Marsha (2001) *Food Safety and the WTO: The Interplay of Culture, Science, and Technology*. The Hague: Kluwer Law International.

Epps, Tracey (2008) *International Trade and Health Protection*. Cheltenham, UK: Edward Elgar.

Frontard, Raymond (1997) "Standards-Related Activities: The Global View." In *Friendship Among Equals*, edited by Jack Latimer. Geneva: ISO Central Secretariat.

GATT Committee on Technical Barriers to Trade (GATT-TBT) (1989) Minutes of the Meeting Held on 16 June 1989 (TBT/M/31) (August 18). http://www.wto.org/gatt_docs/English/HAZPDF/M31.pdf.

General Agreement on Tariffs and Trade (GATT) (2006) "GATT Digital Library: 1947–1994." Stanford University Libraries and Academic Information Resources. http://gatt.stanford.edu/ (accessed May 23, 2009).

Goldstein, Judith (1993) "Creating the GATT Rules." In *Multilateralism Matters: The Theory and Praxis of an Institutional Form*, edited by John Gerard Ruggie. New York: Columbia University Press.

Helfer, Laurence R. (2004) "Regime Shifting." 29 *Yale Journal of International Law* 26–45.

International Organization for Standardization (ISO) (2005) *Historical Record of ISO Membership Since Its Creation*." Geneva: ISO Central Secretariat.

Josling, Timothy, Donna Roberts, and David Orden (2004) *Food Regulation and Trade*. Washington, D.C.: Institute for International Economics.

Jupille, Joseph and Duncan Snidal (2006) The choice of international institutions. Manuscript, University of Colorado and University of Chicago (July).

Kay, David (1976) *The International Regulation of Pesticide Residues in Food*. St. Paul, Minn.: West.

Knight, Jack (1992) *Institutions and Social Conflict*. New York: Cambridge University Press.

Krasner, Stephen (1991) "Global Communications and National Power: Life on the Pareto Frontier." 43 *World Politics* 336–66.

Latimer, Jack, ed. (1997) *Friendship Among Equals*. Geneva: ISO Central Secretariat.

Levi, Jeffrey, Laura M. Segal, and Serena Vinter, et al. (2009) *Keeping America's Food Safe*. Washington, D.C.: Trust for America's Health and Robert Wood Johnson Foundation.

Mansfield, Edward and Marc Busch (1995) "The Political Economy of Nontariff Barriers." 49 *International Organization* 723–49.

Mattli, Walter and Tim Büthe (2005) "Global Private Governance." 68 *Law and Contemporary Problems* 225–62.

———. (2003) "Setting International Standards." 56 *World Politics* 1–42.

Murphy, Craig and JoAnne Yates (2008) *The International Organization for Standardization*. London: Routledge.

Pauwelyn, Joost (1999) "The WTO Agreement on Sanitary and Phytosanitary (SPS) Measures as Applied in the First Three SPS Disputes: EC-Hormones, Australia-Salmon and Japan-Varietals." 2 *Journal of International Economic Law* 641–64.

Poli, Sara (2004) "The European Community and the Adoption of International Food Standards Within the Codex Alimentarius Commission." 10 *European Law Journal* 613–30.

Pollack, Mark and Gregory Shaffer (2009) *When Cooperation Fails: The International Law and Politics of Genetically Modified Foods*. New York: Oxford University Press.

Post, Diahanna (2005) Food fights: Who shapes international food standards and who uses them? PhD diss., University of California, Berkeley.

Ray, Edward John (1987) "Changing Patterns of Protectionism." 8 *Northwestern Journal of International Law and Business* 285–327.

Rosman, Lewis (1993) "Public Participation in International Pesticide Regulation." 12 *Virginia Environmental Law Journal* 329–65.

Ruggie, John (1983) "International Regimes, Transactions, and Change." In *International Regimes*, edited by Stephen D. Krasner. Ithaca, N.Y.: Cornell University Press.

Singh, Jaswinder P. (2006) "The Evolution of National Interest." In *Negotiating Trade: Developing Countries in the WTO and NAFTA*, edited by John S. Odell. New York: Cambridge University Press.

Spruyt, Hendrik (1994) *The Sovereign State and Its Competitors*. Princeton, N.J.: Princeton University Press.

Steinberg, Richard (2002) "In the Shadow of Law or Power? Consensus-Based Bargaining and Outcomes in the GATT/WTO." 56 *International Organization* 339–74.

Tarullo, Daniel (2000) "The Relationship of WTO Obligations to Other International Arrangements." In *New Directions in International Economic Law:*

Essays in Honour of Professor John H. Jackson, edited by Mario Bronckers and Reinhard Quick. The Hague: Kluwer Law International.

Tilly, Charles (1975) "Western State-Making and Theories of Political Transformation." In *The Formation of National States in Western Europe,* edited by Charles Tilly. Princeton, N.J.: Princeton University Press.

Trebilcock, Michael J. and Robert Howse (2005) *The Regulation of International Trade,* 3rd ed. New York: Routledge.

United Nations/Economic Commission for Europe (UN/ECE) (2009) "UNECE Agricultural Quality Standards: Acceptances." UN/ECE. http://www.unece.org/trade/agr/info/accept.htm.

———. (2006) *Terms of Reference and Rules of Procedure of the Economic Commission for Europe,* 4th rev. ed. Geneva: United Nations.

Veggeland, Frode and Svein Ole Borgen (2005) "Negotiating International Food Standards." 18 *Governance* 675–708.

Victor, David (2004) "WTO Efforts to Manage Differences in National Sanitary and Phytosanitary Policies." In *Dynamics of Regulatory Change: How Globalization Affects National Regulatory Policies,* edited by David Vogel and Robert Kagan. Berkeley and Los Angeles: University of California Press.

———. (1997) "The Operation and Effectiveness of the Codex Alimentarius Commission." In Effective multilateral regulation of industrial activity. PhD diss., Massachusetts Institute of Technology.

Vogel, David (1995) *Trading Up: Consumer and Environmental Regulation in a Global Economy.* Cambridge, Mass.: Harvard University Press.

Wilson, John and Victor Abiola, eds. (2003) *Standards and Global Trade.* Washington, D.C.: World Bank.

Woodward, Richard (2009) *The Organization for Economic Cooperation and Development.* London: Routledge.

Agreement Cited

World Trade Organization (WTO). Agreement on the Application of Sanitary and Phytosanitary Measures (SPS) (1994), April 15, Marrakesh Agreement Establishing the World Trade Organization, Annex 1A, pmbl., Legal Instruments, Results of the Uruguay Round. 1867 U.N.T.S. 493.

Chapter 6
Import Safety Rules and Generic Drug Markets

Kevin Outterson

President Woodrow Wilson decried secret diplomacy in the wake of the First World War and famously called for "open covenants of peace, openly arrived at" as the first of his Fourteen Points. Woodrow Wilson is studiously ignored today in global trade negotiations. At the dawn of the twenty-first century, democratic governments still negotiate thousand-page trade agreements in secret, without transparent accountability for the interests being represented. Complex rules—many that affect import safety and public health—are negotiated and implemented without resort to the kind of public notice and comment provisions that apply to many domestic lawmaking processes around the world. The result is too often trade and health policy making by stealth, with significant potential for rent-seeking by powerful companies lobbying for particular outcomes. The policies pursued by these governance mechanisms do little to assist in the cause of assuring that only safe medicines cross international borders but have much to do with protecting intellectual property (IP) rights with spurious connections to import safety.

Consumers are poorly represented at trade talks. They are underrepresented in powerful lobbying institutions and must rely on the general democratic process, mediated through layers of administrative and political intermediaries. In the United States, "fast track" trade promotion authority has frequently prevented Congress from amending trade deals, deepening the democracy deficit. Negotiations occur in diplomatic secrecy, as if the participants were discussing troop movements or royal succession in Metternich's Europe. These models are completely inappropriate for health and trade policy in modern democracies.

Not everyone is unrepresented at these negotiations. As Susan K. Sell (1998; 2003) has aptly noted, the global intellectual property industry has been central to the formation, operation, and extension of global IP rules, especially through the World Trade Organization's Agreement on Trade-Related Intellectual Property (TRIPS). Indeed, she concludes that U.S. and European IP industries were the primary impetus for TRIPS, with the film and music industries leading the way on copyright, the pharmaceutical industry on patent, and the information technology industries supporting both. Unlike consumer representatives, industry actors have direct access to these talks through the trade advisory committee process in the United States and other countries, but public health representatives have been excluded, despite litigation from public health groups calling for representation (Shaffer and Brenner 2005).

Laurence Helfer (2004) and others have noted the "regime shift" that occurred when IP industry leaders became frustrated with the lack of enthusiasm for extensions of global IP rules at the World Intellectual Property Organization (WIPO). The new forum for discussion became the WTO, with IP issues relabeled as "trade-related." But the TRIPS Agreement also has its discontents. One significant casualty of the TRIPS process was public health, which was afforded inadequate attention prior to adoption. Even some global IP industries are not satisfied with TRIPS, despite many successes, such as binding international dispute resolution, early implementation by most developing nations, and many successful negotiations to add TRIPS-plus provisions to bilateral and multilateral trade agreements. Notably, the pharmaceutical industry and the United States Trade Representative (USTR) have strongly opposed actions by Brazil and Thailand to exercise rights reserved to them regarding compulsory licenses of patents under Article 31 of TRIPS. Although the USTR has complained loudly and threatened unilateral sanctions, if Washington took this issue to the WTO Dispute Settlement Body, Brazil and Thailand would be heavily favored to win (Outterson 2009). IP industry leaders now express frustration with the dispute resolution mechanism of the WTO—widely regarded as one of its strongest provisions—and have begun to create new institutions to ramp up enforcement of global IP rights without the restrictions of the WTO. Regime shifting begets regime proliferation.

This chapter examines recent attempts to strengthen border enforcement procedures against counterfeit goods, often under the guise of import safety. Recent examples include the proposed (but secret) Anti-Counterfeiting Trade Agreement (ACTA) and a related anti-counterfeiting effort, the International Medical Product Anti-Counterfeiting Taskforce (IMPACT). The chapter focuses on one particular category of imported goods for which safety concerns have been aired: patented pharmaceuticals. The primary concern is that secret trade negotiations may be used to delay global access to generic drugs, with a potentially significant impact on public health. Regime shifting, diplomatic secrecy, and rent-seeking all converge in ACTA and IMPACT, and in this environment companies may be able to achieve goals that would not otherwise be feasible, such as the suppression of the important and legitimate global trade in generic medicines. Global access to low-cost generic drugs is a major public health issue. Paul Hunt, the former United Nations Special Rapporteur on the right to health, has estimated that "almost 2 billion people lack access to essential medicines. . . . Improving access to existing medicines could save 10 million lives each year" (Khosla and Hunt 2009: 2).

Recent seizures of generic medication by Dutch customs officials highlight the danger from overzealous border protection regimes based on IP. Brazilian officials have identified over a dozen incidents in which authorities have confiscated generic drugs in transit passing through Dutch ports in 2008 (Azevêdo 2009; KEI 2009). Most notably, in November 2008, AIDS medications purchased by the Clinton Foundation through UNITAID, an international organization dedicated to purchasing disease-fighting medications, were confiscated on the grounds that the shipments contained "counterfeit" goods, when there was neither misrepresentation as to source nor patent infringement (Pandeya 2009). The drugs were manufactured in India and en route to Nigeria, where they would have been able to treat 166 HIV-positive individuals for three months (HAI et al. 2009; Pandeya 2009). These generic drugs are legitimate products, prequalified for quality by WHO, and fully compliant with patent and trademark laws in India, Nigeria, and under TRIPS (UNITAID 2009). A Dutch patent holder instigated the seizure, even though the drugs were not being marketed in Europe but merely being transshipped through Schipol airport on their way to Nigeria. This action has been strongly condemned (HAI et al. 2009; UNITAID 2009). As one HAI official said, "This is a grave situation. If the shipment is not allowed to pass, HIV positive Nigerians will miss out on critical treatment. We're concerned about what appears to be confusion between counterfeit medicines that kill people and generic medicines that save lives" (HAI et al. 2009: 1).

This incident was followed by the confiscation of 500 kilograms of the generic blood pressure medication losartan potassium in December 2008 (ICTSD 2009a). The drug was en route from India to Brazil and is not under patent in either country, yet it was seized while in port by Dutch officials at the request of the company that supposedly holds the patent rights to the drug in the Netherlands (ICTSD 2009b). These drugs were held for thirty-six days and sent back to India on their release (Azevêdo 2009). Whether a drug is under patent in the country of transit is "utterly irrelevant" (ICTSD 2009a) to whether the product is legitimate, which is why these seizures have sparked such controversy.

Dutch officials claim these seizures are authorized under EC Regulation No. 1383/2003, which allows IP right holders to petition customs officials to act "when goods are suspected of infringing an intellectual property right" (EU 2003; MSF 2009: 1). This regulation goes beyond what TRIPS requires of customs officials. Article 51 of TRIPS sets out what actions border officials must take when dealing with suspected counterfeit or pirated goods, and in a footnote states, "it is understood that there shall be no obligation to apply such procedures to imports of goods put on the market in another country by or with the consent of the right holder [i.e., parallel traded or grey market goods], or *to goods in transit*" (emphasis added) (WTO 1994: Art. 51). Enforcement of this regulation is particularly problematic in light of the Doha Declaration's mandate that TRIPS "can and should be interpreted and implemented in a manner supportive of WTO members' right to protect public health and, in particular, to promote access to medicines for all" (WTO 2001: para. 4). Many countries lack pharmaceutical manufacturing facilities, and rely on imports from other countries. Seizure of in-transit goods for alleged patent infringement threatens their access to generic medicines (MSF 2009: 1–2).

As we can see, trade policy and health policy intersect at the border. Drug companies have found that "fear moves the needle of consumer perception" (DeLauro 2003); the recent activity of IMPACT and ACTA highlights the need to ensure the pharmaceutical industry is not able to reduce access to medicines by confusing unsafe drugs with legitimate generics and parallel imports. Under the guise of import safety, IP customs enforcement rules may hinder the flow of life-saving generic medicines. As this chapter argues, the root of these difficulties can be traced to recent attempts to expand what constitutes a "counterfeit" drug. Indeed, the term *counterfeit drug* should be limited to deliberate violations of trademark law, and not expanded to include other IP disputes such as alleged patent infringement. Import safety and IP law serve different interests and should not be conflated.

A Lexicon for Pharmaceutical Import Safety

In the context of medicines, many different meanings are attached to the words *fake, substandard,* or *counterfeit.* These terms are often used in a way that encompasses everything from safe and effective drugs from legitimate Canadian pharmacies to drugs that are criminally contaminated with poisons. Patent, trademark, and drug safety issues are unnecessarily conflated. As a result, the language and principles of patent law have been applied to the problem of import safety, where they do not belong. To help ensure a safe, effective supply of medication across international borders, it is important to understand these problems as distinct issues (MSF 2008a; Outterson and Smith 2006).

Counterfeit Medicines

The term *counterfeit* should be reserved for goods that violate trademark laws, misrepresenting the source of the goods. The classic definition of counterfeit under U.S. law focuses exclusively on violations of trademark law and does not concern itself with patent or copyright infringement (Trademark 15 USC sec. 1127; Tariff Act 19 USC sec. 1526[e]). Some luxury goods are prone to counterfeiting—including perfumes, expensive watches, designer handbags, and famous label clothing. The key complaint is that consumers have been misled as to the source of the goods through the use of a spurious trademark.[1] Counterfeit drugs are falsely sold under the trademark of a branded product. These drugs defraud consumers, whether or not the product would otherwise meet regulatory standards.

The prevailing definition from the WHO adopts this approach in its first sentence but sows some seeds of confusion in the remainder of the definition:

> A counterfeit medicine is one which is deliberately and fraudulently mislabeled with respect to identity and/or source. Counterfeiting can apply to both branded and generic products and counterfeit products may include products with the correct ingredients or with the wrong ingredients, without active ingredients, with insufficient active ingredients or with fake packaging. (WHO 2009a, para. 10; WHO/IFPMA 1992)

The second sentence is best understood as a list of problems one could encounter with counterfeit medicines. In other settings, the WHO clearly distinguishes counterfeits from substandard medicines (Park 2009: 3; Shashikant 2009; WHO 2009b, para. 10). TRIPS also follows suit, defining counterfeit goods as violating trademark law:

> Any goods, including packaging, bearing without authorization a trademark which is identical to the trademark validly registered in respect of such goods, or which cannot be distinguished in its essential aspects from such a trademark, and which thereby infringes the rights of the owner of the trademark in question under the law of the country of importation. (WTO 1994: art. 51, n. 14)

Thus, in accordance with TRIPS, the term *counterfeit* refers only to goods that bear an identical or indistinguishable trademark without authorization of the trademark holder. In this respect, TRIPS is quite similar to U.S. law (Trademark 15 USC sec. 1127; Tariff Act 19 USC sec. 1526[e]). Current U.S. law, the TRIPS Agreement, and the historic WHO definitions all agree: To be considered counterfeit, drugs must bear a false trademark.

Substandard, Contaminated, or Adulterated Medicines

Substandard, contaminated, or adulterated medicines are a health risk, whether through substandard manufacturing processes, improper marketing authorizations, or inadequate attention to supply chain issues. These drugs threaten public health as a regulatory risk, without any necessary connection to IP law. Import safety rules should focus assiduously on these safety issues rather than IP disputes. Daniel Cahoy (2008: 428–32) calls for nuanced responses to the drug quality problem. National drug regulatory authorities may need more resources, and manufacturers may be required to invest in quality control procedures in their plants and throughout the supply chain.

Global pharmaceutical companies with impeccable credentials may nevertheless face manufacturing problems resulting in substandard drugs (Essential Action 2008: 2). Drugs sold in the United States may contain incorrect levels of active ingredients, and many are produced using raw materials manufactured in India, China, or other countries where the U.S. Food and Drug Administration (FDA) has not historically inspected manufacturing facilities adequately (Essential Action 2008: 2). Confusing these drugs with criminal counterfeits bearing a false trademark does nothing to further legitimate discussion of these important public health issues. From a public health perspective, the focus should be on removing all substandard medication from the supply chain, counterfeit or not, and on efforts to help improve the quality of legitimate pharmaceutical products (Cahoy 2008: 428–32; Caudron et al. 2008: 1070). This is a drug regulatory and import safety issue, not an IP problem.

That some counterfeit drugs also present safety issues does not alter this conclusion. It is, of course, likely that drugs with deliberate trademark infringement (counterfeits) may have heightened safety risks. These medicines are more likely to have been produced in a manufacturing facility that was not operating under good manufacturing practices (GMP), and the supply chain will almost necessarily be less secure. But the same cannot be said for medicines that are only subject to patent disputes and do not bear a deliberately false trademark. These medicines are produced openly, in facilities that are inspected by the FDA. The patent dispute is likely to be a battle over entry by a reputable generic company, seeking to compete once the patent has expired. That drug is likely to be just as safe as any other in the U.S. market. By comparison, criminally adulterated or substandard drugs are unlikely to involve a patent dispute, especially if the active ingredient is missing.

The Safety and Efficacy of Generic Drugs

When imprecise terms like *fake* are used, or terms like *counterfeit* or *substandard* used imprecisely, some drugs with positive public health effects are improperly lumped with criminal operations (MSF 2008a). The primary error is to conflate alleged patent infringement with deliberate counterfeiting of a trademark. The generic drug trade in the United States is entirely legal, delivering high-quality drugs at a fraction of branded prices. While reliable data are not available, theoretical models predict fewer counterfeit products within the U.S. generic sector, because generic prices are much lower and few are sold under branded trademarks (Outterson 2005). The generic drug industry is frequently sued on patent infringement grounds, but these suits are part of the typical process for generic entry. If a drug is legally generic in both the country of production and the destination market, customs authorities in third countries should not impound it during transit. And yet this is exactly what happened in the case of the Dutch seizures discussed above.

In a second situation called parallel trade, the brand owner places a drug on the market in one country at a lower price, but complains if consumers or wholesalers resell the drug in other countries, where higher prices prevail. Parallel trade in pharmaceuticals is entirely legal within Europe. In no sense are these drugs counterfeit. They fully comply with all applicable laws, including TRIPS (Outterson 2005), and significant safety issues have not been reported. Parallel trade is generally legal in the United States, but drug safety legislation outlawed parallel trade in medicines. For example, a U.S. citizen who purchases drugs from a Canadian pharmacy and brings those drugs back into the United States violates federal law. But unlike criminally counterfeit or contaminated products, these Canadian drugs are just as safe and effective as those sold in the United States. Moreover, they may actually be, in a certain sense, more effective than their U.S. counterparts because they are cheaper, making it more likely patients will comply with their prescribed drug regime. This trade is driven not by criminals but by consumers who need affordable medicines. The primary harm of this activity is lost pharmaceutical patent rents, not damage to patient health (Outterson and Smith 2006: 533). This trade may improve social welfare by increasing access to medication and may have an overall positive effect if U.S. patent rents are supra-optimal (Outterson 2005). Still, these drugs could conceivably pose significant import safety issues, especially if purchased over the Internet without proof of the actual source. In recent congressional legislation, bills to encourage drug importation would legalize some of this parallel trade; these bills also feature enhanced import safety provisions.

Unlicensed generic antiretroviral drugs for AIDS provide a final example. These drugs may be made under compulsory license, through voluntary agreements, or without a license, but they provide an affordable way to treat some of the millions suffering from AIDS. Many of these drugs are prequalified by the WHO, approved by the FDA, and paid for with U.S. government funds, yet would still violate patent law if sold in the United States (Outterson and Smith 2006: 534). These rules are not related to safety at all but are solely focused on protecting the patent rents of the pharmaceutical industry. Promoting pharmaceutical innovation is a legitimate policy option but should not be confused with import safety or public health.

Limiting the Traditional Definition of Counterfeit Medicines

The traditional WHO definition of counterfeit focuses on trademark issues of drugs "deliberately and fraudulently mislabeled with respect to identity and/or source" (WHO 2009a, para. 10), but some patent-based drug companies are now attempting to expand the definition to include any violation of any IP right, however technical or arcane. For example, a United Nations Interregional Crime and Justice Research Institute report recently defined counterfeiting as "illegal reproduction or imitation of products, given that this illegality is the result of a violation of *any type of intellectual property rights*" (emphasis added) (Park 2009: 2; UNICRI 2007). Likewise, ACTA is reported to apply to any violation of IP rights, broadly interpreted. While this is advantageous to pharmaceutical companies seeking to enhance IP rights beyond what TRIPS requires, it does nothing to further the public health and may harm the public health by making it more difficult to access medicines. This shift illustrates the need for a transparent and accountable process in IMPACT and ACTA.

A second example of IP expansion is criminal penalties for counterfeiting. While TRIPS requires criminalization of deliberate trademark counterfeiting, member countries are under no obligation to criminalize other acts of trademark infringement or infringement of other IP rights (Park 2009: 8–14). The distinction between criminal counterfeiting and civil trademark infringement is especially important in the context of pharmaceuticals. Civil trademark infringement disputes are common between generic pharmaceutical manufacturers and their brand-name counterparts. Generic drugs are often given names derived from the international nonproprietary name (INN) of the medical ingredient, names that occasionally sound similar to the drug's brand name (Park 2009: 12). These generic drugs improve access to medication and pose no risk to public health. Generics should not be confused with criminal counterfeits.

Under TRIPS, the only conduct that must be criminalized is "willful trademark counterfeiting or copyright piracy on a commercial scale" (Park 2009: 14; WTO 1994: art. 61). This distinction is also found in U.S. law (Rierson 2008). Nothing in TRIPS requires criminalization of patent infringement (Park 2009: 18), and given the frequency with which pharmaceutical patents are found invalid or not infringed in suits against generic manufacturers, there is a strong argument against criminalizing alleged patent infringement (Park 2009: 19). Furthermore, the Doha Declaration's mandate that TRIPS be interpreted in a way "supportive of WTO Members' right to protect public health and, in particular, to promote access to medicines for all" (WTO 2001: 1) suggests that IP laws should not interfere with access to generic medicines and parallel imports. Criminalizing unintentional acts of infringement by generic manufacturers will likely limit entry of affordable generic drugs into the market (Park 2009: 16–19).

The Unreliability of Statistics on Counterfeiting

Statistics on counterfeit medicine are widely distributed but are neither reliable nor transparent (Outterson and Smith 2005: 527). Estimates on the scope of the counterfeit drug problem vary greatly. Estimates on prevalence in various countries range from 1 to 50 percent of the drug supply, with reports of 40, 30, 17, and 10 percent (Bird 2008: 389). Recently, IMPACT estimated the prevalence of counterfeit medicines to be less than 1 percent of sales in developed countries—even though the potential profit of criminal counterfeiters is highest in these countries—and between 10 and 30 percent in developing countries, where the profit potential is lower. These estimates do not come from peer-reviewed journals, and many actually come from the pharmaceutical companies themselves (Park 2009: 23–24).

In many of these studies, substandard, adulterated, parallel-traded, and generic drugs have been improperly conflated with deliberate violations of trademark law (counterfeits), often under the imprecise catch-all category of "fake." The few studies that did differentiate found the majority of the problematic drugs bore genuine trademarks but were substandard. For example, in India it has been estimated that between

8.19 and 10.64 percent of drugs are substandard (but apparently bearing a proper trademark), while only between 0.24 and 0.47 percent are actually counterfeit in the trademark sense (Outterson and Smith 2006; Park 2009: 25). The primary health issue appears to be drug quality with the original manufacturer, not criminal counterfeiting.

For the most part, drug companies are hesitant to release information on counterfeit drugs, as this information could harm the reputation of their branded products (Essential Action 2008: 2; Outterson and Smith 2006: 527). The Pharmaceutical Security Institute (PSI), an industry organization formed by major drug companies, maintains the most comprehensive global database of counterfeit drug information, but researchers (Outterson and Smith 2006: 527), the WHO, health authorities, and the public are not given access to this database.

Several proposals have been put forward to remedy the problem of insufficient data. The federal government could fund surveillance to ensure the integrity of the U.S. drug market (Outterson and Smith 2006: 529). The WHO has begun some limited surveillance studies in developing countries (WHO 2009a: para. 27; WHO 2009b: Annex, para. 4). Surveillance requires randomized purchases within a market and testing the drugs for compliance with drug regulatory procedures. The results of these studies should be made widely available and performed in a manner that supports accurate cross comparisons. Other proposals would require pharmaceutical companies to report potentially problematic drugs to the regulatory agencies, which would then work to confirm the report and decide whether to alert law enforcement personnel and the public (Cockburn et al. 2005; CDEA 2003: sec. 3[b]; Maybarduk 2007: 5).

With respect to truly counterfeit products, TRIPS requires member states to "promote the exchange of information and cooperation between customs authorities with regard to trade in counterfeit trademarks" (WTO 1994: art. 69). It appears no country has yet required pharmaceutical companies or PSI to disclose information to the public under Article 69 (Maybarduk 2007: 5). However, in 2003, U.S. pharmaceutical companies entered into a voluntary agreement with the FDA to report instances of counterfeit drugs within five days (Cockburn et al. 2005). These data are not available to the public.

Rent-Seeking Regime Shifts: IMPACT and ACTA

The efforts with the Anti-Counterfeiting Trade Agreement were preceded by a public-private organization. IMPACT seeks to expand border enforcement against drugs subject to IP disputes. This effort goes well beyond the TRIPS, WHO, and U.S. definitions of counterfeit, and may reduce access to desirable generic drugs or cheaper brand-name drugs parallel traded from other countries. This section examines the norm-setting activities in IMPACT since 2006, before turning to ACTA. Both efforts seek new IP and customs enforcement rules for an expanded array of products. These expanded definitions may serve the interests of patent-based drug companies, but the impact on public health is less sanguine.

IMPACT

IMPACT is a voluntary organization including international organizations, governments, and private business associations. Participants include the WHO and the International Federation of Pharmaceutical Manufacturers Associations, the global lobbying arm of the patent-based drug companies. IMPACT was unveiled at a conference that took place in Rome on February 16–18, 2006 (WHO 2009b: para. 6). During 2008, a significant controversy arose regarding the relationship between IMPACT and WHO. IMPACT promoted itself as a WHO project involving all 193 WHO member states. In late 2008, developing countries blocked a WHO resolution supporting IMPACT's work, wary of its IP and public health implications (Third World Network 2008: 21). In April 2009, the WHO clarified its role in IMPACT and began to offer more transparency on the process (WHO 2009b).

One IMPACT norm-setting project is the Model Elements for National Legislation, which would strengthen IP protection beyond TRIPS requirements (Third World Network 2008: 24–27). If adopted, the Model Elements may create nontariff barriers to generic medicines. The Model Elements also fail to explicitly recognize parallel importation and TRIPS flexibilities such as compulsory licensing, which provide a legal method of improving access to medication (Third World Network 2008: 24–27). WHO is the primary UN agency for health and is ideally suited to balance the dual health imperatives of drug safety and access to essential medicines. To date, it does not appear that WHO has discussed this issue at IMPACT. A more transparent process might broaden the scope of the inquiry and draw other voices into the discussion.

Industry officials have a strong incentive to discourage the use of TRIPS flexibilities by confusing these drugs with criminal counterfeits, and it appears they are using IMPACT to pursue this agenda (Sell 2008: 13). It seems that members of the private sector were heavily involved in drafting the Model Elements, while many WHO member states had little input (Third World Network 2008: 25).

IMPACT has also had some success in pushing developing countries to adopt laws providing for stronger IP protection. Kenya's recently enacted Anti-Counterfeiting Act provides several measures aimed at targeting the general availability of counterfeit goods in the country (HAI Africa 2008; MSF 2008b). While the bill does have some positive aspects, it also contains several provisions that could hamper the government's ability to provide access to essential medicine to the estimated 1.4 million or more Kenyans living with HIV/AIDS (UNAIDS 2008). The bill needlessly confuses counterfeiting with violations of nontrademark IP rights (HAI Africa 2008; MSF 2008b). The bill also weakens existing Kenyan legislation allowing parallel imports (HAI Africa 2008). Uganda, where about 5 percent of the adult population is infected with HIV/AIDS (UNAIDS 2008), is also considering a similar bill (Mathew 2009). The Ugandan legislation reportedly calls for the death penalty for drug "counterfeiters"; the mixture of imprecise definitions and capital punishment may chill legitimate markets in generic drugs.

In another norm-setting project, IMPACT has proposed modifying the traditional WHO definition of counterfeit:

> A medical product is counterfeit when there is a false representation in relation to its identity and/or source. This applies to the product, its container or other packaging or labeling information. Counterfeiting can apply to both branded and generic products. Counterfeits may include products with correct ingredients/components, with wrong ingredients/components, without active ingredients, with incorrect amounts of active ingredients, or with fake packaging.
>
> Violations or disputes concerning patents must not be confused with counterfeiting of medical products. Medical products (whether generic or branded) that are not authorized for marketing in a given country but authorized elsewhere are not considered counterfeit. Substandard batches of, or quality defects or non-compliance with, Good Manufacturing Practices/Good Distribution Practices in legitimate medical products must not be confused with counterfeiting. (WHO 2008)

This proposed definition partially addresses the confusion between patent infringement, drug registration, and trademark counterfeiting, but also raises several concerns. Although the definition states that patent disputes must not be "confused" with counterfeiting, it does not say patent violations *are not* counterfeiting. Notably, the definition fails to say if counterfeiting must be done deliberately or even whether criminal intent or careless behaviors are necessary elements. The distinction between civil and criminal violations of trademark has a long history under U.S. law, and is also expressed in TRIPS. Significant modifications to these principles should not be made in obscurity.

The definition is unclear whether the term *identity* refers to the INN (the "international non-proprietary name") or the generic name, a global standard that cannot be trademarked. In the proposed definition, the term is described nonexhaustively to *include* any "misleading statement with respect to name, composition, strength or other elements." Generic drugs often appear similar to their brand-name counterparts with regard to taste, shape, or color. IMPACT expands the definition of counterfeit to include false representations of identity or source applied to "the product, its container or other packaging or labeling information." This raises the possibility that generic versions of off-patent drugs could be considered counterfeit on the basis of similar trade dress or drug labeling (Third World Network 2008: 36–39).

The goal of any legal reforms in this area should be to remove goods bearing deliberately false trademarks (counterfeits) from the supply chain, while encouraging legitimate low-cost generic drug markets. A troubling aspect of IMPACT is that norms are being set that potentially will alter common law and statutory rules in many countries, and those changes may occur without much democratic debate. IMPACT's working groups are not accessible to the public, nor are public health groups with knowledge of IP laws invited to participate. The process is driven by the patent-based pharmaceutical companies that stand to benefit financially from hindering generic competition.

The Anti-Counterfeiting Trade Agreement

In addition to the legislative changes being encouraged by IMPACT, international laws on counterfeit goods may soon be dramatically altered by the Anti-Counterfeiting Trade Agreement. ACTA is being negotiated by thirteen countries, led by the United States and the EU (Kaminski 2009: 247). It is difficult to say anything definitive about ACTA because the negotiations are taking place in secret, and no verified draft of the agreement has been circulated (Kaminski 2009: 247, 251). A purported draft is available on the Internet, on Wikileaks, which represents the only publicly available detailed information on ACTA.

ACTA is designed "to bridge the gap between laws on the books and strong enforcement on the ground" (USTR 2008). Given recent seizures of generic medications suspected of violating patent laws, it will be important to watch the development of this agreement and to examine the potential impact it could have on legitimate trade in generic medications and parallel imports.

Several points are notable in the leaked drafts, which we can only assume are authentic. First, the ACTA texts from May and June 2008 covered only trademark and copyright (ACTA 2008a, 2008b; Kaminski 2009); in the text from July 2008, the scope was expanded to cover all IP rights described in TRIPS (ACTA 2008c: art. 2.7 [1]). This is precisely the expansion of IP rights criticized with respect to IMPACT. Second, ACTA proposes to modify existing criminal standards and sanctions (ACTA 2008d: sec. 3), as well as border measures, giving customs officials more authority to seize and destroy infringing shipments and to disclose information to right holders on those shipments (ACTA 2008b: sec. 2; Kaminski 2009: 251–54). One proposal by Japan would expand the definition of "counterfeit" well beyond the accepted bounds of "willful trademark counterfeiting" to include criminal penalties for "trademark infringement caused by confusingly similar trademark goods" (ACTA 2008d: art. 2.14[1]). These changes could expose generic manufacturers to significant risks without justification. Third, the United States proposed that ACTA cover "in-transit" shipments as well as import and export (ACTA 2008b: art. 2.6[1]), the precise issue raised by the Dutch seizures. Fourth, the September 2008 proposal from the EU requires the parties to "ensure that, where a judicial decision is taken finding an infringement of an IP right, the judicial authorities may issue against the infringer an injunction" (ACTA 2008e: art. 2.7). After the recent U.S. Supreme Court decision in *Ebay, Inc. v. Mercexchange* (2006), modification of U.S. law may be required, which would be a very controversial move. Finally, the Canadian "non-paper," dated June 9, 2008, discusses the creation of the ACTA Oversight Council, with institutional powers and capacities, including dispute resolution. Clearly, a new international organization is being formed.

It is important not to be too distracted by the details in ACTA, because we are speculating in the shadows rather than engaging in a transparent and robust debate. But it certainly seems plausible that public health concerns are raised by some of the provisions of ACTA, and should be fully vetted with open and democratic processes. Both Canada and the European Parliament have called for transparency in the ACTA negotiations, but reportedly the U.S. government is blocking disclosure as a national security secret (Geist 2009). Perhaps the Obama administration will say "Yes We Can" to fuller disclosure and public debate.

Conclusion

Drugs that bear a deliberately false trademark must be kept out of the market. But removing counterfeits will not eliminate all problems with substandard, contaminated, and adulterated drugs, as many unsafe drugs are not counterfeits. Moreover, an overly expansive definition of the term "counterfeit" (especially one that expands beyond trademark law to include patent disputes) may impede access to medication by reducing access to generic medications. Recent attempts to conflate these categories damage public health and confuse issues of import safety with patent policy.

Equally significant is the recent strategy to create additional global institutions as regime-shifting fora to expand IP enforcement, diverting import safety resources to serve the IP goals of patent-based drug companies. Given the significant public health issues at stake, these efforts should not proceed without transparency and significant democratic engagement. Recent seizures of generic drugs, suspected of infringing patents in a transit country, highlight the need to ensure the definition of counterfeit is not stretched beyond what TRIPS requires to criminalize legitimate, socially desirable behavior.

Acknowledgments

I thank Paige Goodwin (Boston University Law, 2009), who provided research assistance, and Aly Dudkowski (Boston University Law, 2008), who assisted with editing. I am grateful for comments from Stacey Dogan, now a professor at Boston University Law; Robert C. Bird, Assistant Professor and Ackerman Scholar in the Department of Marketing and Law, University of Connecticut; Peggy E. Chaudhry, Associate Professor of Management and Operations in the Villanova School of Business; the editors of this book; the other participants at the workshop at the University of Pennsylvania Law School; and the participants in a seminar chaired by Susan K. Sell at the Institute for Global and International Studies at George Washington University.

Note

1. Trademark violations are also possible even if the original purchaser knew the item was counterfeit. An example would be a consumer who knowingly bought a cheap watch bearing a false Rolex trademark. In that case, the original consumer was not deceived, and yet a trademark violation may be found on other grounds, such as confusion to other consumers.

References

Azevêdo, Roberto (2009) "Statement by Brazil at TRIPS Council: Public Health Dimension of TRIPS Agreement." Knowledge Ecology Notes. http://www.keionline.org/blogs/2009/03/04/brazilian-intervention-at-trips-council/.
Bird, Robert C. (2008) "Counterfeit Drugs: The Global Consumer Perspective." 8 *Wake Forest Intellectual Property Law Journal* 387–406.

Cahoy, Daniel R. (2008) "Addressing the North-South Divide in Pharmaceutical Counterfeiting." 8 *Wake Forest Intellectual Property Law Journal* 407–32.

Caudron, J.-M., N. Ford, M. Henkens, C. Macé, R. Kiddle-Monroe, and J. Pinel (2008) "Substandard Medicines in Resource-Poor Settings: A Problem That Can No Longer Be Ignored." 13 *Tropical Medicine & International Health* 1062–72.

Cockburn, Robert, Paul N. Newton, E. Kyeremateng Agyarko, Dora Akunyili, and Nicholas J. White (2005) "The Global Threat of Counterfeit Drugs: Why Industry and Governments Must Communicate the Dangers." 2 *PLoS Medicine*, March 14.

DeLauro, Rosa L. (2003) "Imported Drugs: FDA Suddenly Gets 'Concerned'." *L.A. Times*, November 5, sec. B.

Essential Action (2008) Essential Action to Rachel S. Bae, Director for Intellectual Property and Innovation, Office of the United States Trade Representative. Letter (on file with author).

Geist, Michael (2009) "Anti-Counterfeiting Treaty Talks Heat Up." *Toronto Star*, March 30, sec. B.

Health Action International (HAI) Africa (2008) "Kenya Anti-Counterfeit Bill 2008 Poses Threat to Access to Essential Medicines." Nairobi, Kenya: HAI Africa.

Health Action International (HAI), Oxfam International, and Knowledge Ecology International (2009) "Seizure of UNITAID/Clinton Foundation Antiretroviral Medicines by Dutch Customs Authorities 'Unacceptable.'" Press release.

Helfer, Laurence R. (2004) "Regime Shifting: The TRIPS Agreement and New Dynamics of International Intellectual Property Lawmaking." 29 *Yale Journal of International Law* 1–84.

International Center for Trade and Sustainable Development (ICTSD) (2009a) "Fight over Generic Drug Seizure Takes Centre Stage at TRIPS Council Meeting." 13 *Intellectual Property Program*, March 11.

———. (2009b) "Dutch Seizure of Generic Drugs Sparks Controversy." 13 *Intellectual Property Program*, January 25.

Joint United Nations Programme on HIV/AIDS (UNAIDS) (2008) *Report on the Global HIV/AIDS Epidemic 2008*. http://data.unaids.org/pub/GlobalReport/ 2008/JC1510_2008GlobalReport_en.zip.

Kaminski, Margot (2009) "The Origins and Potential Impact of the Anti-Counterfeiting Trade Agreement (ACTA)." 34 *Yale Journal of International Law* 247–56.

Khosla, Rajat and Paul Hunt (2009) *Human Rights Guidelines for Pharmaceutical Companies in Relation to Access to Medicines: The Sexual and Reproductive Health Context*. Essex, UK: Human Rights Centre, University of Essex.

Knowledge Economy International (KEI) (2009) "NGO Views: World Health Organization (WHO) Voice on Issue of Medicines in Transit to Developing Countries?" http://www.keionline.org/blogs/2009/03/13/who-silence-goods-in-transit/.

Mathew, Joe C. (2009) "Ugandan Move on Patented Drugs' Import Worries Indian Companies." *Business Standard*, March 6.

Maybarduk, Peter to Robert Weissman (2007) Listserv post July 20 (on file with author).

Médecins sans Frontières (MSF) (2009) "Médecins sans Frontières to Mr. László Kovács, European Commissioner for Taxation and Customs Union, and Baroness Catherine Ashton, European Commissioner for Trade." http://www.msfaccess.org/main/access-patents/letters-to-ec-on-netherlands-customs-seizure/.

———. (2008a) "Counterfeit, Substandard and Generic Drugs." http://www.msfaccess.org/main/access-patents/counterfeit-substandard-and-generic-drugs/.

———. (2008b) "Fatal Confusion: How Kenya's 2008 Anti-Counterfeiting Bill Endangers Access to Medicines." http://www.msfaccess.org/fileadmin/user_upload/medinnov_accesspatents/2008%2010%20Fatal%20Confusion%20 20-%20Kenya%20Counterfeits%20Final.pdf.

Outterson, Kevin (2009) "Disease-Based Limitations On Compulsory Licenses Under Articles 31 and 31 bis." In *Research Handbook on Intellectual Property Law and the WTO*, edited by Carlos Correa. Cheltenham, UK: Edward Elgar.

———. (2005) "Pharmaceutical Arbitrage: Balancing Access and Innovation in International Pharmaceutical Markets." 5 *Yale Journal of Health Policy, Law, & Ethics* 193–291.

Outterson, Kevin and Ryan Smith (2006) "Counterfeit Drugs: The Good, the Bad and the Ugly." 15 *Albany Law Journal of Science and Technology* 525–43.

Pandeya, Radhieka (2009) "UN Agency Protests Dutch Seizure of Indian HIV Drugs." *Live Mint* (*Wall Street Journal India*), March 6.

Park, Chan (2009) "Defining 'Counterfeit Medicine' from the Public Health Perspective." WHO (on file with author).

Rierson, Sandra L (2008) "Pharmaceutical Counterfeiting and the Puzzle of Remedies." 8 *Wake Forest Intellectual Property Law Journal* 433–58.

Sell, Susan K. (2008) The Global IP Upward Ratchet, Anti-Counterfeiting and Piracy Enforcement Efforts: The State of Play. Paper, George Washington University, June 9.

———. (2003) *Public Power, Private Law: The Globalization of Intellectual Property Rights*. Cambridge: Cambridge University Press.

———. (1998) *Power and Ideas: North-South Politics of Intellectual Property and Antitrust*. Albany, N.Y.: SUNY Press.

Shaffer, Ellen and Joe Brenner (2005) "Corporations Dominate Trade Panels That Set Global Health Policy. Public Health Groups Sue U.S. Government for Fair & Democratic Representation." Center for Policy Analysis on Trade and Health. http://www.cpath.org/id4.html.

Shashikant, Sangeeta (2009) "Dr. Margaret Chan willing to drop 'counterfeit,' stresses on substandard." Third World Network IP Info, IP Health listserv, May 26.

Third World Network (2008) "Unpacking the Issue of Counterfeit Medicines." May 1 (on file with author).

UNITAID (2009) "UNITAID Statement on Dutch Confiscation of Medicines Shipment." http://www.unitaid.eu/index.php/en/NEWS/UNITAID-statement-on-Dutch-confiscation-of-medicines-shipment.html.

United Nations Interregional Crime and Justice Research Institute (UNICRI) (2007) *Counterfeiting: A Global Spread, a Global Threat*. http://www.unicri.it/news/0712-3_Counterfeiting_CRT_Foundation.php.

U.S. Trade Representative (USTR) (2008) "Trade Facts: Anti-Counterfeiting Trade Agreement." Office of the U.S. Trade Representative. http://www.ustr.gov/assets/Document_Library/Fact_Sheets/2008/asset_upload_file760_15084.pdf.

World Health Organization (WHO) (2009a) *Access to Medicines.* http://www
.who.int/mediacentre/news/statements/2009/access-medicines-20090313/
en/index.html.

———. (2009b) *Counterfeit Medical Products: International Medical Products Anti-
Counterfeiting Taskforce.* Report by the Secretariat, A62/14. http://apps.who
.int/gb/ebwha/pdf_files/A62/A62_13-en.pdf.

———. (2008) Counterfeit Medical Products: Report by the Secretariat, December 18. http://www.who.int/gb/ebwha/pdf_files/EB124/B124_14-en.pdf.

WHO/International Federation of Pharmaceutical Manufacturers (IFPMA)
(1992) *Counterfeit Drugs: Report of a WHO/IFPMA Workshop.* Geneva: WHO.

Case Cited

Ebay, Inc. v. Mercexchange, LLC, 547 U.S. 388 (2006).

Statutes, Regulations, and Agreements Cited

Anti-Counterfeiting Trade Agreement (2008a) Japan-U.S. Joint Proposal (20
May).

Anti-Counterfeiting Trade Agreement (2008b) Japan-U.S. Joint Proposal (25
June).

Anti-Counterfeiting Trade Agreement (2008c) EU Proposal (7 July).

Anti-Counterfeiting Trade Agreement (2008d) Japan-U.S. Joint Proposal (16
October).

Anti-Counterfeiting Trade Agreement (2008e) EU Proposal (23 September).

Counterfeit Drug Enforcement Act (CDEA) (2003) H.R. Res. 3297, 108th
Cong.

European Union (2003) Council Regulation (EC) 1383/2003 of 22 July 2003,
OJ (L 196).

World Trade Organization (WTO), Agreement on Trade-Related Aspects of
Intellectual Property Rights (TRIPS) (1994), 33 I.L.M. 81.

World Trade Organization (WTO), Ministerial Declaration of 14 November
2001 (Doha Declaration) (2001), 41 I.L.M. 746.

Trademarks, 15 U.S. Code sec. 1127.

Tariff Act, 19 U.S. Code sec. 1526(e).

Part III
Toward Smarter Regulation

Chapter 7
Forecasting Consumer Safety Violations and Violators

Richard Berk

Responding to reports from China of infant formula contaminated with melamine, the U.S. Food and Drug Administration (FDA) issued a health information advisory in September 2008 stating that there was no known threat of contamination in infant formula manufactured by companies complying with U.S. regulations. The FDA also stated that no companies selling infant formula in the United States were using milk-based ingredients from China but that, nevertheless, there would be ongoing testing of food items imported from China that could contain significant amounts of milk or milk proteins.

The melamine incident is one illustration of the systematic oversight of the safety of consumer products that can be the responsibility of any number of federal, state, and local agencies. Such oversight requires resources, and with an almost limitless number of venues and actors, those resources are guaranteed to be insufficient. A sensible response is to be smart about how oversight resources are allocated. And being smart can depend substantially on the collection and analysis of data that allow administrators to anticipate where the impact of their oversight activities will be most cost effective. This can be very demanding because to anticipate impact, one must look into the future.

Forecasts have long played an important role in a variety of decision making, especially in criminal justice. They have been used to inform the need to build prisons, allocate police personnel to certain neighborhoods, and anticipate the amount and mix of crime. But perhaps the most common use of forecasts has been to aid in making decisions about individuals convicted of crimes. Forecasts of future behavior can at least implicitly affect sentencing decisions by judges (U.S. Sentencing Commission 2006), housing decisions made by prison officials (Berk et al. 2006), release decisions made by parole boards (Glaser 1987), and supervisory decisions made by probation or parole officers (Berk et al. 2009b). The overall success of these forecasting exercises is certainly open to debate, but there is no doubt that some recent statistical developments have begun to produce predictions of useful accuracy and that still better forecasting skill is on the horizon (Berk 2008a).

The goal of this chapter is to provide a translation of forecasting a wide range of criminal behavior to forecasting economic behavior that puts consumers at risk, whether from a drive for profits or just innocent errors. The justification for both applications is much the same. Forecasts can help in the prevention of misconduct, the determination of appropriate punishment for misconduct, the allocation of scarce enforcement resources, and the selection of effective remedies for the consequences of misconduct. Forecasts can also be used in a forensic manner to identify malfeasance that has already occurred. How these applications play out for consumer safety oversight is considered in the rest of this chapter, and we will see that many important lessons from forecasting criminal behavior carry over well to consumer protection.

Examples of Forecasts and Their Roles in Law Enforcement

The forecasting addressed in this chapter is related to other empirical activities. In particular, the kinds of forecasting discussed here are sometimes characterized as "profiling." From a set of attributes that some might call a profile, projections are made. For example: advertisers construct consumer profiles to forecast what certain individuals might be convinced to buy. Colleges construct applicant profiles to forecast who will do well academically. Medical researchers construct profiles of patients and their symptoms to forecast treatments likely to work well.

More immediately relevant here, profiling is common in law enforcement. Parole boards, for instance, construct profiles of prison inmates using information about their past crimes and behavior behind bars to forecast how they will fare under supervision in their communities. Perhaps the best known instances in law enforcement involve profiles of crimes and criminals used to determine which pedestrians and drivers to stop for questioning. In theory at least, police officers are trying to apprehend individuals who have committed crimes or who may soon do so.

Profiling implies forecasting. Behavior is imputed that has not been observed, either because it occurred elsewhere, outside of view, or because it has not yet occurred. One important implication is that the construction and use of profiles should conform to the same statistical principles as conventional forecasting. This emphasis on forecasting also helps to distinguish the procedures discussed in this chapter from "risk assessments" sometimes undertaken in criminal justice settings or when the safety of consumer products is a concern. For example, risk assessments are often undertaken for households in which domestic violence is suspected (Dutton and Kropp 2000), and also for a wide variety of food product contaminants, as described by Zach and Bier in chapter 8 of this volume. The essential goal of a risk assessment is to establish cause and effect relationships between causal variables and some outcome of interest. One must bring to bear, therefore, all of the usual concerns about causal inference (Holland 1986; Rubin 1986). Careful thought must be given to defining the appropriate counterfactual conditions for each causal variable. Thus, for foods stored at a temperature that risks bacterial contamination, the analyst needs to consider what is the appropriate temperature to which the suspect temperature should be compared.

When accurate forecasts are the goal, cause and effect are formally unnecessary. Consequently, the conceptual and statistical tools can differ dramatically (Granger 1989). In particular, the primary criterion for evaluating forecasts is their forecasting accuracy. Whether the variables used to make the forecasts have any sensible causal interpretation is at best a secondary concern. It follows that, in forecasting as opposed to risk assessment, addressing uncertainty centers on the the overall values forecasted, not the role of individual predictors. In practice, however, one can at times find forecasts that have been made implicitly from risk assessments and also at times find causal interpretations that have been given to forecasting predictors. When this happens, there is a mismatch between the tools being used and the goals of the research, and misleading conclusions can follow.

To explain further how forecasting works, as well as provide a basis for drawing lessons for using forecasts in the realm of consumer product safety, we can now turn to four criminal justice applications —domestic violence, probation and parole, incarceration, and environmental crimes—to show how the issues are often very similar to those in consumer protection.

Domestic Violence

One of the key decisions that police officers make in domestic violence incidents is whether to arrest the alleged perpetrator or just try to restore order. An important factor in that decision is a forecast of whether, in the near future, police will again need to be dispatched to that household. If the chances they will have to return are good, police might quite properly decide to employ a more intrusive intervention. Police officers on domestic violence calls routinely make such forecasts in an informal manner using their experience with similar cases in the past. But it is possible to do better.

With a data set of several hundred domestic violence cases, one can in principle link a number of readily available predictors to the chances of another incident involving the same individuals and to the seriousness of that repeat incident. For example, past police dispatches to the same household are, not surprisingly, a good predictor of more dispatches in the future. Likewise, injuries that in the past have required medical attention anticipate subsequent life-threatening violence. When police later confront domestic violence cases, they can exploit such information to make formal forecasts that in turn can be used to inform decisions about what should be done. Just such a procedure was developed for the Los Angeles County Sheriff's Department (Berk et al. 2005). The strong predictors were organized into a checklist. The more checks, the greater the probability of a repeat call. This information helped to inform police officers' actions.

This is an example of forecasts used to prevent unwanted behavior in the future. When the probability of unwanted behavior is sufficiently high, police can choose to intervene in a more intrusive manner. They can try to prevent undesirable outcomes by incapacitating the likely perpetrator through an arrest and incarceration, trying to aggressively mediate the dispute, ordering the perpetrator from the premises for several hours as a "cooling down period," or threatening unpleasant sanctions in the future. Some of these options (and others) can also be usefully combined with each other. The general point is that law enforcement resources can be more effectively allocated if police officers have the ability to make more reliable predictions of future behavior.

Probation and Parole

Approximately 50,000 individuals a year are supervised by the Philadelphia Adult Probation and Parole Department (APPD). This supervision is costly and, most would argue, not effectively deployed. About a quarter of the probationers or parolees fail to meet the conditions set by the authorities and are sent or returned to prison. One possible explanation for the high rate of failure is that supervisory resources are not being allocated efficiently. For example, individual probationers and parolees can differ dramatically in the probability they will re-offend and in how serious the new offenses are likely to be. If one could forecast, at a useful level of accuracy, the risk to public safety an individual poses, it might then be possible to reallocate resources away from low-risk individuals toward high-risk individuals.

Just such an exercise is well under way. Recent research has shown that it is possible, using information routinely available at intake, to forecast with considerable skill which individuals under supervision by the APPD will commit a homicide or attempted homicide within two years after supervision begins (Berk et al. 2009a). That work has now been expanded. Using similar statistical procedures and data, forecasts of at least equal accuracy have been constructed for individuals at the other extreme: parolees and probationers who pose no serious risk to public safety (Berk et al. 2009c). This has, in turn, led to a third forecasting exercise in which there are three outcome classes: (1) a new arrest for a serious crime; (2) a new arrest for any other crime; and (3) no new arrest. Once again, forecasting accuracy has been satisfactory and supervisory resources are now being reorganized in response to needs those forecasts imply.

Incarceration

Yet another forecasting study within the same spirit was conducted for the California Department of Corrections (Berk et al. 2006). The outcome to be forecasted was serious misconduct in prison. "Serious misconduct" was defined as a violation that would be considered a felony if committed on the outside: homicide, attempted homicide, assault, rape, drug trafficking, and such. For prisons, a particularly dear resource is the availability of prison beds in high-security facilities. High-security facilities have per-inmate yearly costs comparable to Ivy League tuition and each new cell built can easily cost six figures. High-security placements, therefore, should only be made for inmates who really need them. Sufficiently accurate forecasts were produced, using information regularly available at admission, that would have routinely made more informed placement decisions possible. Unfortunately, several system-wide crises intervened and, to date, the forecasting procedures have not been used.

Environmental Crimes

The international purse-seine fishery for tuna in the Eastern Pacific is responsible for about a quarter of the total catch of yellowfin tuna. By international treaty, boat captains are required to abide by a number of fishing regulations and, in particular, employ fishing practices that do not kill dolphins. Dolphin mortality can lead to a variety of sanctions imposed on fishing operations, including the loss of all revenues from tuna caught when the dolphins were killed. Moreover, tuna caught when dolphins are killed cannot be sold with the "dolphin safe" label, which effectively eliminates many markets in Europe and North America.

To enforce the fishing regulations, the Inter-American Tropical Tuna Commission, which supervises the fishery, places observers on many of the fishing boats. The observer's job is to report on each tuna set in substantial detail. (A set refers to the large net deployed in the ocean to encircle and then draw in a school of tuna.)

Observers are required to record whether any dolphins are killed in the fishing process, and, if so, how many. A problem with this approach is that captains have strong incentives to bribe observers because, with a stroke of an observer's pen, tens of thousands of dollars can be saved. Indeed, there have been allegations that some observers have falsified data and, in a few such cases, observers have been caught and fired.

The statistical challenge is to identify which observers are likely to be corrupt, using just patterns in the available data. The solution, in brief, has been to develop a model of the purse-seine process that provided figures for expected dolphin mortality under different fishing conditions. For example, dolphins are likely to become entangled in nets when wind, currents, and the speed of the retrieval lead to a folding over of some parts of the net. Problems with the net are routinely recorded and thus can be used as predictors.

If an observer frequently reported no mortality when the model indicated there should have been some, that observer's credibility is undermined. A follow-up investigation is then initiated. The approach was validated with earlier data on observers who were identified as corrupt using other, investigative means. The statistical procedures correctly found most of those individuals—after the fact—with very few false positives.

In short, the statistical forecasts of dolphin mortality, coupled with what was actually reported, allowed the Inter-American Tropical Tuna Commission to develop profiles of corrupt observers. When these profiles were applied to observers' reports, they would trigger investigations that usually proved to be productive. In addition to several other benefits, the statistical procedures aided in the allocation of investigative resources. Rather than trying to investigate all observers, only the "suspicious" observers were investigated (Lennert-Cody and Berk 2007).

Making the Translation

The tasks undertaken for the kinds of criminal justice applications just described are much the same, at least broadly characterized, as the tasks that would need to be undertaken for consumer product safety forecasting. Just as with police interventions in cases of domestic violence, regulatory officials charged with consumer safety depend on cost-effective prevention initiatives. Probation and parole authorities employ oversight that may be especially intrusive once past offenses have been proved and that varies as individual profiles change over time, especially if undesirable behavior persists. Regulatory officials could proceed in a similar fashion. In addition, if these officials choose to rely increasingly on third-party auditors to address import safety problems, they will face the same question raised by the tuna fishing illustration: Who will audit the auditors? We turn now to a summary of the tasks inherent in criminal justice forecasting that carry over into oversight of consumer product safety.

Design Decisions

The first and perhaps most important step is to develop a research design, beginning with the processes that are to be examined and the observational units. For example, if there are concerns about imported pharmaceuticals, one could try to forecast defective products at any of several different steps in the supply chain: from the raw materials used to the products coming off the assembly line; from shipments before leaving the factory to shipments arriving at their destinations; and from wholesale distributors to retail establishments. The units could be individual doses of the medications, single packages of the medications, or entire shipments from certain places and at certain times.

Consider an example involving food safety. Figure 1, obtained from the FDA website, is a simplified flowchart of how peanut products from a given processor are distributed. The flowchart was constructed after reports emerged of salmonella contamination of peanut products by the Peanut Corporation of America (PCA). The public health consequences materialize after the events on the far right side of the flowchart. Salmonella contamination occurs on the far left side of the flowchart. Flowcharts similar to Figure 1 apply to virtually all consumer products, whether from the United States or abroad.

For illustrative purposes, suppose Figure 1 applied to a large number of peanut product manufacturers, and the goal was to construct procedures from which to forecast salmonella contamination. Also suppose, for simplicity, that salmonella contamination gets carried along largely undisturbed. For example, assume there are no production processes in the distribution chain that heat the peanut products to very high temperatures. Under these conditions, it would not matter much at which link in the distribution chain the forecasts of salmonella concentrations were targeted.

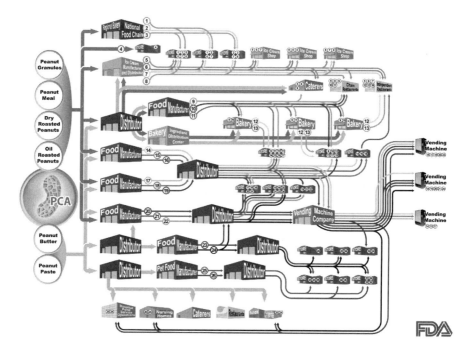

Figure 1. Simplified peanut product distribution pattern from Peanut Corporation of America (PCA) to point of sale. The circled numbers represent products that were made using at least one ingredient originating from PCA's peanut processing facility in Blakely, Georgia. (Reproduced from the FDA website.)

Developing any forecasting procedure for processes like those represented in Figure 1 would require a large sample of peanut products with measures of salmonella concentrations for each. Predictors would need to be derived from information that would ordinarily be available. Otherwise, they could not be used at the time when forecasts were desired. The precise nature of those predictors would depend in part on the stage in the distribution process. Some predictors might come from the size and design of the production or distribution facility, from past inspections of the entities in question, or even from their recent financial circumstances. For example, it might turn out that smaller facilities, using older technology, and under significant economic pressure have been more likely to have salmonella problems in the past. And if so, one might anticipate more salmonella problems for such establishments in the future.

The quality of the data is very important. Key predictors and outcomes must be well measured, and the data must on their own capture a population of interest or a proper sample from such a population. For example, before any forecasts can be used, one needs to determine to what population of observational units they should apply. Would forecasts derived from a distribution chain such as Figure 1 apply to salmonella contamination for all firms making peanut products, or would they apply ten years into the future when the production technology may have changed? At the same time, these kinds of technical concerns do not stand alone. They must respond to the goals of stakeholders. Stakeholder intentions motivate the research. As the famous statistician John Tukey purportedly said, "If it's not worth doing, it's not worth doing well."

To illustrate, consider that the work undertaken for the Inter-American Tropical Tuna Commission had three goals: (1) allocating investigatory resources, (2) preventing record falsification, and (3) punishing offenders. The analysis rested on a population of administrative records that were themselves of interest. The commission was pursuing its three goals with respect to the actions represented in those administrative data. The focus was on the production step in which tuna were netted. The unit of observation was the set. The outcome of dolphin deaths was apparent, given the policy concerns. Extensive administrative data were readily available, which included a number of predictors with at least strong face validity.

Different policy concerns could have led to a dramatically different research design. For example, had the concern been mercury concentrations in tuna, the observational unit could have been individual tuna and the meat that people consume. The outcome variables and predictors would also have been entirely different, and there would have been no need to collect data on fishing boats. Data collected as the fish entered processing plants would probably have been of better quality and easier to obtain.

One key lesson is that the design decisions must respond to the needs, opportunities, and constraints of each situation. There can be no design, or even small set of designs, that will properly apply to all settings. For example, an approach that was effective in an earlier setting may subsequently stumble because some key information becomes proprietary. Likewise, sometimes designs can rely on data that are already available, and sometimes they will need to anticipate the collection of data that otherwise would not exist or the establishment of procedures by which the requisite data will be collected in an ongoing manner.

Another lesson is that any design should be driven by both technical and substantive matters. Both sorts of expertise must be represented among those who are planning the work. And both require specialization. In the pharmaceutical illustration, one would need the team to include expertise on the production processes, legal matters, and the most relevant local and international politics. Such expertise would inform how much effort should go into the data collection. For some purposes, "quick and dirty" will suffice. For other purposes, one would need a "full court press."

Taking Forecasting Errors into Account

One must appreciate from the start that forecasting errors will be made. Perfect foresight is the stuff of science fiction novels and movies (e.g., *Minority Report*). There are no costs from such errors in themselves. There can be enormous costs when those errors are acted on.

For categorical outcomes, such as whether an observer has been taking bribes, the forecasting errors will be of two kinds: false positives and false negatives. For the dolphin analysis, a false positive would falsely identify an observer as a suspect. A false negative would fail to identify an observer as a suspect who was in fact taking bribes. In product safety, a categorical outcome might be whether the presence of health hazards exceeded some medical threshold or not. A false positive would be incorrectly asserting that the threshold had been exceeded. A false negative would be failing to assert that the threshold was exceeded when it actually had been. A possible cost of a false positive would be a product recall in error. A possible cost of a false negative would be the deaths of several infants that could have been prevented. Sometimes there will be tradeoffs between false positives and false negatives, in the sense that research strategies to eliminate one of these types of errors might increase the possibility of the other type. How to make such tradeoffs is a policy decision.

Categorical variables are sometimes called "nominal" variables. Observations are placed into categories that are exhaustive and mutually exclusive. Categorical variables with two categories are most common, but more than two is certainly permitted. For example, baby formula can be made unsafe by several different kinds of contaminants. Then, false positives and false negatives should be considered for each type of contaminant.

In practice, one only needs to determine the *relative* costs of false positives and false negatives. In the study done for the California Department of Corrections, prison officials determined that it was far more costly to have a very high-risk inmate not be accurately identified as high risk than to have a low-risk inmate incorrectly identified as high risk. Ten "over-incarcerations" were treated as if they had the same costs as one "under-incarceration." The cost ratio of false negatives to false positives was 10 to 1.

There are often several sets of relative costs. Different stakeholders will value the relative costs of false positives and false negatives differently. There are then at least two options. Some overarching body or procedure can force a compromise ratio. Or, different sets of forecasts can be provided for the different cost ratios. Ideally, the cost ratios are similar enough so that the forecasts are similar as well. Alternatively, that overarching body or procedure will determine which forecasts to use.

If the relative costs of false negatives and false positives are not explicitly introduced, equal costs are the usual default. This is likely to be a mistake. For the Department of Corrections, equal costs would have produced far less useful and very different forecasts from those that were being sought. In the baby formula example, if the costs of several avoidable infant deaths are much higher than a false-alarm product recall, the forecasts will by design increase the false-positive rate relative to the false-negative rate. That is, the procedure will accept weaker evidence that a product recall is needed than it would if the relative costs were not so extreme, let alone if infant deaths were valued less than a formula producer's economic well-being.

When the response being forecasted is quantitative, constructing useful forecasts can be more technically demanding. For example, one may be interested in forecasting the concentration of a given contaminant in baby formula. Then, the forecasting errors will be overestimates or underestimates of those concentrations. The direction and the size of the forecasting error matters, and asymmetric costs are common. For example, overestimates or underestimates of contaminant concentrations with no medical or economic implications may have zero costs because no actions are required. But the costs of larger underestimates may increase in an increasing fashion, while the costs of larger overestimates may increase in a constant fashion. Building these kinds of complexities into a forecasting procedure can be challenging, and a full treatment of how to do so is beyond the scope of this chapter. A useful discussion and application can be found in the recent paper by Kriegler and Berk (2009).

Analysis of the Data

The available data must be analyzed so that associations between predictors and the outcomes to be forecasted are established. "Predictors" are sometimes called regressors, independent variables, or exogenous variables. Outcome variables are sometimes called response variables, dependent variables, or endogenous variables.

The data used for such purposes are often called "training data" because algorithms linking predictors to the response are "trained." For example, in the study done for the APPD, the training data consisted of a random sample of 30,000 individuals whose supervision began in 2006 and whose behavior on probation or parole was followed for two years. Among the many predictors were each individual's past criminal record. The key response was a homicide or an attempted homicide.

Mad cow disease provides an illustration for consumer product safety. On January 9, 2007, the FDA announced that it was

> requiring that manufacturers and processors of human food and cosmetics that are manufactured from, processed with, or otherwise contain, material from cattle establish and maintain records sufficient to demonstrate that the human food or cosmetic is not manufactured from, processed with, or does not otherwise contain, prohibited cattle materials. . . . FDA [required] recordkeeping because manufacturers and processors of human food and cosmetics need records to ensure that their products do not contain prohibited cattle materials, and records are necessary to help FDA ensure compliance with the requirements of the interim final rule. (FDA 2007)

These requirements were imposed so that there would be a database with which to monitor beef production and other products from cattle. The information sought had been identified using training data from earlier epidemiological studies that linked the content of certain cattle feed to bovine spongiform encephalopathy. Particular feed constitutes (e.g., the brain, skull, eyes, trigeminal ganglia, and spinal cord from uninspected cattle) would then serve as predictors to identify suspect cattle that were not to be imported or were to be destroyed. Other predictors could include the temperatures used in any rendering process and whether as young calves the cattle were fed infected protein supplements.

One must always evaluate the performance of the forecasting procedures. This requires "test data" that are a probability sample from the same population as the training data. The test data must contain the same predictors and outcomes as employed with the training data. Then, the procedures developed from the training data are applied to the test data. Ideally, the forecasts using the test data are sufficiently accurate for the purposes at hand. For the Philadelphia parole study, 26,000 (or so) individuals not included at random in the training data became the sample for the test data. For all practical purposes, the forecasting model built with the training data performed equally well in the training data and the test data.

It is important to understand that the common practice of evaluating forecasting performance using the training data is usually a mistake. One is not assessing forecasting skill. One is assessing goodness of fit. Goodness of fit refers to how well the statistical model accounts for the data on hand. Forecasting performance refers to how accurately the procedure forecasts with data not used to construct the forecasts (i.e., new data). Goodness of fit statistics will generally provide an inappropriately optimistic sense of forecasting skill because real forecasts are not undertaken. The development of a powerful forecasting algorithm will capitalize not just on systematic patterns in the data, but also patterns resulting from noise. The result is "overfitting." Because in a new data set the noise patterns will likely be quite different, forecasting algorithms generally perform better on the data used to build the algorithm than on new data. So, honest evaluations of forecasting performance require test data.

Honest forecasting assessments also should provide information on uncertainty. The basic problem is this: If the study were done again, the results would almost certainly differ, at least a bit. Some of the difference would result from unsystematic variation in the data that, for purposes here, can be considered "noise." It follows that a summary of the impact of that noise should be attached to any forecasts. "Error bands" representing the "margin of error" is one illustration.

Within the usual modeling paradigm used in forecasting, uncertainty is built into the model. That is, one imposes theory about the sources of uncertainty. It is then possible to construct overall measures of consequences of that uncertainty. The algorithmic methods favored in this discussion (described shortly), which can perform better than conventional models, provide special challenges when uncertainty is considered. The issues are quite technical, but substantial progress is being made. An important insight from that work is the uncertainty assessments from conventional forecasting approaches are often on less solid ground than many practitioners realize (Leeb and Pötscher 2005, 2006, 2008). All existing approaches to uncertainty calculations can be significantly compromised (Berk et al. 2009b).

The forecasting procedures must be ported to the setting in which they will be used. This step may be trivial if the forecasting procedures were developed within the system in which they will be used in practice. Commonly, however, this is not the case and the challenges can be daunting. For example, for both the Department of Corrections study and the probation/parole study, forecasting had to be available rapidly in real time as intakes occurred. This meant having forecasting capacity at a large number of desktop computers in many field offices. One approach is to link each desktop to a single server. An alternative approach is to install the forecasting tools necessary on each desktop. In both settings, the server option was chosen.

Forecasting Algorithms

In the past decade, there have been dramatic advances in the statistical tools from which one can construct forecasts. Conventionally, a "model" is formulated from past research or extant theory. The model is essentially a simplified description of how the data came to be. That model is then applied to the data and some very specific statistical features of the model are computed from the data. The main weakness of this approach is that the forecasts are highly model dependent. If the model is not a good one, the accuracy of the forecasts can suffer dramatically. In recent work, however, much less about the model needs to be specified in advance. Many of the model's key features are arrived at inductively from the data. It now seems increasingly clear that there are a large number of situations in which this is a far better way to proceed.

A brief summary will show why this is so. As was noted, a model is a quantitative theory of the processes responsible for generating the data —that is, a model is a quantitative explanation of how the data on hand came to be. To take the linear regression example, one is interested in understanding how nature produced an outcome, often denoted by y_i, from a set of predictors, often denoted by $x_{i,p}$. One can think of $x_{i,p}$ as input and y_i as output. Then,

$$y_i = \beta_0 + \sum_{p=1}^{P} \beta_p x_{i,p} + \varepsilon_i$$

where $\varepsilon_i \sim NIID(0, \sigma^2)$, there are P predictors $x_{i,p}$, and $i = 1,2,3, \ldots, N$ cases. For each of the N cases, nature multiplies the values of each of the P predictor variables $x_{i,p}$ by its constant β_p, adds up these products, adds the value of constant β_0, and then adds an independent random perturbation ε_i, which is a random realization of a normal distribution having a mean of 0.0 and a variance of σ^2.

The primary goal of this model is to represent how nature works —how nature generated the outcome. It may turn out that the model also produces usefully accurate forecasts, but that is usually a secondary concern if the intent is to capture the data generation process. The same holds for more general models such as

$$y_i = f(X_i) + \varepsilon_i$$

where X_i is a set of predictors, and as before, $\varepsilon_i \sim NIID(0, \sigma^2)$. We are no longer limited to a linear combination of the predictors. The function of X_i is to be determined by the data.

In this canonical context, it is easy to forget that the goal of forecasting is to forecast accurately. The goal is not to identify important causal variables, let alone develop an explanatory model, although such by-products can be desirable on other grounds. In conventional econometric language, an "astructural" model will suffice, and forecasting accuracy should not be sacrificed so that "structural" models can be developed. Thus, if there is a predictor that adds forecasting skill even if it is not in any way responsible for generating the values of y_i, it should be allowed to contribute. If the shoe size of a peanut factory's manager helps to forecast the level of salmonella contamination, it should be included among the predictors.

Focusing on forecasting skill alone can be quite liberating. In a single-minded fashion, one can bring any technology to bear that produces good forecasts. It will also be clear which approach to use; forecasting accuracy will separate the winners from the losers.

Over the past decade, a wide variety of new data analysis procedures have been developed by statisticians and computer scientists that can be called "model free." They can be used without any concerns about whether the data-generating mechanisms are being properly represented. Called "statistical learning" by most statisticians and "machine learning" by most computer scientists, their intent is to search extensively through the data to find how a set of predictors is associated with a response. An earlier generation of statisticians would call the approach "exploratory data analysis." Consider the following set of steps as an example:

1. Fit a regression model to the data. If the outcome is binary, that regression model might be logistic regression.
2. Determine which outcome observations are accurately identified and which are not. In an epidemiological study of bovine spongiform encephalopathy, are the infected cows identified as such? Likewise, are the uninfected cows identified as such?
3. Reweight the data. Give more weight to observations that were classified incorrectly.
4. Repeat steps 1–3 a large number of times (e.g., 1,000).
5. For each case, compute a weighted average of the class designated by the model. The weights come from the models. The better a given model fits the data, the more weight given to its output when the average is computed.

The steps just outlined have much in common with a machine-learning procedure called boosting. Boosting is one of the new kinds of inductive procedures that can perform much better than conventional parametric models (Berk 2008b; Hastie et al. 2001). The $f(X)$ is determined as part of the fitting process. It is not specified in advance. The danger is that the algorithm will be too responsive and build on idiosyncratic features of the data. Insofar as this happens, overfitting is the result. Forecasting performance can degrade substantially when applied to new data. The remedy is to have a test data set from which honest measures of forecasting accuracy can be obtained.

Boosting is one especially popular technique (actually a set of procedures) within a machine/statistical learning framework. Two popular competitors, with at least comparable forecasting performance, are random forests and support vector machines. For the problems at hand, all of these procedures can be seen as ways to arrive at the $f(X)$ inductively. Looked at in this manner (and there are other ways to look), machine/statistical learning has much in common with the older tradition of smoothing. The generalized additive model (Hastie and Tibshirani 1990) is probably the closest analog. The usual regression equation of

$$y_i = \beta_0 + \sum\nolimits_{p=1}^{P} \beta_p x_{i,p} + \varepsilon_i$$

is replaced by

$$y = \beta_0 + \sum\nolimits_{p=1}^{P} f_p(x_{i,p}) + \varepsilon_i$$

Each predictor has its own inductively produced functional relationship with the response, which are then combined in an additive fashion.

Although the main goal in profiling is to forecast accurately, many machine/statistical learning procedures can provide measures of the forecasting contribution of each predictor. The basic idea is to compute how much less accurate a forecast is when any given predictor is not allowed to contribute to the forecasting exercise. Then, predictors may be ordered by their forecasting "importance."

It is also possible to show the inductively generated functional form linking each predictor to the response. For example, Figure 2 shows how the age of individuals on parole or probation is related to the likelihood that they will commit a homicide or attempted homicide, with other predictors held constant. The technical details need not concern us here. When the parolee or probationer is under 20 years of age, the risks are the highest. The risk drops precipitously up to about age 30, after which age seems to have virtually no relationship to the outcome. Thus, although a difference in age between an individual of 18 and 25

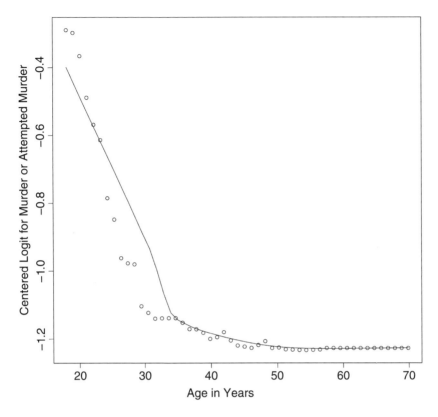

Figure 2. Relation between the age of individuals on parole or probation and the likelihood that they will commit homicide or attempted homicide.

can be very important, the difference in age between an individual of 28 and 35 hardly matters at all.

Some might worry whether it is "fair" to use age. The same holds for gender, which is also a very important predictor. Prospective murderers have no control over either variable. And if there are causal links to homicide perpetration, they are not well understood. But, this is not a statistical decision. On ethical, legal, or political grounds, one has to determine if the loss in accuracy is worth it. For example, in a city like Philadelphia, if age and gender are not used to forecast homicides, there could easily be 50 homicides a year that would have otherwise been prevented. There will be trade-offs because most homicides are committed by young men. Moreover, background variables are already used informally in probation and parole decisions. At least in a forecasting model, no one is hiding the ball.

It is likely that similar issues will arise in profiling of consumer safety violators. What sorts of predictors are legitimate? For example, can one use as a predictor the country in which a food processor is located? In the instance of bovine spongiform encephalopathy, should all processed beef from Canada have been prohibited? Such decisions would depend on the forecasting importance of a given predictor and the potential trade-offs if it were not used.

As noted briefly earlier, forecasts should be combined with assessments of uncertainty. For algorithmic methods, the usual approaches to uncertainty do not apply. The basic problem is that inductive methods violate a key assumption of conventional statistical inference (Barnett 1982). For such inference, the model must be known before the data are examined. However, relatively simple resampling procedures can be used to, in effect, simulate what would happen if the study were repeated. The result is a useful assessment of how stable one's forecasts really are. How different would the forecasts likely be if the study were repeated?

The Benefits—and Limits—of Forecasting

In principle, the motivations driving forecasting in criminal justice settings can apply to consumer product safety concerns, and the same kinds of benefits can follow. Looking forward, forecasts can help determine how to allocate scarce oversight resources. Product safety "hot spots" can be identified and subjected to especially close scrutiny. Concentrating oversight where it is most needed may help identify problems in a more cost-effective manner. One consequence can be a more efficient search for defective products and those responsible for them.

Better still is the prospect of prevention. Prevention implies an intervention before the product safety is compromised. Clearly, prevention cannot be undertaken without a forecast of what would happen if nothing were done. However, prevention too can be costly. One of the benefits of usefully accurate forecasts is that prevention resources can be concentrated where they are most needed.

Forecasting can help deliver important benefits in the long run. Knowledge that more effective oversight is in place can serve as a deterrent. It is widely believed that deterrence is a function of the probability of apprehension and severity of punishments that follow. It is also widely believed that the probability of apprehension is the more important of the two. Effective product safety oversight—made possible through carefully developed statistical forecasts—speaks directly to that probability.

Finally, it is important to emphasize that forecasts of the sort considered in this chapter are meant to help inform decisions. They are not intended to wholly determine the decisions made. Even very accurate forecasts should be ignored if acting on them leads to undesirable outcomes. There needs to be a separation between the information that the forecasts can provide and what is done with that information.

Acknowledgments

Thanks go to Cary Coglianese and Adam Finkel for very helpful comments on an earlier draft of this chapter.

References

Barnett, Vic (1982) *Comparative Statistical Inference.* New York: John Wiley and Sons.

Berk, Richard A. (2008a) "Forecasting Methods in Crime and Justice." In *Annual Review of Law and Social Science,* edited by John Hagan et al. Palo Alto, Calif.: Annual Reviews.

———. (2008b) *Statistical Learning from a Regression Perspective.* New York: Springer.

Berk, Richard A. et al. (2009a) "Forecasting Murder Within a Population of Probationers and Parolees: A High Stakes Application of Statistical Learning." 172 *Journal of the Royal Statistical Society, Series A* 191–211.

———. (2009b) Statistical inference after model selection. Working paper (under review), University of Pennsylvania.

———. (2009c) When second best is good enough: A comparison between a true experiment and a regression discontinuity quasi-experiment. Working paper, University of Pennsylvania.

———. (2006) "Forecasting Dangerous Inmate Misconduct: An Application of Ensemble Statistical Procedures." 22 *Journal of Quantitative Criminology* 131–45.

———. (2005) "Developing a Practical Forecasting Screener for Domestic Violence Incidents." 29 *Evaluation Review* 358–82.

Dutton, Donald G. and P. Randall Kropp (2000) "A Review of Domestic Violence Risk Instruments." 1 *Trauma, Violence, and Abuse* 171–81.

Glaser, Daniel (1987) "Classification for Risk." In *Prediction and Classification,* edited by D. M. Gottfredson and M. Tonry. Chicago: University of Chicago Press.

Granger, Clive W. J. (1989) *Forecasting in Business and Economics,* 2nd ed. New York: Academic Press.

Hastie, Trevor and Robert Tibshirani (1990) *Generalized Additive Models.* New York: Chapman and Hall.

Hastie, Trevor, Robert Tibshirani, and Jerome Friedman (2001) *The Elements of Statistical Learning: Data Mining, Inference, and Prediction.* New York: Springer.

Holland, Paul W. (1986) "Statistics and Causal Inference." 81 *Journal of the American Statistical Association* 945–60.

Kriegler, Brian and Richard A. Berk (2009) Estimating the homeless population in Los Angeles: An application of cost-sensitive stochastic gradient boosting. Working paper (under review), UCLA, Los Angeles.

Leeb, Hannes and Benedickt M. Pötscher (2008) "Model Selection." In *The Handbook of Financial Time Series*, edited by Torben G. Anderson et al. New York: Springer.

———. (2006) "Can One Estimate the Conditional Distribution of Post-Model-Selection Estimators?" 34 *The Annals of Statistics* 2554–91.

———. (2005) "Model Selection and Inference: Facts and Fiction." 21 *Econometric Theory* 21–59.

Lennert-Cody, Cleridy E. and Richard A. Berk (2007) "Statistical Learning Procedures for Monitoring Regulatory Compliance: An Application to Fisheries Data." 170 *Journal of the Royal Statistical Society, Series A* 671–89.

Rubin, Donald B. (1986) "Which Ifs Have Causal Answers?" 81 *Journal of the American Statistical Association* 961–62.

U.S. Sentencing Commission (2006) *Final Report on the Impact of The United States v. Booker on Federal Sentencing.* Washington, D.C.: United States Sentencing Commission.

Regulation Cited

U.S. Food and Drug Administration (FDA) (January 9, 2007) 21 CFR Parts 189 and 700, [Docket No. 2004N-0257], RIN 0910-AF48.

Chapter 8
Risk-Based Regulation for Import Safety

Lorna Zach and Vicki Bier

To deal adequately with import safety, we need to improve our ability to assess risks quantitatively throughout the life cycles of imported products, from the foreign point of production to the end use by consumers in the importing nation. This includes developing a better understanding of the sources of risk in exporting countries (as a basis for deploying limited monitoring, inspection, and interdiction resources, and prioritizing training and capacity-building efforts), as well as understanding which imported goods pose the greatest risk (as a basis for prioritizing inspection resources at the border). Such a risk-based approach would allow producers, importers, and regulators to focus their attention on the parts of the production process or supply chain that pose the greatest risk, and thereby would create the possibility of win-win situations (increased testing of the most risk-critical processes or ingredients, coupled with a decreased regulatory burden for less risk-significant parts of the supply chain). We believe that using risk analysis in both standard-setting and enforcement can complement and enhance management-based regulatory approaches (good-practice standards in production and manufacturing) as well as performance-based approaches (finished-product testing).

Some Background on Import Safety

Achieving safety for imported food, drugs, and consumer products will likely require a shift in governance strategies to a framework based at least in part on a more systematic understanding of and response to the magnitude of actual and potential hazards (IWGIS 2007). International trade agreements, such as the sanitary and phytosanitary measures (SPS) of the World Trade Organization (WTO), have codified the idea that a demonstration of increased domestic health risk (e.g., through a risk assessment) is the only acceptable basis for barriers to international trade in food (Scott 2007; WHO/FAO 2006). In addition, domestic food regulators are increasingly being required to demonstrate the cost-effectiveness of their efforts in achieving risk reduction (Lammerding and Paoli 1997: 484). This opens up the treatment of import safety to a broader set of analytic and policy tools than has been used in the past.

Among these tools, quantitative risk assessment (QRA) has become the most prominent method in use worldwide to determine whether products and processes present nonzero but presumptively "acceptable" levels of harm. QRA may be especially useful for issues like import safety, where a brute-force approach—monitoring everything or inspecting everyone—is clearly infeasible. QRA can be applied at many different scales of activity, and can be used to make decisions not only about how stringently to control particular hazards, but also about which hazards justify more detailed risk assessment. Moreover, QRA can be used to set priorities not only between multiple sources of the same risk, such as multiple avenues for bacterial contamination of meat products, but also among wholly disparate risks. Finally, QRA can be implemented by individual producers, at the level of an entire industry sector, by state or federal agencies with responsibility for multiple industry sectors, or by transnational organizations.

In this chapter we will focus on risk-based regulation for imported food products. We believe that similar issues arise with respect to risk-based regulation of imported pharmaceuticals, medical devices, and consumer products. However, because in most countries such products are regulated by different agencies, with differing types of legal authority, we have chosen to focus primarily on food to simplify the presentation of our ideas. Moreover, the way has been paved for risk-based governance in the food sector to a greater extent than in other sectors. Examples of such groundbreaking efforts include international work done by the Codex Alimentarius Commission (Codex) (WHO/FAO 2006; Dawson 1995), quantitative microbial risk assessments (QMRA) performed by the Food Safety Inspection Service (FSIS) of the U.S. Department of Agriculture (USDA), and the U.S. Food and Drug Administration (FDA) (USDA/FSIS 1998; FDA 2002; ILSI 1996), and European regulatory reforms based on risk management (König 2006).

A focus on food also makes sense because the food supply is an example of a public good where trust is critical. The availability of safe and adequate food is an important social value, and as such, the possibility of risk in the food supply is viewed extremely negatively. Food-related risks may be perceived as greater than they actually are; consider the public outcry to the risk of bovine spongiform encephalopathy (BSE) from beef in 1998 (Kasperson et al. 2003: 29). Therefore, consumer confidence in the food supply is a political priority around the world.

In the United States, imported food is inspected at ports and border crossings by two different federal agencies with differing jurisdictions, which results in differing degrees of risk-based governance. The USDA inspects meat, poultry, and egg products, and the FDA inspects all other incoming food products; however, the inspection and upstream regulatory powers extending back into the country of origin are different for the two agencies.

Currently, the USDA is legally empowered to require equivalency of foreign regulatory structures to those in the United States in order for meat, poultry, and egg products to be imported (Fortin 2009: 477–78). This means that a foreign country must apply to the USDA for approval of its regulatory system for a specific meat, poultry, or egg item, and must be specifically approved to export that item to the United States. In this process, the foreign country must demonstrate to the USDA's satisfaction that it provides the same level of public-health protection for a specific food item as is provided in the United States; the USDA then may inspect the foreign regulatory system in the exporting country to verify these claims. As a result, the USDA refers to its border inspections of shipments as reinspection (although only the foreign regulatory structure has been inspected previously, not the specific shipments). Current USDA staffing resources support a "reinspection" rate of 10 to 11 percent (by weight) in 2007 (Fortin 2009: 478; James 2007: 2), and this appears to be reasonably effective, as the rate of recalls for legally imported meat and poultry is low. For one illustration of the stringency of these procedures, as of 2009, Canada is the only country certified to export eggs to the United States (USDA 2009).

By contrast, the FDA (which regulates all other food products, including fish) is statutorily prevented from imposing equivalency requirements on foreign regulatory systems, and is allowed to assure public health and safety only by inspections at the border. Moreover, at current staffing resources and import levels, FDA inspection rates of food imports have decreased to less than about 1 percent (by number of shipments) in 2007 (Nelson 2007: 2). Although FDA inspections are targeted based on at least a rough evaluation of risk—for example, taking into account product documentation and records of previous violations, if available (Buzby et al. 2008; IWGIS 2007: 5)—the U.S. Government Accountability Office (GAO) has consistently found that a 1 percent inspection level is insufficient (GAO 1998; 2001: 7; 2003; 2007: 29–30; 2008). Although the FDA does attempt to apply a risk-based approach to targeting its inspections of import shipments, its ability to do so is limited, because the agency lacks the authority to reach back into the country of origin. Thus, it is unable to inspect sources of hazards and risks in the chain of production, and is also unable to verify the identity of the original exporting company (which might have changed names to avoid heightened rates of inspection triggered by large numbers of violations).

As noted by the IWGIS, "the challenges presented by the increasingly global economy and growing import volumes require a paradigm shift from an intervention, border-focused strategy to a life-cycle approach that stresses a risk-based approach to prevention with verification that identifies high-risk segments of the import life cycle and verifies the safety of products at those important phases" (IWGIS 2007: 11). In proposing a life-cycle approach, the IWGIS is referring to the entire chain of food production, which at its broadest extends from the initial point of production on the farm, through collection, manufacturing, and border crossing, to the retail store, and finally through additional storage and possible cooking in a commercial or consumer kitchen. Moreover, when considering food imports, the life cycle may include consolidation of shipments at a foreign port, transportation to the United States, and approval by U.S. officials for entry into domestic commerce. Problems and violations can occur at several points in a product's life cycle or supply chain. For example, consider the microbial contamination of raspberries sprayed with contaminated water at the producer level (Powell 2000), the use of a potentially unsafe and unregistered process for canning of fruits and vegetables at the manufacturing level (Buzby et al. 2008: iii, 9), and untraceable consolidation of commodities at the broker level before shipment (as in the case of genetically identical salmonella outbreaks caused by imported sprout seeds in Finland and the United States) (Puohiniemi et al. 1997). Features of the regulatory infrastructure of an exporting country can affect the potential for accidental or intentional contamination or adulteration at several points in the life cycle. For example, a fragmented regulatory and oversight structure involving numerous government departments at the national level of the exporting country, and little coordination with lower levels of government (which may have their own, differing standards for food products), may cause problems. Lack of documentation or traceability in the exporting country that may be due to lack of suitable standards and enforcement mechanisms, or a fragmented marketing system dominated by large numbers of small firms handling small volumes of food products, often on a cash basis, can exacerbate the situation. Finally, high levels of corruption in the exporting country can defeat almost any system of regulation or governance.

The SPS empowers the Codex to regulate global trade in food (Scott 2007). The Codex standards are a collection of internationally adopted food standards aimed at protecting consumer health and economic interests worldwide, and ensuring fair practices in the international trade in food. A key element in the development of the Codex standards, especially as they are used for the SPS, is the use of principles of risk analysis and process control to protect human health. According to Dawson (1995), these principles have the advantage of allowing flexibility in the method of achieving a specified quality standard, thereby facilitating use of a wide variety of procedures and approaches that are appropriate to a range of production and processing methods. The Codex has performed risk analyses of the life cycles for a variety of food products, generally described as "farm to fork" or "gate to plate." The results have led to codes of practice and guidelines for dealing with such issues as food additives and contaminants, pesticide residues, residues of veterinary drugs, and hygiene measures.

Risk analysis was further emphasized in the reform of the food-safety system in the European Union (EU) after the crisis involving BSE (König 2006: 133). The BSE crisis, along with an incident in which chicken feed was found to be contaminated with dioxin, highlighted the need for a vertically integrated, life-cycle approach to the governance of animal feed and food safety to address all stages of production from farm to fork, and the need for greater coordination in risk-management measures among EU member states. The goals of the resulting regulatory-reform effort were similar to the goals of current efforts to improve import safety in the United States—namely, to reestablish consumer trust and increase the effectiveness of the food-safety regulatory system. The resulting "general food law" in the EU requires the use of the U.S.-developed Hazard Analysis and Critical Control Points (HACCP) system as a method of self-regulation by food producers. In addition, though, the European Food Safety Authority was given the responsibility of conducting scientific risk assessments of food-safety issues (König 2006: 144), while the European Commission was responsible for coordinating risk-management efforts among EU member states, including the EU-wide rapid-alert system and network for crisis management described by Alberto Alemanno in chapter 9.

In the United States, according to the National Research Council (NRC 1983), risk analysis was initially promoted during the 1970s as an objective scientific basis for environmental planning and decision making by federal agencies, Congress, and the public. Regulatory agencies were expected to demonstrate a transparent connection between an imposed regulation and its expected health benefits or cost-effectiveness (Lammerding and Paoli 1997: 484). QMRA evolved from initial analyses of environmental risks to be applied to food and water safety (Jaykus 1996; Rose and Sobsey 1993). A good example of its initial use by the USDA was to analyze the risks of *Salmonella enteritidis* in eggs and egg products (Baker et al. 1998). In the next section, we provide a more detailed introduction to the concepts of risk, risk assessment, and risk management as a basis for understanding the strengths and weaknesses of risk-based regulation.

Risk Analysis and Its Role in Regulation

In their seminal paper, Kaplan and Garrick (1981) define "risk" as involving "both uncertainty and some kind of loss or damage." More specifically, Kaplan and Garrick note that "risk includes the likelihood of conversion of that source into actual . . . loss, injury, or some form of damage." Thus, fundamentally, risk depends both on the probability or frequency of an adverse outcome, and also on the severity of that outcome. Sage and White state that "risk" refers to the probability of a particular harm and "represents the statistical likelihood of a randomly exposed individual being adversely affected by some hazardous event" (1980: 426). However, the term is also sometimes used to refer to the aggregate consequence of a hazard to a population of individuals (i.e., the sum of the individual risks); for example, the number of cancer cases estimated to result from exposure to a carcinogen in food may sometimes be described as the "risk" of that carcinogen.

Risk Assessment Supports Risk Management

As noted by Zimmerman and Bier (2002), risk assessment is a means to characterize uncertainty to support risk management. Modern methods of probabilistic risk assessment have been applied to a vast array of chemical risks being regulated under dozens of federal environmental and occupational health statutes. For example, risk assessment has been used as the foundation for: setting drinking-water, ambient water-quality, and air-quality standards; review and renewal of pesticide applications; and determining cleanup levels for the remediation of hazardous waste sites.

Risk Assessments Apply Scientific Knowledge to Evaluate Mitigations

According to the NRC, risk assessment refers to "a systematic approach to organizing and analyzing scientific knowledge and information for potentially hazardous activities or for substances that might pose risks under specified circumstances" (1994: 4). The overall objective of risk assessment is to estimate the risk of adverse health or safety effects due to chemicals, biological agents, or physical hazards. Kaplan and Garrick (1981) state that the goal of a risk assessment is to answer three questions: "What can go wrong?" "How likely is it that that will happen?" and "If it does happen, what are the consequences?" However, many risk assessments also include the evaluation of possible risk-reduction measures, so that risk assessment and risk management are integrated, as suggested by the NRC (2008: 5–6, 10–11).

Risk Assessment and Risk Management Should Ideally Be Integrated

Early on, risk assessment and risk management were viewed as separate functions. For example, the NRC's *Risk Assessment in the Federal Government: Managing the Process*, often known as the Red Book (NRC 1983), recommends that regulatory agencies maintain a clear distinction between assessment of risks and consideration of risk-management alternatives (i.e., between the scientific findings embodied in risk assessments and the political, economic, and value judgments that may influence the choice of regulatory strategies). Over time, however, the processes of risk assessment and risk management have begun to merge (Zimmerman 1998). Thus, the NRC (1994, 1996, 2008), the U.S. Environmental Protection Agency (EPA 1996), and the Presidential/Congressional Commission on Risk Assessment and Risk Management (1997) each recommend or assume far more interaction between stakeholders (including agency decision makers) and risk assessors than the approach described in the Red Book.

Good Risk Communication Flows Both Ways

The NRC (1996) defined "analysis" as "the systematic application of specific theories and methods . . . for the purpose of collecting and interpreting data and drawing conclusions about phenomena," and "deliberation" as using "processes such as discussion, reflection, and persuasion to communicate, raise, and collectively consider issues, increase understanding, and arrive at substantive decisions." The NRC (1996: 163) referred to the combination of these two steps as the "analytic-deliberative" process, an iterative process in which "deliberation frames analysis and analysis informs deliberation." For example, stakeholders may provide inputs into the design of the risk assessment by specifying exposure routes or health outcomes to be evaluated. The results of the risk models can then be communicated to interested stakeholders, including not only government regulators but also consumer groups, industry, the scientific community, and the general public (although political and economic considerations can also affect the eventual risk-management decisions).

Health Risk Assessment Involves Hazard Identification, Exposure, and Dose-Response

The general framework presented above is applicable to both health/environmental and engineering risk assessment. However, some of the details of the methodology differ between the two areas, as discussed below (Zimmerman and Bier 2002). In particular, the steps in health risk assessment, which were formalized in 1983 in the Red Book, include hazard identification, exposure assessment, dose-response assessment, and risk characterization. The objective of hazard identification is to determine which hazards to include in the risk assessment. Thus, hazard identification relies on methods such as epidemiology (to identify disease clusters), structure-activity relationships (linking the structure of a chemical to its possible or likely biological effects), and toxicological testing. Exposure assessment estimates the level of a hazardous substance to which people may be exposed, taking into account factors such as the concentration of the contaminant, microbial growth and decay in the life cycle, the frequency and duration of exposure, and (where relevant) the individual's body weight, age, expected lifetime, and susceptibility to the health end point of concern. Dose-response relationships translate the results of the exposure assessment to specific risk levels, constructing a quantitative function that models how the probability or severity of adverse effects (or both) changes as the dose increases. Finally, the NRC (1983) and the ILSI stress the "dynamic and iterative nature of the risk assessment process" (ILSI 1996: 841).

Engineering Risk Assessment Analyzes the Effects of System Failures

Like health and environmental risk assessment, the process of risk assessment for engineered systems begins with hazard identification, followed by the assessment of accident frequencies, and then consequence analysis. Techniques commonly used to structure the set of possible accident scenarios and estimate their frequencies include fault trees and event trees (McCormick 1981). As noted by Paté-Cornell (1984), fault trees start with a hypothesized failure—such as unacceptable levels of pathogens in a food product—and work backward to identify which combinations of failures could give rise to that event; event trees start by hypothesizing an initiating event or departure from normal operations (inadequate heat treatment of a food product, for example), and determining its possible consequences. Available data are used to help quantify the resulting risk model, including initiating-event frequencies, such as the likelihood of inadequate heat treatment, as well as failure rates of subsequent safety steps, such as microbial testing, and the likelihood of human error in the life cycle, using expert opinion when data are sparse. Consequence analysis typically considers both how hazardous products could lead to hazardous exposures, and also the consequences of those exposures for public health and safety.

Risk Models Help to Evaluate the Value of Information and Analyze Potential Mitigations

Once we know how big the risks are, how uncertain they are, and where they arise in the life cycle for a product, we can use this knowledge to prioritize decisions about where to spend our research dollars to reduce risk in the long term, as well as which protective measures should be implemented in the short term. Risk estimates can be used to prioritize inspection resources to focus attention on those firms, processing plants, or parts of the supply chain that are likely to be especially hazardous. Risk estimates can also be used to identify where additional risk-reduction measures are most needed. Thus, risk assessment can be one important input into risk management, by providing technical information to inform decision making. However, risk management is inherently a social and political process, so as was noted earlier, decision makers may wish to take into account a variety of political and economic factors above and beyond estimated risk levels. For this reason, the term *risk-informed regulation* is sometimes used in place of *risk-based regulation*.

Risk Analysis Can Evaluate the Cost Effectiveness of Further Risk-Based Mitigation

The probabilistic risk assessments conducted by the USDA modeled the risk of contamination and growth and decay of *E. coli* O157:H7 in ground beef all the way from the cattle ranch through harvest, processing, manufacturing, packaging, distribution, and finally food service or consumer preparation and consumption (USDA/FSIS 2001). Such life-cycle models can help to ensure that the levels of government effort devoted to different parts of the process correspond to the magnitudes of risk to public health, by identifying the risks of contamination at various points along the farm-to-fork continuum and relating contamination risks to the risk of human illness. Regulators can also use such models to cost-effectively prioritize their efforts according to the size and vulnerability of the affected populations (as was done in the risk assessment of *Listeria monocytogenes* in ready-to-eat foods (FDA 2003), to quantify the likely effects of various risk-mitigation strategies before they are actually implemented, and to determine where more information might be useful. For example, a risk model can be used to predict the likely effects on human health of new meat preservatives or increasing processing temperatures on microbial growth to determine before they are introduced whether such measures are likely to be effective at reducing illness.

Risk-Based Regulation Can Be More Cost-Effective Than Other Approaches

An eventual outcome of the QMRA for ground beef (USDA/FSIS 2001) was the application of a performance-based risk plan for testing for *E. coli* O157:H7 in USDA-regulated facilities (Withee and Schlosser 2008). Until 2003, the USDA had inspected all regulated establishments for *E. coli* O157:H7 at the same frequency, and inspection resources were allocated equally across all establishments, without regard for the number of positive microbial tests that had been observed in the past. Now, a positive test result for *E. coli* O157:H7 in final products is linked to more inspection resources and increased frequency of *E. coli* testing. In other words, the new risk-based sampling plan requires more testing and inspection at those operations estimated as being at higher risk of causing illness so that public health is better and more cost-effectively protected. This risk-based sampling approach to further testing and allocation of inspection resources can be viewed as a form of profiling, as Richard Berk discussed in chapter 7.

Risk Assessment Models Can Attribute Harm to Specific Steps in the Life Cycle

Risk or harm to public health can sometimes be directly measured by the number of cases of food-borne illness linked to a specific food item. This works for microbial contamination, as the consequences of exposure are usually short-term and acute, and can therefore be linked to the offending food, given good surveillance and trace-back. As a result, predictions of the number of cases of disease from well-tuned risk models can be compared with those reported from actual surveillance data, confirmed by public-health departments and attributed to food-borne transmission (Mead et al. 1999: 609–10; USDA/FSIS 2001: 109–13, 122). Therefore, measures of harm to public health can be attributed to specific hazardous steps in the life cycle of a food, potentially creating a political will to find improved alternatives. Further, the risks from imported products could be compared to those of similar domestic products, as done by Tuominen (2009) in estimating the risk of salmonellosis from imported beef and beef-derived foods to be higher than that from domestic beef in Finland.

Risk Assessment Models May Aid Public-Health Decision Making

The risk of harm to public health from long-term chronic threats such as prions (BSE), carcinogens, and chemical contaminants (like mercury or lead) can be difficult to measure empirically, because health effects are typically not immediate. This can be complicated by multiple routes of exposure to a variety of complex mixtures (Callahan and Sexton 2007). In such cases, the role of risk assessment and life-cycle analysis can be even more critical, because public-health decisions may need to be made on the basis of predicted rather than measured outcomes.

Over the past several decades, the track record of QRA has become that of a mature, reliable discipline. Despite the necessity of using models of exposure and dose response rather than exhaustive data, the risk estimates themselves have been shown to be surprisingly reliable, both qualitatively and quantitatively (Allen et al. 1988). Even if some risk estimates have been off the mark (and in general, additional refinement of the estimates has tended to reveal that first-generation estimates underestimated actual risks), risk assessment has brought us many successful decisions, such as the phase-out of lead in gasoline and the virtual elimination of diseases caused by exposure to vinyl chloride and cotton dust in the workplace, to name a few examples. To be sure, risk assessment has trouble addressing some concerns, such as synergies (Ryker and Small 2008), hormesis (Cook and Calabrese 2006), and unusual species-specific responses that would lead to gross overestimation of human risk if not understood and addressed (EPA 1998). However, risk assessment is becoming more attuned to even these complicating factors as the field matures.

Risk Analysis Has Numerous Benefits

Since the Red Book (NRC 1983) and the first use of risk analysis for nuclear power plants (U.S. Nuclear Regulatory Commission 1975), risk analysis has been formalized into a rigorous discipline. According to the World Health Organization (WHO) and the FAO, risk analysis has gained wide acceptance as the preferred way to assess links between hazards in the food supply chain and risks to human health (WHO/FAO 2006). Further, when risk analysis is used to establish standards and controls for management and performance-based governance, the technique can foster comprehensive scientific evaluation, stakeholder participation, transparency of process, consistent treatment of different hazards, and systematic decision making by risk managers (WHO/FAO 2006: xi). Therefore, application of harmonized risk-analysis principles and methods in cooperating countries is perceived as facilitating trade. However, it is important to note that even when all the data sets and methods are harmonized, two agencies or countries can still reach different conclusions about how safe is safe enough, because their goals for risk management may differ.

Concerns About and Limitations to Risk-Based Regulation

The types of risk analyses described in the previous section allow regulators to take a broader, more informed view of the hazards in the import life cycle than has historically been possible. In addition, using QRA, the risks of imports can be compared to those of comparable domestically produced products, if any exist. However, risk analysis is not a panacea. Knowledge gaps, time and resource constraints, and trade-offs between competing objectives may all interfere with the ability of risk analysis to inform regulatory decisions.

As risk often cannot be reliably estimated from sparse and equivocal data, knowledge gaps may result in skewed conclusions. Data gaps can arise at any step of a risk assessment: toxicological or epidemiological studies can be incomplete; exposure measurements can be biased or misleading; and assumptions about the behavioral responses of manufacturers or consumers can be incorrect. Examples of data gaps include the information asymmetries between industry and regulators, as well as possibly flawed assumptions about non-normative consumer behavior in food handling—not cooking frozen food adequately, or microwaving food in non-microwave-safe plastic containers and thereby increasing the rate of migration of bisphenol A from plastic containers into hot liquids (Le et al. 2008). Such assumptions may result in large deviations from estimated risk levels, as ConAgra found in the outbreak of salmonella from frozen chicken pot pies (ConAgra Foods, Inc. 2007; USDA 2007). Further, gaps in the knowledge about exposure pathways and dose-response relationships may interfere with comparisons of model predictions with estimates of illness rates from epidemiological data (Hoel et al. 1988).

Alternatively, risk assessment may be even more critical in deciding how best to protect public health where knowledge of exposures and dose-response relationships are unavailable or difficult to ascertain, such as for low levels of chemical exposure, mixtures, combinations of exposures, and at-risk populations (Callahan and Sexton 2007: 802). As an example, the chemical adulterant melamine may not result in a noticeable public-health outbreak in the short term, because illnesses might progress at a subclinical level unless the dose is high or the melamine is combined with another hazardous chemical (Wong and Chiu 2008: 231). Furthermore, risk assessments may point to the need for more research in areas of particularly great uncertainty. Although risk analysis is most straightforward to apply in situations where the science is mature, where cause and effect relationships are well understood, and where the condition resulting from a contaminant is acute, it can still be used even when the science is rapidly developing, such as in the case of genetically modified foods or nanotechnology. In such cases, though, experts may not even be aware of which health effects to model; moreover, the results of any risk assessments in such cases are likely to be especially contentious.

Time and resource constraints are also significant obstacles to more widespread use of quantitative risk assessment. Risk assessments are resource-intensive. They often rely on complex scientific and mathematical models, and typically need to be modified for different food types, different contaminant vectors, and even different geographical regions (e.g., farming and manufacturing practices may vary from one region to another). A typical food risk assessment may require about a year of effort by highly trained experts, as well as additional resources to communicate the complexities to stakeholders, to update the models as new data and scientific knowledge become available, and to manage the actual risks.

However, in agencies that are prohibited by statute from examining the equivalency of other countries' risk management regulations or that are unable to use QRA methods to develop proactive regulations, alternative, highly resource-intensive epidemiological methods may be needed to react to outbreaks of illnesses associated with imported products. As mentioned earlier, the current FDA testing level of 1 percent (Nelson 2007: 2) is considered too low to pose an effective deterrent to contaminated imports (GAO 1998; 2001: 7; 2003; 2007: 29–30; 2008). Due to the lack of testing resources, and that the FDA is statutorily constrained from imposing equivalency requirements (as the USDA does), the FDA has as one of its only options the epidemiological investigation of illnesses after the fact of an outbreak, including consumption questionnaires for people diagnosed with illnesses, followed by product trace-back through the supply chain. Powell (2000) describes how a consumption questionnaire and effective trace-back was able to tie a specific disease cluster to imported raspberries from Guatemala, after which the U.S. Centers for Disease Control and Prevention was able to match the *Cyclospora* responsible for the disease cluster to *Cyclospora* found in water samples used to spray the raspberries in Guatemala. Only then was the FDA able to block entry of Guatemalan raspberries.

Using consumption surveys and trace-backs to stop imports is not only resource-intensive, but also relies heavily on the ability to trace a product back through the supply chain all the way to the producer. While this was possible in the case of Guatemalan raspberries, numerous difficulties (including identifying the problematic food in the first place, and then tracing it back through the supply chain to identify its origin) were encountered in the 2008 incident involving salmonella-contaminated jalapeno peppers (Produce Safety Project 2008: 1). In addition, the trace-back procedure is slow and cumbersome, giving the public no satisfaction that prompt action is being taken to protect the public health. As more disease outbreaks from imported food occur, proactive risk assessment may begin to be accepted as less costly and more effective than reactive alternatives like trace-back.

In general, compared to the types of traditional regulations promulgated by the USDA for meat and poultry facilities and the prescriptive regulations used by the FDA (e.g., the Pasteurized Milk Ordinance for ensuring uniform sanitation and milk quality across state lines), regulation informed by risk analysis is likely to be more easily adaptable to heterogeneous industries using a wide variety of disparate technologies. Of course, life-cycle risk assessments may suffer from lack of data or suitable default assumptions, and may therefore be subject to disputes by regulated industries and consumers. However, it is important to note that the assumptions in a well-documented risk assessment are at least transparent, and may be revised as part of the risk-communication process, after stakeholder feedback and consultation.

While the ability to relate risky steps in a product's life cycle to eventual harm can create a powerful political will to reduce the risks, this is effective only if the risk estimates are credible and can be adequately and understandably communicated. Moreover, some risky practices may be so widespread, or so integral to the production of a highly desired foodstuff, that there is effectively no political support for challenging them; neither risk analysis nor any other regulatory approach will necessarily motivate regulators and the public to confront such risks.

As we have indicated in this chapter, risk estimates alone are not sufficient to guide sensible decision making. First, there can be a gap between assessed risk and perceived risk (Gigerenzer and Edwards 2003; Slovic 1987). Some of this gap may be due to misinformation on the part of either the "experts" or the public, but some of the gap is also due to qualitative aspects of risk that are important to decision makers, but cannot be easily captured by numerical risk estimates. In addition, "large" risks (whether assessed or perceived) do not, or should not, necessarily always translate directly into high priorities for risk reduction. In particular, risk managers also need to consider the performance and costs of the available control options. Some large but intractable risks may not be readily reducible using current technology, and should perhaps therefore be considered priorities only for future research, while some small but easily addressed risks should perhaps be eliminated or greatly reduced as "low-hanging fruit" (Finkel and Golding 1995).

Risk-Based Regulation and HACCP

Perhaps the most prominent regulatory strategy today for addressing food safety is to mandate that food production facilities implement hazard analysis and critical control point management systems. HACCP systems are used by operational facilities to identify the inherent hazards in ingredients, processes, and final food products, establish steps to control the identified hazards, and monitor those controls. HACCP systems have historically been implemented in qualitative and procedural ways, whereas risk-based regulation is typically quantitative. As such, it might seem that risk-based regulation is quite different than HACCP, but regulations that mandate HACCP are not entirely incompatible with a regulatory approach based on risk analysis, as indeed such analysis can actually improve HACCP's use.

The WHO and FAO have promoted the use of HACCP to food-safety regulators to achieve consumer protection while providing flexibility in the control methods that can be used by industry (WHO/FAO 2006: 27). HACCP clearly recognizes that responsibility for ensuring safe food rests with the food industry, requiring continuous problem solving and prevention by facility operators, rather than relying solely on periodic inspections by regulatory agencies. However, HACCP can facilitate more effective government inspections, as the HACCP system of record-keeping provides a continuous method of ensuring that food workers consistently implement sanitary procedures.

This general approach (although not referred to as HACCP) was successful when promulgated by the FDA for low-acid canning operations in 1974, and virtually eliminated the incidence of botulism associated with canned food produced in the United States. The FDA later adopted HACCP for the seafood industry in 1995 and for the juice industry in 2004, with good results for consumers. HACCP essentially replaced a system of end-product quality-assurance testing, providing in its place a science-based hazard-control system for identifying and preventing potential food-safety problems. However, USDA implementation of HACCP in the meat industry in 1999 faced extensive criticism, with consumer groups claiming that the method was being watered down, and the meat industry claiming that requiring HACCP was beyond the authority of the USDA (Fortin 2009: 244–45).

Although risk-based evaluation was not part of the original conception of HACCP, it has improved the implementation of HACCP. In particular, the 2001 edition of the Food Code (FDA 2001: Annex 5) recommended as one of its seven HACCP principles that risk-based targets be used for control of hazards in the food-production chain. This has resulted in improved priority setting, both within a single establishment and throughout the supply chain. In an HACCP plan, these priorities are typically developed based on a combination of scientific experience, epidemiological data, and information available in the technical literature. As such, the HACCP system as currently implemented effectively incorporates some aspects of risk-based decision making for control of the hazards at critical steps in the food-production chain (FDA 2001: Annex 5.C.2).

Proactive Regulation and Risk Assessment

Overall, risk-based regulation (or more broadly, risk-informed governance) can be a win-win situation, especially in situations where the science is relatively mature and public-health effects are readily observable. In particular, risk-based regulatory enforcement can yield higher levels of safety with less total inspection effort than regulatory approaches that do not rely on careful attention to setting priorities among risks. Thus, risk-based regulation can complement, and increase the effectiveness of, other types of regulation, whether performance-based or management-based. Of course, in situations in which the science is rapidly developing and public-health effects may be difficult to determine (such as nanotechnology and genetically modified foods), risk-based regulation may pose both equity and efficacy issues, because of difficulties in linking the harm to the hazard. In such situations, however, accountability is generally poor for any regulatory method, and societies investing in the potentially risky technology may still be well served by risk-based regulation, even if it only supports the conclusion that more research is needed.

Deciding how to approach problems like import safety is a continuing research task. Shavell found that proactive approaches such as regulation tend to be preferable to retroactive approaches such as liability, "where injurers are unable to pay fully for harm done . . . , if responsibility for harm done cannot be satisfactorily assigned to injurers . . . , and if injurers have little knowledge about risk" (1987: 279–81). Import safety falls precisely into this situation: small foreign producers may be unable to pay fully for harm done, and have little knowledge about the risks posed by their production practices. Moreover, trace-back to identify which of many small foreign producers was responsible for an incident of contamination can be extremely difficult. This would suggest that proactive, regulatory approaches are to be preferred to the retroactive approach of epidemiological trace-back and recall after an outbreak. Shavell also concluded that state-initiated approaches are generally preferable to privately initiated approaches if "victims of dispersed, individually small harms . . . have little incentive to bring suit . . . [and] where a social authority will be expected to possess . . . superior information about risk or the occurrence of harm" (1987: 283) than will the typical victim. Following on the contributions of Shavell and others in developing general theory about regulation, additional research is clearly needed on the merits of different proactive regulatory approaches in the area of food-import safety. Whatever approach is adopted, future regulatory decision making can only be improved by greater attention to and reliance on careful risk analysis.

References

Allen, Bruce C., Kenny S. Crump, and Annette M. Shipp (1988) "Correlation Between Carcinogenic Potency of Chemicals in Animals and Humans." 8 *Risk Analysis* 531–44.

Baker, Arthur R. et al. (1998) "*Salmonella* Enteritidis Risk Assessment: Shell Eggs and Egg Products." Food Safety and Inspection Service/U.S. Department of Agriculture. www.fsis.usda.gov/OPHS/risk/.

Buzby, Jean C., Laurian J. Unnevehr, and Donna Roberts (2008) *Food Safety and Imports: An Analysis of FDA Food Related Import Refusal Reports.* Washington, D.C.: U.S. Department of Agriculture.

Callahan, Michael A. and Ken Sexton (2007) "If Cumulative Risk Assessment Is the Answer, What Was the Question?" 115 *Environmental Health Perspectives* 799–806.

ConAgra Foods, Inc. (2007) "ConAgra Foods Offers Consumer Advisory Regarding Banquet Pot Pies Press Room News Release." http://media .conagrafoods.com/phoenix.zhtml?c=202310&p=irol-newsArticle&ID =1060683.

Cook, Ralph and Edward J. Calabrese (2006) "The Importance of Hormesis to Public Health." 114 *Environmental Health Perspectives* 1631–35.

Dawson, Richard J. (1995) "The Role of the Codex Alimentarius Commission in Setting Food Standards and the SPS Agreement Implementation." 6 *Food Control* 261–65.

Finkel, Adam M. and Dominic Golding (1995) *Worst Things First? The Debate Over Risk-Based National Environmental Priorities.* Washington, D.C.: Resources for the Future Press.

Fortin, Neal (2009) *Food Regulation: Law, Science, Policy, and Practice.* Hoboken, N.J.: Wiley.

Gigerenzer, Gerd and Adrian Edwards (2003) "Simple Tools for Understanding Risks: From Innumeracy to Insight." 327 *British Medical Journal* 741–44.

Hoel, David G., Joseph K. Haseman, Michael D. Hogan, James Huff, and Ernest E. McConnell (1988) "The Impact of Toxicity on Carcinogenicity Studies: Implications for Risk Assessment." 9 *Carcinogenesis* 2045–52.

Interagency Working Group on Import Safety (IWGIS) (2007) *Protecting American Consumers Every Step of the Way: A Strategic Framework for Continued Improvement in Import Safety.* http://www.importsafety.gov/report/report.pdf.

International Life Sciences Institute [ILSI] Risk Science Institute Pathogen Risk Assessment Working Group (ILSI Working Group) (1996) "A Conceptual Framework to Assess the Risks of Human Disease Following Exposure to Pathogens." 16 *Risk Analysis* 841–48.

James, William (2007) "Testimony Before the Subcommittee on Oversight of the House Committee on Ways and Means." http://waysandmeans.house .gov/hearings.asp?formmode=printfriendly&id=6511.

Jaykus, Lee-Ann (1996) "The Application of Quantitative Risk Assessment to Microbial Food Safety Risks." 22 *Critical Reviews of Microbiology* 279–93.

Kaplan, Stan and B. John Garrick (1981) "On the Quantitative Definition of Risk." 1 *Risk Analysis* 11–27.

Kasperson, Jeanne X., Roger E. Kasperson, Nick Pidgeon, and Paul Slovic (2003) "The Social Amplification of Risk: Assessing Fifteen Years of Research and Theory." In *The Social Amplification of Risk*, edited by Nick Pidgeon, Roger E. Kasperson, and Paul Slovic. Cambridge: Cambridge University Press.

König, Ariane (2006) "Governance of Food Safety in the European Union." In *Global Governance of Food and Agriculture Industries: Transatlantic Regulatory Harmonization and Multilateral Policy Cooperation for Food Safety*, edited by Raba A. Carruth. Cheltenham, UK: Edward Elgar.

Lammerding, Anna M. and Greg M. Paoli (1997) "Quantitative Risk Assessment: An Emerging Tool for Emerging Foodborne Pathogens." 3 *Emerging Infectious Diseases* 483–87.

Le, Hoa H. et al. (2008) "Bisphenol A Is Released From Polycarbonate Drinking Bottles and Mimics the Neurotoxic Actions of Estrogen in Developing Cerebellar Neurons." 176 *Toxicology Letters* 149–56.

McCormick, Norman J. (1981) *Reliability and Risk Analysis: Methods and Nuclear Power Applications.* San Diego, Calif.: Academic Press.

Mead, Paul S. et al. (1999) "Food-Related Illness and Death in the United States." 5 *Emerging Infectious Diseases* 607–25.

National Research Council (NRC) (2008) *Science and Decisions: Advancing Risk Assessment.* Washington, D.C.: National Academy Press.

———. (1996) *Understanding Risk: Informing Decisions in a Democratic Society.* Washington, D.C.: National Academy Press.

———. (1994) *Science and Judgment in Risk Assessment.* Washington, D.C.: National Academy Press.

———. (1983) *Risk Assessment in the Federal Government: Managing the Process.* Washington, D.C.: National Academy Press.

Nelson, David (2007) *Diminished Capacity: Can the FDA Assure the Safety and Security of the Nation's Food Supply: Part 2.* Staff Statement, Subcommittee on Oversight and Investigations, Committee on Energy and Commerce, July 12. http://energycommerce.house.gov/cmte_mtgs/110-oi-hrg.071707.Staff-testimony.pdf.

Paté-Cornell, M. Elisabeth (1984) "Fault Trees vs. Event Trees in Reliability Analysis." 4 *Risk Analysis* 177–86.

Powell, Douglas A. (2000) "Risk-based Regulatory Responses in Global Food Trade: Guatemalan Raspberry Imports into the U.S. and Canada, 1996–1998." In *Risk and Regulation*, edited by Bruce G. Doern. Toronto, Ont.: University of Toronto Press.

Presidential/Congressional Commission on Risk Assessment and Risk Management (1997) *Risk Assessment and Risk Management in Regulatory Decision-Making, Final Report*, vol. 2. Washington, D.C.

Produce Safety Project (2008) "Breakdown: Lessons to Be Learned From the 2008 *Salmonella Saintpaul* Outbreak." Georgetown University. http://www .producesafetyproject.org/admin/assets/files/0015.pdf.

Puohiniemi, Ritvaleena, Tarja Heiskanen, and Anja Siitonen (1997) "Molecular Epidemiology of Two International Sprout-Borne *Salmonella* Outbreaks." 35 *Journal of Clinical Microbiology* 2487–91.

Rose, Joan B. and Mark D. Sobsey (1993) "Quantitative Risk Assessment for Viral Contamination of Shellfish and Coastal Waters." 56 *Journal of Food Protection* 1043–50.

Ryker, Sarah J. and Mitchell J. Small (2008) "Combining Occurrence and Toxicity Information to Identify Priorities for Drinking-Water Mixture Research." 28 *Risk Analysis* 653–66.

Sage, Andrew P. and Elbert B. White (1980) "Methodologies for Risk and Hazard Assessment: A Survey and Status Report." 10 *IEEE Transactions on Systems, Man and Cybernetics* 425–45.

Scott, Joanne (2007) *The WTO Agreement on Sanitary and Phytosanitary Measures.* London: Oxford University Press.

Shavell, Steven M. (1987) *Economic Analysis of Accident Law.* Cambridge, Mass.: Harvard University Press.

Slovic, Paul (1987) "Perception of Risk." 236 *Science* 280–85.

Tuominen, Pirkko (2009) "Developing Risk-Based Food Safety Management." PhD diss., University of Helsinki.

U.S. Department of Agriculture (USDA) (2009) Eligible Foreign Establishments. http://www.fsis.usda.gov/regulations_and_policies/Eligible_Foreign_ Establishments/index.asp.

———. (2007) "Missouri Firm Recalls Frozen Pot Pie Products for Possible *Salmonella* Contamination." Recall Release FSIS-RC-044-2007. Washington, D.C.: USDA FSIS.

USDA/FSIS *Escherichia coli* Risk Assessment Team (2001) Risk Assessment of the Public Health Impact of *Escherichia coli* O157:H7 in Ground Beef. http:// www.fsis.usda.gov/OPPDE/rdad/FRPubs/00-023N/00-023NReport.pdf.

USDA/FSIS *Salmonella* Enteritidis Risk Assessment Team (1998) "*Salmonella* Enteritidis Risk Assessment: Shell Eggs and Egg Products." www.fsis.usda.gov/ OPHS/risk/.

U.S. Environmental Protection Agency (EPA) (1998) *Assessment of Thyroid Follicular Cell Tumors.* EPA/630/R-97/002. Washington, D.C.: EPA.

———. (1996) *Strategic Plan for the Office of Research and Development.* Washington, D.C.: EPA.

U.S. Food and Drug Administration (FDA) (2003) *Quantitative Assessment of Relative Risk to Public Health from Foodborne* Listeria monocytogenes *Among Selected Categories of Ready-to-Eat Foods.* http://www.foodsafety.gov/~dms/ Lmr2-toc.html.

————. (2002) *Initiation and Conduct of All "Major" Risk Assessments Within a Risk Analysis Framework.* http://www.cfsan.fda.gov/~dms/rafw-toc.html.

————. (2001) *Food Code.* Annex 5: HACCP Guideline. http://www.fda.gov/Food/FoodSafety/RetailFoodProtection/FoodCode/FoodCode2001/ucm089302.htm.

U.S. General Accountability Office (GAO) (2008) *Food Safety: Improvements Needed in FDA Oversight of Fresh Produce.* GAO-08-1047. http://www.gao.gov/new.items/d081047.pdf.

————. (2007) *High Risk Series: An Update.* GAO-07-310. http://www.gao.gov/new.items/d07310.pdf.

————. (2003) *Bioterrorism: A Threat to Agriculture and the Food Supply.* GAO-04-259T. http://www.gao.gov/new.items/d0247t.pdf.

————. (2001) *Food Safety and Security: Fundamental Changes Needed to Ensure Safe Food.* GAO-02-47T. http://www.gao.gov/new.items/d0247t.pdf.

————. (1998) *Federal Efforts to Insure the Safety of Imported Foods Are Inconsistent and Unreliable.* GAO/RCED-98-103. http://www.gao.gov/archive/1998/rc98103.pdf.

U.S. Nuclear Regulatory Commission (1975) *Reactor Safety Study.* Washington, D.C.

Withee, James and Wayne Schlosser (2008) *Risk-based Sampling for* Escherichia coli *O157:H7 in Ground Beef and Beef Trim.* USDA/Food Safety and Inspection Service. http://www.fsis.usda.gov/PDF/Ecoli_Sampling_RA_ExecSumm_Feb08.pdf.

Wong, S. N. and M. C. Chiu (2008) "The Scare of Melamine Tainted Milk Products." 13 *Hong Kong Journal of Paediatrics* (New Series) 230–34. http://hkjpaed.org/details.asp?id=672&show=1234.

World Health Organization (WHO)/Food and Agriculture Organization of the UN (FAO) (2006) *Food Safety Risk Analysis: A Guide for National Food Safety Authorities.* http://www.who.int/foodsafety/publications/micro/riskanalysis06/en/.

Zimmerman, Rae (1998) "Historical and Future Perspectives on Risk Perception and Communication." In *Risk Research and Management in Asian Perspective: Proceedings of the First China-Japan Conference on Risk Assessment and Management, November 23–26, 1998, Beijing, China.* Beijing Normal University. Colorado Springs, Colo.: International Academic Publishers.

Zimmerman, Rae and Vicki M. Bier (2002) Risk assessment of extreme events. Paper presented at Columbia-Wharton/Penn Roundtable on "Risk Management Strategies in an Uncertain World, Palisades, N.Y., April 12–13. http://www.ldeo.columbia.edu/chrr/documents/meetings/roundtable/white_papers/zimmerman_wp.pdf.

Chapter 9
Solving the Problem of Scale
The European Approach to Import Safety and Security Concerns

Alberto Alemanno

Regulation of import safety in the European Community (EC) involves, as is often the case in the European legal order, a complex interaction among a number of different actors within novel systems of supranational governance that are both relatively new and continuously evolving.[1] The European legislature, assisted by the European Court of Justice (ECJ), has established a set of mechanisms governed by a network of actors bound to participate in the construction of the Community. This embraces not only European bodies but also local authorities in addition to central institutions of the member states. This structure involves many layers of responsibility for the development and administration of Community law.

Of the roughly 1.5 trillion euros worth of third-country goods imported into the European Union (EU) each year, the vast majority escapes systematic control at border inspection posts.[2] Once shippers have satisfied customs formalities, the third-country imports they deliver circulate freely within the Community's internal market, regardless of their origin.[3] As a result, most of the import safety problems in Europe are not detected at the points of entry existing at the EU external border (where it would be a Herculean task to systematically check all incoming shipments). Safety problems tend to arise only later, once the products are already within the territory of the European internal market, where they are subject to member states' controls. Under this model, consumers throughout the Community are therefore entitled to expect that their interests will be protected and taken into account, not simply by their own state but by all member states, regardless of the origin (domestic or international) of the products placed on the European market.

To ensure this outcome, the EU needed to elaborate a regulatory safety framework that, while capable of being applied to all products in free circulation within the Community, remained homogeneous enough to be consistently enforceable throughout Europe. This is crucial since nonuniform policies in relation to imports could have important safety implications as well as lead to serious distortions of trade. Moreover, as illustrated in chapter 4, by Tracey Epps and Michael Trebilcock, the design of a regulatory safety framework by any World Trade Organization (WTO) member (of which the EC counts itself) must conform to its multilateral trade obligations.

Yet there is a significant dose of historical fortuity within the evolution of the EC policy toward product safety. Indeed, although not originally foreseen, the Community has resorted to countless regulatory instruments, which have encompassed the control of all kinds of risk to public health and safety: not only product safety regulation in pharmaceutical law, food law, chemicals and medical devices, but also in wider areas such as safety at work and environmental protection (Alemanno 2008). As illustrated below, the constitutional basis of the Community legislation that regulates product safety is founded on trade considerations; safety is merely a subsidiary consideration. Perhaps this is not entirely surprising from a U.S. perspective to the extent that, as has been said regarding food safety, "regulators in both jurisdictions ultimately derive their legal authority to define and control food safety risks from their constitutional power over the free or interstate movement of goods and both share some aspects of that authority with their constituent states" (Echols 1998: 530).

In the absence of a dedicated import safety regime in Europe, it is crucial, in order to understand how Europe addresses the growing concerns about import safety and security, to examine the European product safety framework as it applies to both domestic and imported products as well as the existing import control mechanisms. Such an examination will be the focus of the first part of this chapter. The chapter then proceeds to identify the main features of the European regime and analyzes its partial reform following the 2007 "summer of recalls" when over 18 million toys were recalled globally because of magnetic parts that posed a choking hazard. The recent melamine dairy scandal will be presented as an interesting case study illustrating the European approach to import safety by exemplifying its reactive rather than proactive nature.

The Emergence of the European Product Safety *Acquis*

Although it might be surprising to any person outside the grip of European law, the foundation on which the Community enjoys competence to legislate in relation to product regulation is based almost exclusively not on a policy of consumer protection but on the facilitation of trade, in particular the free movement of goods, within the context of the creation of the internal European market. The Community's gradual involvement with product safety issues is indeed nothing more than a rather accidental spillover effect of the realization of the common market (Vos 1999: 9). When implementing the prohibition laid down in Article 28 of the Treaty establishing the European Community (ECT) on "quantitative restriction and measures having an equivalent effect," the Commission, helped by the ECJ, derived the right to review the contents of laws as yet not harmonized at Community level (Alemanno 2007: 34). In particular, because product safety concerns might have become a possible source of hindrance to intra-Community trade, the Community had to step in. This process shows why, and also how, the Community was forced to address an import safety issue emerging among its own members well before tackling "external" import safety.

How did the EC tackle "internal" import safety issues? As is well known, the EC enjoys both negative and positive integration powers to attain the treaty-sanctioned imperative of free movement of goods. However, before the 1986 shift to qualified majority vote, Community harmonization required, under Article 94, a unanimous vote in the European Council (Alemanno 2006: 237–58). Against this thorny institutional backdrop, which had led to a sort of regulatory impasse over EC harmonization, the ECJ developed, in its legendary Cassis de Dijon judgment,[4] the principle of mutual recognition. This original principle implies the substitution of "home state control" for "host state control" in the handling of obstacles stemming from interstate regulatory diversity, including different safety standards. According to this principle, once a product has been lawfully marketed in one member state, it should be admitted into any other state without restriction.[5] However, the host country may challenge the presumed equivalent level of protection pursued by the home country's legislation by invoking the exceptions listed in Article 30 of the ECT or the judicially identified mandatory requirements.[6] Home state control prevails in the absence of a sufficiently compelling basis for host state control.

The principle of mutual recognition, while preserving local, regional, and national traditions, allowed the Community to realize an internal market without having to adopt hundreds of "vertical" directives.[7] However, even among European member states, which are relatively similar in terms of regulatory approach, national regulations cannot always ensure equivalent levels of protection. This stems from the different approaches to regulation adopted in each member state, reflecting differences in culture, the specific functioning of their political institutions, and also their different perceptions and attitudes toward the management of risk. As a consequence of the resulting differences in regulation, the goals of free movement could not have been achieved without some form of "positive integration" that came about through agreement on common rules to overcome the obstacles that could not have been tackled solely by the mutual recognition principle (Craig 2002: 12). Thus, the Commission's response in the post-1986 period was to introduce legislation to harmonize the laws of the member states on health and safety, thereby removing these obstacles to trade.

However, to avoid the excessive "Euro-uniformity" of the traditional approach to harmonization, which implied slow negotiations on technical specifications among member states, a "new approach" to harmonization was developed.[8] Under this new approach, legislative harmonization, "a common rule for a common market," was restricted to laying down "essential health and safety requirements" and the formulation of technical specifications (so-called European Norms) to meet these conditions was delegated to private standardization bodies, such as the European Committee for Standardization (CEN), and the European Committee for Technical Standardization (CENELEC).[9] Although these specifications are not binding as such (unlike the essential requirements), member states are obliged to presume that products manufactured in accordance with them comply with the "essential requirements" laid down in the directives (and which are therefore legally binding). As a result, these products can be marked CE (*Conformité Européenne*) by their suppliers (Farr 1996: 5). This new approach, by allowing a manufacturer to show that its products complied with essential safety requirements, even if they did not comply with the Community standards, shifted toward minimum, rather than total, harmonization. As stated, "the EC legislation would set a floor, and the Treaty a ceiling, with member states being free to pursue their own policies within these boundaries" (Craig 2002: 24).

Although the free movement of goods within the internal market is still the primary policy consideration for product safety legislation at the EU level, various provisions of the treaty have been amended in the meantime to specify the need for a "high level of protection" in matters of safety, health, public health, and consumer protection. As a result, when called on to regulate risks regardless of their origin, the EU legislature is caught between two competing treaty-sanctioned goals and must strike a balance between attaining a high level of protection of human health and consumers' interests and ensuring the effective functioning of the internal market.

The Product Safety Law *Acquis*

In parallel with the "new approach" directives, which, combined with the mutual recognition principle, aimed at ensuring the internal free movement of goods within the Community, the EC legislature also developed two separated frameworks for product safety law: one for nonfood consumer products and another for food products. Together, these frameworks make up the body of the EU's product safety law—its *acquis*—which applies to both domestic and imported products.[10]

To reinforce the overall level of consumer protection within the Community, a General Product Safety Directive (GPSD) laying down performance standards was first introduced.[11] This directive establishes a general obligation for manufacturers to place only safe products on the market and establishes conformity assessment criteria and procedures based on manufacturers' self-declaration of compliance (known as the CE marking) (GPSD 2001: art. 17; Lohbeck 1998: xi). Since this obligation covers only manufacturers of nonfood consumer products, the subsequent General Food Regulation (GFR) introduced a similar requirement also for food business operators.[12] Both instruments complement the Community liability regime for defective products, as laid down by Directive 85/374/EEC,[13] which sets out the principle that "the producer shall be liable for damage caused by a defect in his product" (strict liability regime).[14] A producer under this legislation includes not just the manufacturer, but under certain circumstances every link in the supply chain (Cannarsa 2005). While the GPSD and GFR promote safety by acting ex ante, the liability regime ensures compensation for damages, which may stem from both food and nonfood products.[15] Although compensatory in nature, the liability directive is also expected to produce a preventive effect in the end. Under the GPSD, the safety of nonfood products is presumed if production took place according to standardized norms. The same cannot be said of the GFR, where it is explicitly stated that "food shall be deemed to be unsafe if it is considered to be injurious to health and/or unfit for human consumption" (GFR 2002: art. 14[2]).

Even when a product is in conformity with relevant standards, authorities are not barred from taking appropriate measures, such as organizing appropriate checks, introducing warnings, stopping sales, withdrawing products from the market, and recalling them from consumers (GPSD 2001: art. 5; GFR 2002: art. 19). Under both regimes, member states are entrusted with ensuring compliance by producers and distributors in such a way that food or consumer products placed on the market are safe, regardless of their origin (imported or domestic). As a result, they are obliged to establish market surveillance authorities to ensure compliance with general safety requirements. These authorities may adopt interim protective measures and enjoy mandatory recall power (GPSD 2001: art. 8; GFR 2002: art. 54).

Rapid Alert Systems

These national, postmarket enforcement mechanisms, based on national market surveillance, have been strengthened, since the 1980s, by the creation of rapid alert systems: the Rapid Alert System for Non-food Consumer Products (RAPEX) (GPSD 2001: art. 12) and the Rapid Alert System for Food and Feed (RASFF) (GFR 2002: arts. 35 and 50). Both systems have been put in place to provide (national) control authorities with a tool to exchange information about measures taken in response to serious risks detected in nonfood and food products. This coordination adds value to surveillance and enforcement action at the national level to increase the safety of European citizens.

Under both rapid alert systems, the European Commission must be notified of all measures taken to prevent or restrict the marketing of a product adopted by the national authorities or the producer/distributor in relation to a dangerous product. If the examination of the notification conducted by the Commission leads to validation, the relevant information is circulated to the RAPEX/RASFF members in all member states. Notifications are published on a weekly basis on the websites of the Commission.

If we break down the total number of RASFF notifications received in 2007 according to the type of control, it appears that most of them concern official controls on the internal market, whereas the second largest concerns controls at border posts when the consignment was not accepted for import. Almost 60 percent of notifications to the RAPEX system in 2007 concerned third-country products, and 51 percent of these notifications concerned products imported from China. Under RAPEX, China was indicated as the country of origin of the notified product in more than half of the cases in 2007 (52 percent for China including Hong Kong) (RAPEX 2007: 24).

Both RAPEX and RASFF systems may be open to applicant countries, third countries, or international organizations on the basis of reciprocity. In any event, to avoid the recurrence of the problem detected, RAPEX and RASFF inform third countries of origin in a systematic way. As the recent melamine dairy scandal has shown (discussed later), the rapid alert systems represent the internal market's safety net vis-à-vis unsafe products.

Community Action in the Case of "Serious Risk"

Under both the GPSD and GFR, the Commission may adopt temporary (emergency) EU measures in the case of a serious risk to human health, animal health, the environment, and safety of consumers. These trigger the same market surveillance and restrictive measures in all member states with respect to the specified product (GPSD 2001: art. 13; GFR 2002: art. 53). Generally, Community action may occur where the risk cannot be contained satisfactorily by means of measures taken by the member states individually. These measures are normally introduced in full consultation with the member states and on the basis of comitology decisions. They may consist, depending on the origin of the product, in the suspension of the placing on the market or in the suspension of imports of the food or consumer product in question (GPSD 2001: art. 8[1][b]–[f], 13; GFR 2002: art. 53[1][a][b]). In the latter case, which involves commercial policy that falls within the sphere of exclusive Community competence, it is only the Commission that may act to limit imports of third-country products into the Community. To date, five such measures have been adopted at the Community level. Three concerned consumer products (in particular a ban on phthalates in children's toys[16] and on novelty cigarette lighters,[17] and a warning on toys containing or made from magnets[18]), whereas the rest involved food items, notably aflatoxins[19] and melamine in dairy products.[20]

Controls on Imports from Third Countries

Although lacking a dedicated import safety regime providing for systematic controls at the border, the EU has adopted a set of control mechanisms on imports of certain specific products. As a result, these controls are not uniform across sectors but are instead a function of the level of risk: the higher the risk the greater the control. Animal products, for example, are subject to especially stringent checks, due to the very high risks to both public and animal health from unsafe products. Third countries are required to receive formal approval before they are eligible to export high-risk products; the Food Veterinary Office (FVO) routinely carries out a mission to verify on-the-spot compliance with the relevant Community requirements. Similar pre-export listing requirements may be established if necessary by the Commission, assisted by the Standing Committee of the Food Chain, for any specific food, also of nonanimal origin.

The European Approach to Import Safety and Security Concerns

Following the high-profile, worldwide alerts involving key consumer products, the European Commission carried out a thorough review of the product safety law *acquis* in the latter half of 2007. This review focused on existing legislation, enforcement capacity of member states, obligations of economic operators, and cooperation with third countries. The European Commission's analysis suggested that the problems relating to unsafe products were limited (mainly involving nonfood products) and the possible solutions should concentrate on those areas where there are problems, as opposed to developing an overall new system. As a result, a new legislative framework for goods has been developed in response to identified weaknesses in the *acquis*.[21] This new framework builds on and complements the existing system for (nonfood) consumer products under the GPSD so as to substantially realign it with the most recent and effective safety framework for food products (GFR). At the same time, some of these reforms extend also to the food sector.

Customs Authorities: From a Reactive Role to a (More) Proactive Approach

Recognizing the increasing threat to public health and safety posed by imported dangerous products, the EC legislature expressed the need to reform the role played by customs authorities at the points of entry. Data from the member states showed that in the first half of 2007 an average of 9 percent of incoming consignments were controlled. Although this percentage is significantly higher than the 3 percent recommended by the World Customs Organization, it seems inadequate in the light of the new developments, including enlargement and globalization and the role of organized crime. Indeed, under the previous legislative framework,[22] there was no obligation for the customs authorities to initiate specific control checks for unsafe products beyond the standard customs control procedures involving a mere documentary check. Therefore, the role of custom authorities was substantially reactive once an unsafe product had been identified in the course of customs controls. No proactive obligations existed for the customs authorities to carry out controls for unsafe products at EU borders on their own initiative. In the future, following the entry into force of Regulation 765/2008 in January 2010, customs authorities "shall carry out appropriate checks on the characteristics of the products on an adequate scale . . . before these products are released in free circulation" (Regulation 765/2008: art. 27[1]). While the exact scope of this obligation to perform checks on consumer products is likely to become a matter of interpretation, customs authorities maintain the power to suspend the release of a product for free circulation on the Community market (Regulation 765/2008: art. 27[3]). However, their decision is temporary (its validity does not last more than three days) and may be confirmed only by the market surveillance authorities when the product presents "a serious risk" or does not comply with Community authorization (Regulation 765/2008: art. 29). In the former case, national authorities may even destroy or otherwise render inoperable the relevant products (Regulation 765/2008: art. 29[4]).

Traceability for Nonfood Consumer Products

To increase product safety, the EC legislature has introduced traceability as a mechanism that can provide a continuous flow of information and allow for the retrieval of the history and the origin of a product at any point in the supply chain. Although traceability does not itself make a product safe, it is a risk-management tool to be used to assist in containing a product safety problem.

Its primary aim is therefore to ensure product safety and to assist in enabling an unsafe product to be removed from the market, notably by making the recall of a product easier. The system of traceability for nonfood consumer products is based on Article R7 of Decision 768/2008, which requires economic operators to be able to identify any person who has supplied them with a product and other businesses to which their products have been supplied. This approach, which is largely inspired by the traceability system introduced in the food sector, may be defined as a one-step-backward, one-step-forward approach, requiring each operator to know the step before him or her in the food chain and the step after (GFR 2002: art. 18). Everyone involved in the supply chain has to be put in the position of identifying any person responsible for the supply of an unsafe food product. This goal is translated into an operational duty imposed on manufacturers who must ensure that their products bear mandatory information concerning not only the product (type, batch, serial number, etc.) but also their own information (name, registered trade name or trademark, and address) (Annex I of Decision 798/2008, art. R2[5] and [6]).

It is believed that the introduction of such product information will help to make market surveillance simpler and more efficient by ensuring traceability of a product throughout the whole supply chain. Indeed, an efficient traceability system facilitates market surveillance authorities in the job of tracing economic operators who made noncompliant products available on the market.

Obligations of Importers and Distributors in View of Ensuring Traceability

The new legislative framework for the marketing of products has also introduced for the first time a specific set of obligations on importers (performance standards) (Annex I of Decision 798/2008, art. R4). Importers are obliged to place only compliant products on the Community market and, for this purpose, before placing a product on the market, they shall ensure the following: the appropriate conformity assessment procedure has been carried out by the manufacturer; and the product bears the required conformity marking and mandatory information of the product (type, batch, serial number, etc.) and of the manufacturer (name, registered trade name or trademark, and address). Similar obligations have been imposed on distributors, the idea being that both importers and distributors, because they are close to the marketplace, should be involved in market surveillance tasks carried out by national authorities, and should be prepared to participate actively, providing the competent authorities with all necessary information relating to the product concerned.

In addition, the new legislative framework aims to clarify the conformity assessment procedures and to reinforce the quality and use of accreditation to ensure that certification bodies are truly competent to work in support of the application of the Community harmonization legislation.

Increased Cooperation Between Customs and Market Surveillance Authorities

Another important part of the reform aims at improving cooperation between customs (who rely on the Risk Information System, or RIS, in the customs area) and market surveillance authorities (who rely on the rapid alert systems). All customs officials' decisions to block or reject goods at the EU borders for safety reasons must immediately be sent to the domestic market surveillance authority concerned, which in turn will immediately transmit the information to the other member states' customs and market surveillance authorities through the RAPEX (Regulation 765/2008: art. 27[5]) and RASFF systems. At the same time, the rapid alert systems' contact points should also inform their customs authorities of the measures and actions taken by market surveillance authorities relating to imported products that pose a serious risk in order to avoid further imports of the same product into the EU market. Thus, customs authorities, by becoming recipients of all information exchanged through the rapid alert systems, may better target control actions related to a certain type of good (e.g., toys originating from a certain third country). In the meantime, the customs authorities have introduced Commonly Agreed Priority Control Areas (CAPCA), enabling the EU to carry out targeted control actions relating to a specific type of goods.

Besides this reform, the Commission has put forward a proposal to improve toy safety in Europe by replacing and modernizing the 20-year-old toys directive (GPSD 2001). The proposal foresees the introduction of safety-enhancing provisions such as prohibiting the use of carcinogenic chemicals in toys, reducing the use of substances such as lead or mercury, and obliging operators to issue appropriate warnings to prevent accidents.[23]

Europe and the 2008 Melamine Dairy Scandal

The manner in which Europe handled the 2008 melamine dairy scandal provides an overview of the actual practice and functioning of import control mechanisms and procedures in urgent situations.

When the European Commission was made aware that high levels of melamine had been found in infant milk and other milk products in China during the summer of 2008,[24] it initially chose not to act, as imports of milk and milk products originating from China were not allowed into the Community. However, after some reflection, the Commission soon realized that certain composite products (i.e., products that contain at the same time a processed product of animal origin and a product of nonanimal origin) containing processed milk might have reached the EU market, and decided to enact—on the basis of Article 53(2) of the GFR—emergency measures. In a record 24 hours, the Commission adopted, after consulting the Standing Committee on the Food Chain and Animal Health, a decision prohibiting the import into the Community of all composite products from China intended for the nutrition of infants or young children.[25] However, by relying on the advice of the European Food Safety Authority (EFSA),[26] the Commission in 2008 required member states to systematically check all composite products containing at least 15 percent milk products originating from China (Comm. Dec. 2008/757/EC: art. 2). Indeed, according to EFSA's worst-case scenario, children with a high daily consumption of such products might exceed the tolerable daily intake of melamine (0.5

mg/kg body weight). Within the same decision, the Commission, by clearly rejecting a zero-risk approach, established—taking into account the available occurrence data—the level of 2.5 mg/kg as the appropriate one to distinguish between unavoidable background presence of melamine and unacceptable adulteration. It therefore required member states to destroy all products containing higher levels of melamine.

Given that member states are expected to report any unfavorable results of laboratory analyses through the RASFF, the Commission has been regularly reassessing its decision in the light of the results of the controls carried out by the EC member states' authorities.

One month later, in October 2008, member states had reported, via the RASFF system, significant difficulties in establishing the exact milk or milk product content of composite products. This led the Commission to realize that the value of 15 percent was largely irrelevant in deciding whether a consignment is subject to control requirements prior to import. As a result, to streamline and simplify import control procedures, the Commission amended the second part of its previous decision and established the requirement of controls irrespective of the exact amount of milk or milk products in the composite products (Comm. Dec. 2008/798/EC). Moreover, the Commission, building on member states' notifications, decided to introduce, within the amended decision, random checks prior to importing other feed and food products with a high protein content originating from China (Comm. Dec. 2008/798/EC: art. 2[2]).

In the meantime, according to information made available by the member states through the RASFF, high levels of melamine were also found in products containing soya or soya products imported from China, as well as in ammonium bicarbonate, used in the food industry as a raising agent. The Commission therefore considered it appropriate to extend the measures laid down in Commission Decision 2008/798/EC to these products by prohibiting in particular the import of products containing soya and soya products intended for use by infants and young children originating in or consigned from China. It also introduced 100 percent testing of feed and food containing soya and soya products originating in or consigned from China and additive ammonium bicarbonate imported from China. This final decision, 2008/921/EC, has not only amended the previous October 2008 decision but, being confirmative of Community action, is no longer subject to continuous reassessment and is currently in force (GFR 2002: art. 53[1]).

Although representing one of the most challenging food contaminations the world has faced, the melamine dairy scandal did not produce any tangible negative health effects on the European population. Even though this encouraging result cannot be entirely ascribed to the

European product safety *acquis* per se, the European regime, by showing its flexible and reactive nature, certainly contributed to this favorable outcome. On the one hand, the emergency powers entrusted to the Commission have indeed permitted the rapid adoption of an initial import ban coupled with targeted checks. Yet, on the other, the feedback received, via RASFF, by the national authorities in charge of the implementation of these emergency measures, has enabled the Community to update its decision by targeting the right products and fine-tuning its precise reach. The EU reaction substantially contained the damage by preventing recurrences. Notwithstanding the high risk of overreaction facing the authorities in this model scenario of the social amplification of risk, the Community, by relying on its multiactor and multifaceted mechanisms of control, seems to have managed to adopt an approach proportionate to the risk at stake. The Commission, by rejecting a zero-risk policy, struck a fair balance between reaction and overreaction. Finally, it should not be forgotten that the preexisting EU ban on Chinese dairy products has facilitated the containment of the scandal.

Exporting the European Approach to Import Safety

Ensuring that imports are safe presents special challenges as production takes place in third countries, outside the direct control of the member states. However, besides a few exceptions regarding high-risk products (such as animals and animal products), the regulation of import safety in the Community is not the focus of direct legislative attention. As a result, import safety in Europe is pursued not through the application of special conditions governing the import of third-country products, which would impose systematic checks at the external borders, but rather through the decentralized enforcement by member states' market surveillance authorities of a harmonized set of product safety regulations: the European product safety *acquis*. This multilevel and multiactor regulatory framework, which is applicable to all products that seek to gain access to the Community market and then circulate within it, applies to both domestic and imported products.

While its enforcement is decentralized at the member states' level,[27] any action taken by national market surveillance authorities and customs officials within the Community framework must be communicated to the European Commission, which, in accordance with the existing rapid alert systems (RAPEX and RASFF), centralizes this information before transmitting it among all national authorities. Following the recent reform, national authorities' activities and findings will be communicated also to the customs authorities, who by becoming recipients of all information exchanged through the rapid alert systems, may better target control actions related to a certain type of goods (e.g., toys originating from a third country). This exchange of information facilitates authorities' tasks of ensuring product safety within the European market and enables the European Commission, whenever national intervention is not adequate to achieve a declared safety goal, to act for the entire EU. This shared allocation of responsibility, which is made possible by the rapid alert systems, is one of the distinguishing features of the European approach to import safety.

By not providing systematic checks at the external border, the European regulatory approach to import safety is substantially reactive: it is only once an unsafe product has been identified in the course of random customs controls or internal market surveillance that either the relevant member state or the Commission will act. Indeed, no proactive obligation exists for the customs authorities to carry out controls on unsafe products at the EU border on their own initiatives. Instead, they confine themselves to a documentary check, which might be supported by a certification scheme. However, as illustrated by the recent handling of the melamine scandal, the European framework, although substantially reactive, is capable, once triggered, of becoming preventive and even precautionary, allowing EC action even in a situation of scientific uncertainty.

While it is true that Commission action was not *in casu* triggered by alarming findings of its own inspection authorities but rather by media reports, it was speedy enough to effectively coordinate customs and market surveillance authorities' reactions vis-à-vis those products. The introduction of an obligation on customs authorities to perform controls "on an adequate scale" before imported products can be released in free circulation might reasonably be interpreted as a sign suggesting that there has been a shift by the European regime toward more prevention at the external borders. However, notwithstanding this apparent willingness of the Community to strengthen checks at the external border of nonfood products, the EU approach toward import safety is not expected to change in its essence (EC Reg. 2008: art. 27 [1]). The EU, aware that systematic controls at the border are not a realistic option, seems likely to shift its regulatory focus to where the source of a possible safety issue is located: the country of origin. Indeed, the Community is currently focusing its efforts in extending its reactive "safety-net" regulatory model beyond its borders, thus inevitably giving rise to an interesting legal export of its own approach to import safety. In particular, it recently developed the RAPEX-China system, which establishes a regular and rapid transmission of data between the EU's and China's product safety administrations. Under this newly created rapid alert system, the Commission provides the Chinese authorities with information on consumer products originating from China that have been identified as dangerous and consequently banned or withdrawn from the EU market. Under the terms of the agreement, China investigates all the notifications it receives and, when necessary, adopts measures limiting further exports of the notified dangerous products to the EU. To date, after the first two years of operation, 669 RAPEX notifications have been investigated by China (out of 3,338 stored in the database) and in 353 investigated cases appropriate preventive measures were adopted either by the Chinese government or voluntarily by the Chinese manufacturer or exporter. In most of the other investigated cases (47 percent), no measures were taken—mainly because China could not find the company responsible for manufacturing and/or exporting dangerous products to the EU.[28] EU and Chinese authorities are currently cooperating to extend the EU RASFF system to China to also cover food products.

The immediate gain from including China in the EU rapid alert systems is to prevent further imports into the EU of dangerous products without crossing jurisdictional lines. Once more, this confirms the reactive nature of the EU approach to import safety while showing at the same time it has the aptitude to quickly adopt preventive measures in an emergency. Yet, the major success of extending these alert systems to China has been to familiarize the local authorities with an original cooperation mechanism that they did not hesitate to choose as a blueprint for the creation of their own rapid alert systems. RAPEX and RASFF are both likely to be instrumental in establishing the foundations of market surveillance culture in China and beyond (RASFF 2008: 46).

Notes

1. Although the European Community (EC, or, the Community) and the European Union (EU) are not identical entities, these terms will be used interchangeably here.

2. Only some high-risk products are subject to systematic controls at border inspections posts, such as live animals and animal products (Comm. Dec. 2007/275/EC).

3. This is a direct consequence of the Community being a customs union (Molle 1990: 12).

4. In Case 120/78, *Rewe-Zentrale AG v. Bundesmonopolverwaltung für Branntwein* ECR 649 (1979), involving review of a German rule prescribing minimum alcohol content for fruit liqueurs, the European Court stated that where a product "suitably and satisfactorily" fulfills the legitimate objective of a member state's own rules (public safety, protection of the consumer or the environment), the importing country cannot justify prohibiting its sale in its territory by claiming that the way it fulfills the objective is different from that imposed on domestic products.

5. This formulation was developed for the first time by the communication of the Commission concerning the consequences of the judgment given by the Court on February 20, 1979 in Case 120/78 *Rewe-Zentrale AG v. Bundesmonopol-verwaltung für Branntwein* (Cassis de Dijon), ECR 649 (1979).

6. This concept was introduced by the ECJ to soften its expansive interpretation of Article 28 of the ECT and it is used by the same court as a flexible tool to balance the sometimes competing interests of market integration and market regulation.

7. This new approach to harmonization was launched by the European Commission in its White Paper on the Completion of the Internal Market, COM (85) 603, 7, published in June 1985. It eventually became the cornerstone of the 1992 Programme (Mattera 1992: 80).

8. Under the new approach, the EC institutions, apart from legislating only on "essential requirements," have also delegated the determination of more detailed standards to quasi-public European Standards organizations and then coordinated quasi-public national bodies in charge of assessing the conformity of products produced in any one member state for sale throughout the EC market (Shaffer 2002: 33).

9. Concerns have been formulated that business interests would have been predominant in the standardization bodies (Whetherill 1990: 578).

10. This distinction is increasingly questioned today and has recently been defined as a "disadvantageous dichotomy." The objectives pursued by both regimes are indeed common: to protect consumer health and safety and to ensure the proper functioning of the internal market (Brack 2009: 173–98).

11. Originally, it was Directive 92/59/EEC (Coun. Dir. 1992), which was later replaced with Directive 2001/95/EC (GPSD 2001). This directive covers fully those consumer products that are not subject to sector-specific legislation (e.g., child-care products, furniture, and lighters) and complements sector-specific legislation by applying to products covered by sectoral legislation (e.g., toys, chemicals, pharmaceuticals, cosmetics, machinery, and electric products) for those safety risks not addressed in that legislation.

12. Regulation (EC) No. 178/2002 (GFR 2002) sets forth the general principles and requirements of food law, establishes the European Food Safety Authority, and articulates procedures in matters of food safety.

13. Council Directive 85/374/EEC of July 25, 1985 on the approximation of the laws, regulations, and administrative provisions of the member states concerning liability for defective products, O.J. (L 210, p. 29), as amended by Directive 1999/34/EC, 1999 O.J. (L 141, p. 20).

14. Article 1 of this directive provides for absolute liability for damage caused by any defect (subject to a number of exceptions that are not relevant here).

15. An amendment to the directive has clarified that this product liability legislation includes all food as well as nonfood products. This change in the scope of this directive reflects the outbreaks of diseases and food safety concerns which occurred in the 1990s.

16. Commission Decision (1999/815/EC) adopted measures prohibiting the distribution of toys and childcare articles made of soft PVC-containing phthalates.

17. Commission Decision (2006/502/EC) required member states to take measures to ensure that only lighters that are child-resistant are allowed to be sold, as well as to prohibit the sale of novelty lighters.

18. Commission Decision (2008/329/EC) required member states to ensure that magnetic toys placed or made available on the market display a warning about the health and safety risks they pose.

19. Commission Decision (2006/504/EC) governs certain foodstuffs imported from certain third countries due to contamination risks of these products by aflatoxins. Aflatoxins are highly toxic and carcinogenic secondary fungal metabolites and have been detected in various food commodities including pistachio nuts.

20. Commission Decision (2008/757/EC) imposes special conditions governing the import of products containing milk or milk products originating in or consigned in China.

21. See, in particular, EC Reg. (2008: 21) and Joint Dec. 2008/768/EC.

22. Council Regulation No. 339/93 (EEC Reg. 1993) on checks for conformity with the rules on product safety in the case of products imported from third countries.

23. Proposal for a Directive of the European Parliament and the Council on the Safety of Toys, COM (2008) 9 final.

24. Melamine is a chemical intermediate used in the manufacture of amino resins and plastics and is used as a monomer and as an additive for plastics. High levels of melamine in food can result in very severe health effects. See chapter 2 by Jacques deLisle for a detailed discussion of the melamine scandal.

25. Commission Decision (2008/757/EC: art. 1, p. 10) imposes special conditions governing the import of products containing milk or milk products originating in or consigned in China.

26. EFSA received a request on September 19, 2008 from the European Commission's Health and Consumers Directorate requesting urgent scientific advice on the risks to human health due to the possible presence of melamine in composite food products imported from China into the EU.

27. Member states are responsible for carrying out checks of their conformity and, when doing so, they are subject to common rules to avoid any distortion that might adversely affect safety and health.

28. Further improvement can be expected as a result of recently adopted EU requirements that the name and the address of the manufacturer and the importer must be provided. However, continued efforts are still needed to ensure effective international traceability.

References

Alemanno, Alberto (2008) "The Shaping of Risk Regulation by Community Courts." Jean Monnet Working Paper, New York University, 18/2008.

———. (2007) *Trade in Food: Regulatory and Judicial Approaches in the EC and the WTO*. London: Cameron May.

———. (2006) "Food Safety and the Single European Market." In *What's the Beef? The Contested Governance of European Food Safety*, edited by Christopher Ansell and David Vogel. Cambridge, Mass.: MIT Press.

Brack, Anthony (2009) "A Disadvantageous Dichotomy in Product Safety Law: Some Reflections on Sense and Nonsense of the Distinction Food-Nonfood in European Product Safety Law." 20 *European Business Law Review* 173–98.

Cannarsa, Michel (2005) *La responsabilité du fait des produits défectueux: Étude comparative*. Milan: Giuffré.

Craig, Paul (2002) "The Evolution of the Single Market." In *The Law of the Single European Market: Unpacking the Premises*, edited by Catherine Barnard and Joanne Scott. Oxford: Hart.
Echols, Marsha (1998) "Food Safety Regulation in the European Union and the United States: Different Cultures, Different Laws." 4 *Columbia Journal of European Law* 525–44.
Farr, Stephan (1996) *Harmonization of Technical Standards in the EC*. New York: Wiley.
Lohbeck, Dave (1998) *CE Marking Handbook, A Critical Approach to Global Safety Certification*. Woburn, Mass.: Newnes.
Mattera, Alfonso (1992) *Le marché unique européen*. Paris: Jupiter 80.
Molle, Willem (1990) *The Economics of European Integration*. Dartmouth, N.H.: Ashgate.
Rapid Alert System (RAPEX) (2007) *Annual Report* 2007.
RASFF (2008) RASFF *Connecting with the World*. Annual Report.
Shaffer, Gregory (2002) "Reconciling Trade and Regulatory Goals: The Prospects and Limits of New Approaches to Transatlantic Governance Through Mutual Recognition and Safe Harbor Agreements." 9 *Columbia Journal of European Law* 29–78.
Vos, Ellen (1999) *Institutional Frameworks of the Community Health and Safety Regulation: Committees, Agencies and Private Bodies*. Portland, Ore.: Hart.
Whetherill, Stephan (1990) "The Evolution of the Single Market: Harmonisation or Liberalisation?" 53 *Common Market Law Review* 578.

Case Cited

Case 120/78 *Rewe-Zentrale AG v. Bundesmonopolverwaltung für Branntwein* (Cassis de Dijon), ECR 649 (1979).

Commission Decisions, Regulations, and Agreements Cited

Commission Decision (Comm. Dec.) 2008/798/EC of October 14, 2008 imposing special conditions governing the import of products containing milk or milk products originating in or consigned from China. 2008 O.J. (L 273/18).
Commission Decision (Comm. Dec.) 2008/757/EC of September 26, 2008 imposing special conditions governing the import of products containing milk or milk products originating in or consigned from China. 2008 O.J. (L 259/10).
Commission Decision (Comm. Dec.) 2008/329/EC of April 21, 2008 requiring member states to ensure that magnetic toys placed or made available on the market display a warning about the health and safety risks they pose. 2008 O.J. (L 114/90).
Commission Decision (Comm. Dec.) 2007/275/EC of April 17, 2007 concerning lists of animals and products to be subject to controls at border inspection posts under Council Directives 91/496/EEC and 97/78/EC. 2007 O.J. (L 116/9).
Commission Decision (Comm. Dec.) 2006/504/EC of July 12, 2006 on special conditions governing certain foodstuffs imported from certain third coun-

tries due to contamination risks of these products by aflatoxins. 2006 O.J. (L 199/21).

Commission Decision (Comm. Dec.) 2006/502/EC of May 11, 2006 requiring Member States to take measures to ensure that only lighters which are child-resistant are placed on the market and to prohibit the placing on the market of novelty lighters. 2006 O.J. (L 198/41).

Commission Decision (Comm. Dec.) 1999/815/EC of December 7, 1999 adopting measures prohibiting the placing on the market of toys and childcare articles intended to be placed in the mouth by children under three years of age made of soft PVC containing one or more of the substances di-iso-nonyl phthalate (DINP), di(2-ethylhexyl) phthalate (DEHP), dibutyl phthalate (DBP), di-iso-decyl phthalate (DIDP), di-n-octyl phthalate (DNOP), and butylbenzyl phthalate (BBP). 1999 O.J. (L 315/46).

Council Directive (Coun. Dir.) 1992/59/EEC of June 29, 1992 on general product safety. 1992 O.J. (L 228/11/08).

Council Directive (Coun. Dir.) 1985/374/EEC of July 25, 1985 on the approximation of the laws, regulations and administrative provisions of the member states concerning liability for defective products. 1985 O.J. (L 210/7.8).

Council Regulation (EEC Reg.) No. 339/93 of February 8, 1993 on checks for conformity with the rules on product safety in the case of products imported from third countries. 1993 O.J. (L 040).

General Food Regulation (GFR) (178/2002) of the European Parliament and of the Council Regulation (EC) No. of 28 January 2002 laying down the general principles and requirements of food law, establishing the European Food Safety Authority and laying down procedures in matters of food safety. 2002 O.J. (L 31/1).

General Product Safety Directive (GPSD) (2001/95/EC) of the European Parliament and of the Council of December 3, 2001 on general product safety. 2002 O.J. (L 11/4).

Joint Decision (Joint Dec.) 768/2008/EC of the European Parliament and of the Council of July 9, 2008 on a common framework for the marketing of products, and repealing Council Decision 93/465/EEC, L218/82. 2008 O.J. (L 218/82).

Regulation (EC Reg.) No. 765/2008 of the European Parliament and of the Council of July 9. 2008 setting out the requirements for accreditation and market surveillance relating to the marketing of products and repealing Regulation (EEC) No. 339/93. 2008 O.J. (L 218/30).

Part IV
Leveraging the Private Sector

Chapter 10
Importers as Regulators
Product Safety in a Globalized World

Kenneth A. Bamberger and Andrew T. Guzman

In the wake of recent scandals involving lead toys, toxic toothpaste, poisonous pet food, and other dangerous products, policy makers have proposed a variety of strategies that purport to address safety concerns. Though many of these proposals would have salutary effects on consumer product safety, they do not provide, either individually or collectively, a full solution to the problem. This chapter offers a different proposal for addressing the challenges that global production poses for state-centered regulation of import safety. We argue that regulators should structure administrative penalties to make private importers regulate the foreign manufacturing processes from which they benefit.

Specifically, we make the case that where U.S. regulators expect a threat to consumer protection from foreign goods and services, they should augment the legal penalties imposed against foreign and domestic partners in international trade that are within the reach of American authorities. This enhanced threat of legal liability would serve to ensure that these parties act as de facto regulators of the foreign activity from which they benefit, even when those activities themselves are beyond the reach of American law. Trade in domestic goods and services would not trigger the same penalties because these products face regulation of the production process that, in principle, achieves the desired level of safety.

The goal of this enhanced regulation is to motivate American firms (or others within the reach of the American legal system) trading in imported goods and services to take into account the safety of those products. In other words, we propose that these firms assess the effectiveness of the legal, social, and economic forces that are at play in the production and marketing of these items and then supplement those forces as necessary to protect consumer safety. Increased penalties for harmful products can ensure that private parties internalize the costs of reduced consumer safety and, therefore, balance it against the savings available through lower production costs.

Our proposal could apply, in concept, just as well to importing countries other than the United States. It is designed in response to the particular reality of regulation in the presence of global trade. Domestic authorities have a wide range of tools available to regulate domestic producers, but only a subset of those are available to deal with global production. This fact distinguishes the regulation of domestic products from the regulation of imported products. To the extent that domestic production is regulated using tools that are unavailable for foreign production, an alternative regulatory strategy is needed for imported goods.

It is useful to divide the available regulatory options into two categories. The first focuses on "outcomes"—characteristics of the final product or service affecting its level of safety. These regulations typically set safety standards, and create an apparatus for inspecting finished products, coordinating recalls, forcing disclosure to affected consumers, and imposing administrative penalties through enforcement actions. Importantly, this form of regulation requires no information beyond what can be gleaned from the product itself. We refer to this approach as "outcome-based regulation" or the "outcome lever."

The second type of regulation constrains firm behavior during the process of production, seeking to increase safety by addressing the way in which goods and services are made. When outcome-based laws mandating the safety of U.S.-made goods prove insufficient—when, for example, noncompliance is difficult to detect through ex post inspection or before consumer harm has actually occurred, or when harm may become apparent only long after use of the product—the production process itself is regulated. Specifically, regulators can mandate that private firms adopt internal procedures and assessments intended to prevent risks before they occur, or they oversee production processes directly through inspection, monitoring, reporting, and licensing to ensure a high level of safety before goods ever leave the plant or reach the market. We refer to this approach as "production-based regulation" or the "production lever."

One could debate the relative merits of outcome-based and production-based regulation in the domestic context. Our task in this chapter, however, is different. We are interested in how best to regulate foreign production, given the existing choices regarding the regulation of domestic production.

The central dilemma facing regulators thinking about imported products is that production regulation is largely unavailable. This is so because of the legal and practical limits on the extraterritorial reach of government power. Lacking regulatory authority in foreign states, or the resources to ensure comprehensive monitoring, reporting, or inspection of production processes, American regulators cannot hope to regulate the process by which imports are produced comparably to the way they govern domestic production. Regulators cannot easily place themselves, in a literal or figurative sense, in a foreign producer's delivery bay to keep an eye on the inputs being purchased, on the factory floor to monitor production, or in the information-processing center to ensure that sensitive personal data is kept secure. Thus, in the very context that policy makers might ordinarily turn to production-based regulation, the production lever is largely unavailable.[1]

Importers, however, are better positioned to monitor the safety of their products. Although they are often not themselves the producers of those products, given appropriate incentives they are in a position to demand assurances about safety and to choose their business partners with safety in mind. Providing importers with appropriate incentives ensures that they will compete with one another to sell products that are not only inexpensive but also safe.

Two Modes of Domestic Consumer-Safety Regulation

Outcomes Regulation

The most pervasive form of government involvement in the regulation of domestic goods and services uses the outcome lever. This form of regulation wields a variety of instruments, including rules requiring or prohibiting particular outcomes, inspections of finished products, ex post agency enforcement actions, and the imposition of penalties. The Consumer Product Safety Commission (CPSC), for example, promulgates regulations governing outcomes—such as those limiting the use of lead paint and setting standards for toys intended for young children. It possesses the authority to bring civil and criminal enforcement actions against those who violate specific legal mandates (FDCH Regulatory Intelligence Database 2004, 2001) and it can impose penalties of up to $15 million on companies that fail to inform the agency when they discover unsafe toys on the market (Consumer Product Safety Improvement Act of 2008, sec. 217[a][1][B]).

After the finding of a violation or an increased risk of consumer harm, outcome regulation may also require ameliorative measures. For example, the CPSC has a program designed to encourage the reporting of unsafe goods and coordinate their recall. Alternatively (or perhaps in addition), responsible parties may be forced to publicize the risk they have created, as is the case of the 38 states with laws requiring notification of data breaches to affected consumers (Berinato 2008; Schwartz and Janger 2007). The outcome lever, moreover, operates at all levels of government; various forms of food-safety testing, for example, are carried out by both federal and state officials (Sparks 2007). And the governance of outcomes extends beyond administrative regulation: tort law, too, may impose liability for physical harms actually caused by unsafe products or behavior (Keeton et al. 1984: 677–724).

The success of these formal legal mandates frequently rests in part on the presence of a variety of social and economic factors promoting compliance. These include the normative commitments of firms, advocacy of consumer-protection groups, threat of more comprehensive government regulation, operation of standards bodies, and, perhaps most important, reputational constraints (Bardach and Kagan 1982; Gunningham et al. 2003). These forces serve to encourage compliance by domestic manufacturers with both legal mandates and voluntary standards promulgated by groups such as the American National Standards Institute and the American Society for Testing and Materials (ASTM 2008).

For a number of reasons, however, policy makers may conclude that in a given context the outcome lever is insufficient to achieve consumer-safety objectives. Performance outcomes may be difficult to identify in advance or to assess contemporaneously (Bamberger 2006: 388–91). This is the case, for example, if the harm from a defective product is observable only after a long period of time (as with certain health effects), or the harm is diffuse and difficult to associate with specific products (as with some environmental effects). Similarly, outcome-based measures may be difficult to implement if product failures are themselves hard to observe (as with information databases that are inadequately secured).[2]

Nonlegal incentives for compliance with consumer-protective outcomes, moreover, may vary by context. The same informational difficulties that undermine outcome regulation's direct efficacy can undermine social safety norms and reputational mechanisms. Furthermore, if it is difficult for consumers or consumer groups to assign blame for unsafe products—perhaps because it is difficult to observe each step in a long supply chain—the incentive effect of these informal mechanisms is weakened. If consumers have difficulty identifying the risks posed by products, and if consumer groups are difficult to organize, these problems will be exacerbated (Gunningham et al. 2004).

Production Regulation

For any of these reasons, policy makers may decide that production-based approaches—alone or in concert with outcome-based approaches —should be employed to reduce the incidence of harmful or defective products, or achieve a given level of consumer protection more efficiently (Coglianese 2002).[3]

The case of food and drugs provides an illustration. In this context, regulators govern and monitor the process of product manufacturing extensively. The U.S. Department of Agriculture (USDA) and the U.S. Food and Drug Administration (FDA) Hazard Analysis and Critical Control Point (HACCP) programs governing food safety compel firms to assess food-safety hazards and to identify points in the production process at which they can be eliminated, minimized, or reduced to an acceptable level (Coglianese and Lazer 2003: 696–98; FDA 1995; USDA 1996). They also establish procedures to measure and address risks at those points through corrective action. Furthermore, those same agencies have developed programs for testing and inspecting during the production process to ensure safe outcomes, such as the USDA on-site inspections of meat processing facilities (Federal Meat Inspection Act 2000; Poultry Products Inspection Act 2000) and the FDA quality-control inspections of drug manufacturing plants (FDA 2001: sec. 210.1).

Indeed, as the U.S. Department of Health and Human Services (HHS) 2004 Task Force on Drug Importation has described, "a fundamental principle of drug regulation is that quality cannot be tested into a product," but must instead be "built into the product through the manufacturing process" (HHS Task Force on Drug Importation 2004: 21). Chemical testing of finished products might "verify if the active ingredient is present"; yet it is insufficient to identify the product's safety and potency, or whether it was manufactured pursuant to best industry practices, was stored improperly, has expired, or is counterfeit (HHS Task Force 2004: 21).

Challenges for Product Safety Regulation in a Globalized World

Challenges for Regulating Outcomes

When producers are located abroad, enforcement mechanisms are hindered. Extraterritorial application of U.S. safety norms, such as through administrative proceedings or tort liability, is significantly constrained as against foreign defendants, and may run into jurisdictional problems. Even when a plaintiff can obtain an American court judgment, it may be difficult or even impossible to enforce (Clarke 2004).

Moreover, the volume of imports and the challenges inherent in ex post testing limit the efficacy of inspecting geared toward measuring compliance with outcome-based regulation. Approximately 9.1 million imported food shipments enter the United States annually (Kaufman 2007). But in 2006, the FDA visually inspected only 115,000 shipments, and sent 20,000 samples for laboratory analysis (Barrionuevo 2007). Toys—87 percent of which are produced overseas (Public Citizen 2007) —currently undergo no testing at all by regulators. No technology exists to test completed drugs effectively at the border, a reality underscored by the recent incident in which nineteen patients died from contamination of heparin, a blood thinner produced by drug manufacturer Baxter International (Harris and Bogdanich 2008). While routine testing indicated that the manufactured product contained a "heparin-like" ingredient, it did not detect the counterfeit element, which proved fatal before its recall. Indeed, even if the means existed, the task of testing pharmaceutical imports would be, in the words of the HHS, "logistically impossible" and "prohibitively expensive" (HHS Task Force on Drug Importation 2004: 21).

Moreover, extra-legal incentives for compliance by foreign parties may not exist or may not operate in the same way as in the domestic context. Local safety norms may be different in foreign states, and local consumer groups may not exist or may not be concerned with exports. The producing firm may also face slight or nonexistent reputational constraints because it is several links down in the supply chain—and possibly thousands of miles away from consumers. Certainly, a brand-name product may suffer negative reputational consequences when a hazardous product finds its way to the market, and even a supplier that is invisible to consumers may suffer if intermediaries or sellers recognize that the supplier's products are unsafe. Yet when supply chains stretch across countries and continents, these reputational effects are muted at best. For example, a supplier's reputation may not spread from buyers in one country to another, and purchasers may not be able to observe whether a new supplier is the same or different from an existing supplier with a poor reputation.

Challenges for Regulating Production

In the domestic context, when the outcome lever proves insufficient, regulators can elect to supplement it with the production lever. With respect to imported goods and services, however, the production lever will normally operate less effectively than it does in the domestic context, and will often be entirely unavailable. Simply stated, while U.S. regulation frequently purports to subject imported goods and services to the same set of legal regulations as those produced or performed entirely within the United States, significant functional barriers obstruct the exercise of the production lever against foreign production and service provision. As a practical matter these barriers often leave the outcome lever as the only relevant tool, reducing the effectiveness of the regulation of imports.

Imported drugs and food illustrate the way in which foreign production disables the production lever. In the drug context, manufacturers in India and China supply an ever-increasing share of the U.S. drug market, particularly generic and over-the-counter medications. India exported $800 million worth of 350 varieties of antidepressants, heart medications, antibiotics, and other drugs to the United States in 2006, up from just eight generic drugs a decade ago, and Chinese manufacturers sold $675 million in drug ingredients and products in 2006, a figure that more than doubled in five years (Kaufman 2007). Drug industry analysts trace 20 percent of finished generic and over-the-counter drugs to India and China, as well as more than 40 percent of the active ingredients in American-made medications (Kaufman 2007).

All drug-ingredient manufacturers, whether foreign or domestic, ostensibly face the same regulatory regime. They must register drug ingredients and other information with the FDA. The FDA both approves new drugs and regulates the manufacture and distribution of brand-name and generic medicines (FDA 2001: secs. 207.20 and 207.37) by providing minimum good manufacturing guidelines and conducting quality-control inspections (FDA 2001: sec. 210.1). However, because FDA regulators do not have the authority to enter foreign factories unannounced, as they do in the United States, they must schedule inspections in advance through an American-based agent of the foreign company (FDA 2001: sec. 207.40). And, due to resource constraints, foreign inspections are dramatically less frequent than those conducted in the United States. In 2006, for example, the agency performed 32 quality-assurance inspections in India and 15 in China—but over 1,000 in the United States (Kaufman 2007). Moreover, some of the inspections conducted abroad were related to the initial drug approval, rather than to manufacturing procedures, and others involved inexpensive HIV/AIDS drugs that would not be sold in the United States.

Similar practical constraints limit the exercise of the production lever to ensure the use of safety-enhancing processes in the foreign production of food. For example, foreign processors that ship fish or fishery products to the United States are formally required to operate in conformance with the FDA's seafood HACCP regulations (FDA 1995). But FDA inspection trips to foreign countries simply cannot ensure worldwide compliance. The chance of any one processor being subject to administrative inspection is extremely low (FDA 2008), and regulators change targets, and even countries, year by year. Accordingly, should an inspection take place it is virtually certain that it will be a

long time before any further inspections occur. With regard to manufactured goods, the CPSC lacks broad jurisdiction to test a product's
safety before it reaches the market (CPSC 2009).

Seeking Regulatory Solutions

The discussion in the prior section frames a challenge for public regulators. While the outcome lever remains an important part of the regulatory system, it is insufficient to achieve consumer safety objectives
and, in any event, is weaker in the context of imports than in the context of domestic production. The production lever, used domestically to
address the shortcomings of the outcome lever in the domestic context,
is severely disabled when it comes to foreign production. How, then,
should the importing countries go about protecting their consumers
from unsafe imports? Many recent legislative proposals approach the
problem by attempting to bolster the ability of domestic regulators to
extend the traditional outcome or production levers they use domestically to foreign activity as well. But these proposals are not likely to
succeed. Instead, policy makers should seek to foster the creation of
surrogate regulators who can exercise the traditional regulatory functions more effectively.

Legislative Proposals for Addressing the Global Challenge for Product Safety: State-Regulator-Centered Approaches

Several recent policy proposals have suggested enhancing both outcome-based inspections and the production-based component in U.S.
regulation of foreign activity (Agence France-Presse 2007). One option
is to increase postproduction inspections. This could certainly yield
benefits in some important contexts, but it provides at most an incomplete response. Approximately $2 trillion of products were imported
into the United States in 2006, from more than 150 countries (U.S.
Census Bureau 2008). More than 825,000 importers brought shipments
into the United States through more than 300 ports, border crossings, and postal facilities (Barrionuevo 2007). Furthermore, the value
of imports is increasing over time. A system of inspections could never
achieve the scale and scope necessary for the comprehensive regulation
of such an enormous volume of imports.

A second option would seek to extend the reach of American production-based regulation. For example, an Interagency Working Group
on Import Safety (IWGIS) convened by President George W. Bush,
called for an increased presence overseas to inspect goods before they
enter the United States, and to integrate inspections of processes into

the regulatory framework (IWGIS 2007a, b).[4] Former FDA Commissioner Andrew C. von Eschenbach proposed an initiative called "FDA Without Borders," through which FDA inspectors and technical advisers would be based in China, India, the Middle East, and three other regions (FDAnews 2008). He also requested that the State Department approve a permanent FDA presence at the U.S. Embassy in Beijing and two American consulates in China (Kaufman 2008). More generally, the FDA has explored requiring inspections of foreign plants before foreign-manufactured active drug ingredients are allowed in FDA-approved prescription medication (U.S. Congress 2008).

One problem with such proposals is the sheer size that a program of extraterritorial inspections and regulations would have to achieve to be effective. The resources required to achieve an important presence in all the places from which the United States imports products and services are simply not available. Even if the United States were to focus only on China, an effective regulatory team in that country would need a much larger staff than would be required for similar tasks here in the United States. This is so both because China is much larger than the United States and because its political, social, and economic context is different. There is, moreover, reason to believe that American inspectors and officials operating in China would be less effective than those operating domestically, simply because they would lack the language and cultural skills to navigate Chinese society and to understand local business practices. This phenomenon is evidenced in the case of the 2008 heparin deaths, in which FDA inspectors thought they had inspected the Chinese plant that manufactured the fatal contaminant, but later learned that they had been taken to a different pharmaceutical plant with a similar name (Kaufman 2008).

The high cost of this regulatory approach would be borne by American taxpayers, and would not be reflected in product prices. When decisions are made about where to produce or source goods and services, this cost will be ignored, creating a distortion in such decisions. That distortion would be economically inefficient and costly to the United States.

Furthermore, even if American authorities were to discover a violation of a production standard abroad, they often would have difficulty enforcing any relevant sanction. To begin with, if a supposed violation concerns products that have not yet entered the United States, there may not yet have been any violation of any American legal requirement, even if as a practical matter the products were destined for the United States.

All of these problems make it easier and cheaper for foreign producers to ignore American laws. Production-based regulation is poorly designed to reach production outside the United States. Attempts to extend it will remain too expensive to represent a practical solution, not to mention the political and diplomatic constraints on any effort to extend American regulatory requirements abroad. Turning to out-come-based alternatives is also likely to be a poor solution. Whatever reason motivated regulatory authorities to use production-based rather than outcome-based regulation for domestic production applies to for-eign production, and makes it unlikely that an outcome-based solution is available.

Reduced regulatory effectiveness lowers the cost borne by produc-ers when unsafe products find their way to store shelves and consumers. This, in turn, reduces firms' incentives to comply with U.S. standards. The lower the expected sanction for conduct inconsistent with Amer-ican requirements, the less reason they have to adjust their behavior. The obvious result is that, unless some substitute for American produc-tion-based regulation is available, imported products will be less safe than comparable goods made within the United States.

A Mechanism for Making Importers Regulate

The solution is to establish more appropriate incentives for private par-ties within the reach of the American regulatory system. Of course, not all imported products represent high safety risks. For some products, the relevant local (non-U.S.) authorities may have regulatory measures in place that ensure adequate levels of safety, especially if regulatory practices in the exporting state are comparable to American regulatory practices. Where this is the case, our proposal for enhanced penalties would not apply, and these products should continue to be regulated as they currently are. On the other hand, where existing regulatory struc-tures fail to ensure satisfactory consumer-protection levels for imported goods, existing regulatory strategies must be supplemented by or substi-tuted with the strategies we propose.

Our proposal operates within the confines of existing regulatory authority. Domestic regulators in importing countries like the United States would still retain three important regulatory tools. First, even when regulators cannot exercise power over foreign parties, the ac-tivity of concern almost always will involve some entity in the role of importer, outsourcer, distributor, or seller within the reach of the im-porting country's laws. These parties may not be those most culpa-ble for consumer harm, and may not be optimally situated to promote safety. Yet they are the ones on whom the importing country's system can credibly impose regulatory obligations and penalties, and are in-volved in the stream of commerce at some point prior to the final purchase by the consumer. They are also typically in a better position than the regulator to ensure appropriate safety levels. Second, an importing country's regulators would retain the ability to use the outcome lever to observe, regulate, and punish outcomes in the form of services or finished products that threaten or cause harm to citizens within their borders. Finally, they would retain control over rules governing liability for violations of outcome restrictions, and—perhaps most important—over associated penalties.

Our proposal builds on these three important regulatory powers. In its simplest terms, it suggests that regulators should use liability standards and penalties directed against American parties (or at least parties within reach of the U.S. legal system) to achieve appropriate levels of safety. U.S. partners in international trade should be subject to *additional* outcome-based regulatory penalties for safety and other consumer protection violations beyond those imposed on those who engage in purely domestic activity.[5] This system of discriminatory penalties should be structured to ensure that U.S. partners in international trade internalize the full cost of harmful products. This, in turn, will motivate them to monitor the production process and outputs of their trading partners to ensure that those partners pay proper attention to safety issues. These private parties become de facto regulators, pursuing the same objectives as domestic regulators, while influencing foreign activities in ways that domestic regulators cannot. These additional obligations would be "strict" regulatory obligations on importers and sellers in the sense that they would operate without regard to what the party in question knows, should have known, or even could have known about the process of production and service provision.

Recall that a key goal of regulation is to establish sufficient incentives at each stage of the chain of production to realize optimal levels of consumer safety. The optimal level of safety is the level of safety that would be chosen by a producer or consumer who internalizes the full costs and benefits of a product. When imports escape regulatory obligations that domestic producers must satisfy, or when they avoid extra-legal pressures to increase safety, foreign producers do not internalize the cost of harmful products as fully as their domestic counterparts. Foreign producers, then, have weaker incentives to produce safe products.

At root, our proposal is a fairly straightforward application of the existing literature on tort law and its behavioral effects, combined with the recognition that imported products often must be regulated entirely through the outcome lever. In the tort context, for example, the imposition of strict liability forces actors to internalize the full cost of defective or harmful products. Penalties, moreover, should be set at the level necessary to ensure that the costs of harmful behavior are internalized by relevant actors. Those actors then have an incentive to take action to reduce this risk up to the point where the cost of further reductions exceeds the benefit of reduced liability.

The same strategy of strict liability is proposed here, although in the context of outcome-based sanctions. Those participants in the stream of commerce that are within the reach of American authorities and that bring imported products to market should be subject to penalties for regulatory noncompliance regardless of the level of care they take, or their actual knowledge about product safety.[6] The associated penalties, moreover, should be set at levels that force actors within the reach of domestic authorities to internalize the full social costs of increased risks to consumer welfare. Specifically, penalties should make up for the discount provided by engaging in more harmful behavior while escaping the domestic costs of safety they would otherwise face under domestic regulation.

In this way, the system would encourage importers and sellers to become de facto regulators. The potential of liability for products that fail to meet outcome requirements represents a cost. Importers and sellers may not have direct control over this cost, and, indeed, they may not even have knowledge of the relevant risks or production methods. The threat of liability, however, will provide these parties with the incentive to achieve some level of control over the quality of the product, or to find a way to shift liability to parties that do have such control. Thus, even if importers and sellers themselves do not know the quality of individual imported products, the liability scheme will encourage them to take action to ensure that the quality is of a sufficiently high level to protect them from undue costs.

For importers or sellers to manage their exposure to liability, they must therefore estimate the risk of liability with respect to a particular product and adjust their behavior to reflect that potential cost. This can be achieved in any number of ways. A firm could, for example, acquire the producer, allowing it to manage quality issues directly. Or it could enter into a joint venture with the producer, ensuring that it could manage and monitor quality. Other options include inspecting imports before they reach the American market, seeking producers from jurisdictions that ensure high-quality products through regulation of their own, or even contractual specifications to increase the quality and safety of the product. It could also take actions that resemble production-based regulation as practiced by governments; it might require on-site inspections, specify the inputs to be used and where they are to come from, and demand that the producer adopt better internal practices and procedures to reduce the risk of a hazardous product being produced.

The importer or seller could demand that such contractual obligations be enforceable, either through local courts in the country of the producer—if those are thought to be reliable and unbiased—or through arbitration.

One way or another importers and sellers can generate enforcement through contractual mechanisms (including the choice of whom they contract with) that may be impossible for domestic regulatory authorities to achieve directly. The threat of legal sanctions, in turn, may lead to the creation of an industry of intermediaries able to certify the quality of products or suppliers, or an insurance industry willing to offer coverage against this form of legal obligation. As with the proposal by Tom Baker in chapter 11, the intermediary or insurance company would then take action to reduce the risk of unsafe products reaching the market.

Focusing on firms within the reach of American authorities also addresses the problem of fly-by-night foreign enterprises, which engage in production until a problem arises and then simply close up shop only to appear later under a different name. Domestically based private parties are much better situated than regulators to identify and avoid such operators.

If, after considering whichever of the above strategies (or others) provides the best way to manage the risk of liability, it remains impossible to get the expected cost of liability to a point at which the importer or seller can expect to earn a profit, the importer or seller will simply decline to participate in the process of bringing the product to market. The importer or seller will instead seek other producers of the product, perhaps from the United States or perhaps from countries where the liability issues can be managed more effectively. This private decision to exclude the product represents a regulatory success (assuming the level of liability is set correctly). Because the importer or seller has internalized the expected cost of harm from the product, its decision not to participate reflects that the potential safety issues are large enough that importing the product represents a net harm to the United States.

Appropriate administrative penalties, then, both align the interests of regulators and domestic partners in global trade, and enlist the party with superior oversight and decision-making capacity. This strategy satisfies the need to ensure safe products while allowing foreign producers to supply the American market with affordable goods and services. The regulator is concerned about damage caused by harmful products. The importer or seller comes to have this same concern if its expected penalty is equal to the cost of the relevant harm. And while domestic regulators are constrained in their ability to assess accurately which foreign actors should be allowed to engage in trade that affects domestic consumer well-being, importers and sellers have a different set of tools that accord a much greater ability to influence quality, identify sellers with appropriate safeguards in place, or avoid certain transactions altogether.

In sum, by enlisting private parties to fill the role of de facto regulators of their foreign business partners, this strategy seeks to permit domestic firms to compete on the cost of consumer protection, rather than on the level of safety.

Two Possible Concerns

International Trade Rules

Importers and sellers facing higher expected costs from our proposed system of discriminatory regulation will try to reduce costs by improving safety, but they may also pass these costs along to consumers by raising prices. Raising the domestic price of imports obviously serves to make domestic production more competitive relative to imports. This discrimination between domestic and foreign producers raises the question of whether our proposed system would be permitted under existing international trade treaties and, in particular, the rules of the World Trade Organization (WTO).

We begin with an analysis of Article III of the General Agreement on Tariffs and Trade (GATT). This rule, known as the national treatment obligation, prohibits states from imposing regulations on imports that are "less favorable than that accorded to like products of national origin" (GATT 1947: art. III.4). If a measure fails to meet this requirement, it is nevertheless permitted if it satisfies any one of several available exceptions. The exception of interest in the case of our discriminatory regulation proposal can be found in Article XX(d) of GATT, which provides an exception for measures "necessary to secure compliance with laws or regulations which are not inconsistent with the provisions" of GATT.[7]

The discriminatory liability regime we propose distinguishes products based on whether they are produced domestically or abroad, which immediately makes them suspect under Article III. Mere differences in treatment, however, are not enough to conclude that a measure is inconsistent with Article III (WTO 2000, 2001). Imports and domestic products may be treated differently as long as the outcome-liability scheme we propose does not cause imports to receive "less favorable" treatment than that applied to domestic products.

It is clear that if one looks at the outcome-based liability component of the regulatory system in isolation, ignoring the production-based obligations faced by domestic producers, then imposing higher penalties on foreign producers would be a violation of Article III.4. And while it makes more sense to examine the production and outcome-based liability schemes together, even if one does so, it is likely our proposal is inconsistent with the requirements of Article III.4.

The problem is that our proposed outcome-based liability scheme imposes larger penalties on imports even if safety levels are the same as for domestic products. Suppose, for example, that domestically produced products achieve a given level of safety primarily because they are subject to rigorous quality control and inspection protocols mandated by government regulation. Though some outcome-based obligations exist, including penalties, assume that it is the production lever that determines the ultimate level of safety. This is exactly the sort of situation in which we propose discriminatory regulation in the form of higher outcome-based penalties on imports than on domestic products.

Imagine that a foreign producer chooses to mimic the quality control and inspection system required of American producers. Suppose that this foreign producer puts these systems into place and achieves the same level of safety (at the same cost) as do American producers. Now imagine that an unsafe product makes it to the market despite these safety efforts. If the product is from the American producer, the penalty will be smaller than if it is from the foreign producer. The foreign producer, then, even if it behaves in exactly the same way as the American producer, faces a higher cost from unsafe products. This amounts to discrimination in contravention of Article III.4.

Our proposed discriminatory regulation is saved, however, by the already mentioned Article XX(d). Our proposal is intended to secure compliance with laws or regulations governing safety and quality, and the latter are quite clearly consistent with the provisions of the GATT. The question is whether such measures are "necessary." The question of whether the discriminatory penalties are "necessary" to secure compliance invokes a well-developed GATT jurisprudence. In general, the relevant WTO cases have concluded that the necessity of a measure under GATT XX(d) must be judged based on a balancing of relevant factors, including (1) the relative importance of the interest the regulation seeks to protect; (2) the extent to which the measure contributes to compliance with the regulation; and (3) the impact on international trade (WTO 2000). The central thrust of this article has been that regulators have almost no choice in the tools they use to address the safety of imports.[8] Furthermore, we advocate discriminatory regulation only when other, less-trade-distorting alternatives are unavailable or ineffective, including regulation by a foreign government and self-regulation. We also propose the use of discriminatory regulation only where existing regulatory structures aimed at domestic producers are unable to provide appropriate incentives to foreign producers.

A system of discriminatory regulation, then, should be used only when it is the only practical response available. Needless to say, if no other option exists, discriminatory regulation is also the least trade-restrictive approach. The protection of safety is acknowledged by the WTO as being of paramount importance, placing considerable weight on the scale in favor of the legality of our proposal (WTO 2001). Moreover, we have shown both that discriminatory regulation serves the goal of promoting compliance with relevant safety requirements, and that it is the only way to ensure that foreign producers internalize the full cost of harm from dangerous products. In this sense, the measure contributes directly to compliance with relevant safety regulations. The three-factor balancing test mentioned above, then, is satisfied by our proposed system of discriminatory regulation: the measure at issue addresses an interest of vital importance, contributes directly to compliance with relevant safety regulations, and is the least trade-restrictive alternative available to decision makers. The exception provided by Article XX(d) requires, in addition to the above, that the relevant measure not be a means of "arbitrary or unjustified discrimination between countries where the same conditions prevail" or be a "disguised restriction on international trade."

Suffice it to say that the use of discriminatory regulation as we have described it does not constitute an abuse of the GATT Article XX(d) exception of a sort likely to cause difficulty under the "chapeau" of Article XX, as these provisions are called. The regulation is neither arbitrary nor unjustified; as discussed previously, it is only used when no other alternatives are available.[9] Finally, to meet the requirements of the WTO, the outcome-based penalties imposed on foreign products must be calibrated to reflect the social harm from dangerous products. This is precisely what we have proposed. Larger penalties would trigger concerns that the measure is a "disguised restriction on international trade" or not "necessary" under the Article XX(d) exception.

Financially Weak Firms

Imposing liability on importers or sellers may fail to generate appropriate incentives if those parties are damage-proof or nearly so. The problem is more acute when one realizes that importers and sellers could organize themselves in such a way as to shield assets from potential liability. Rather than operating as a single large importer, for example, a firm could establish a large number of relatively small corporations, each of which imports a single specific product or a small group of products. These corporations would hold minimal assets so their exposure to liability would be quite limited.

This is a reasonable concern, but it is not unique to this proposal: the same problem exists for any regulation that relies on sanctions or penalties, including regulation of domestic production. It is perhaps somewhat more acute in the context of imports because production may require a certain scale and sufficient assets to reduce the risk that a firm is damage-proof but an importer has no such needs. Alternatively, the distribution of products within the United States often requires a large entity, as does the sale of products under familiar brand names. These concerns are legitimate ones, but they are problems that come up in this or other regulatory contexts under existing rules. Where they have come up, they have not proved fatal to the enactment and effective use of regulation. Furthermore, whatever challenges these concerns pose, and even if they prevent the application of a perfect regulatory regime, they do not change the fact that a system of discriminatory liability provides better incentives for foreign producers than is the case under the status quo.

Import Safety Warranties: A Complementary Proposal

Tom Baker, in chapter 11, has proposed a system under which importers of goods thought to pose a potential danger would face a statutory obligation to warrant that those products do not contain undisclosed harmful substances. Breach of that warranty would trigger liability. Importers would also be required to post a bond equal to the value of the goods to increase the likelihood that they will have the ability to pay any penalties incurred.

Baker's proposal is similar to our own, at least in terms of its general effect. His proposal and ours seek to hold importers and sellers accountable for unsafe imports—in both cases seeking a party in the supply chain that is within the reach of American authorities. Both proposals also serve to increase the exposure of imports to domestic liability. Our proposal would increase the sanctions imposed on imports that prove to be unsafe. Baker's proposal would do essentially the same thing, but relies on warranties made by importers rather than increased sanctions.

To be sure, there are differences between the proposals. Baker's reliance on a bond posted by importers, for example, imposes a cost on every importer. Our own proposal, because it relies on ex post liability rather than an ex ante bond, imposes costs only in the event of a violation. Baker's proposal also requires the construction of a new regulatory system and the associated private markets needed to provide the bonds that importers would require. However, the bonding system greatly reduces the problem of how to deal with importers that lack the resources to pay the sanctions they incur under our system.

Though we naturally have a preference for our own proposal over Baker's, the more important point is that both proposals adopt essentially the same strategy of forcing importers to bear the risk of harmful products. Adoption of this general approach would represent a significant and healthy change from the approaches that have so far dominated policy deliberations. For this reason, rather than debating the relative merits of our proposal as compared with Baker's, we prefer to think of them together as representing a more sensible and productive way to increase the safety of imported goods.

Competition Without Compromising Safety

We have shown that conventional regulatory strategies are insufficient to address the safety challenges of importing products from foreign jurisdictions. When goods and services are provided abroad, producers and suppliers can evade the importing country's regulatory obligations and extra-legal pressures that increase consumer safety. In particular, they can avoid measures that protect consumers by preventing unsafe products before production is completed. Accordingly, foreign producers will not internalize the cost of harmful products as fully as their domestic counterparts, and will, therefore, invest less in ensuring the safety of their products.

Moves to remedy this imbalance through increased oversight, inspection, and enforcement by domestic regulators can improve consumer protection, but will provide only a partial solution in the face of imports on a massive scale. Moreover, the increased cost of safety in foreign activity would be borne by domestic taxpayers, while individual firms would continue to reap the benefits of offshore outsourcing.

A liability scheme aimed at parties within the reach of domestic authorities can help address this problem. Where alternate mechanisms are unavailable for preventing the production of unsafe goods, the domestic firms that benefit from foreign activity should be forced to internalize the domestic costs of their activity through increased penalties for the violation of consumer protection norms. In this manner, these domestic firms' superior capacity for oversight, monitoring, risk shifting, and decision making about location, organizational form, and activity level can be brought to bear in the very context in which domestic regulators are impeded by lack of information, resources, and jurisdiction.

Implementation of our proposal would require some delicate judgments about which products from which countries should be subject to the higher liability scheme. Yet from the perspective of domestic consumers, our proposal has the great advantage of ensuring appropriate levels of safety while encouraging healthy competition among domestic and foreign producers and suppliers, competition that should be focused on improving quality and lowering price, but doing so without compromising safety.

Acknowledgments

A more extended discussion of our proposal appears in Bamberger and Guzman (2008).

Notes

1. To be sure, importing countries could articulate requirements intended to govern the extraterritorial production of goods, but mechanisms for enforcing such mandates (such as foreign government oversight or third-party certification) will in many contexts prove unreliable or underdeveloped regulatory substitutes (Bamberger and Guzman 2008: 1422–29).

2. Cary Coglianese (2002: 2) has discussed those contexts in which outcomes are "undesirable to rely upon as the sole basis for a regulatory standard."

3. It is possible to debate the desirability of using production-based regulation either in general or specific cases. For the purposes of this chapter, however, we simply take the use and effectiveness of this form of regulation as given. We do so because reviewing the full debate about the merits of production-based regulation would serve only to distract from the focus of this chapter.

4. The Working Group included the heads of the Departments of Agriculture, Commerce, HHS, Homeland Security, Justice, State, Transportation, and Treasury, as well as the Director of the Office of Management and Budget, U.S. Trade Representative, Administrator of the Environmental Protection Agency, and Chairman of CPSC. The FDA, Customs and Border Protection, and USDA Food Safety and Inspection Service were active participants in the Working Group as well.

5. Importantly, we do not here advocate changes to substantive safety requirements. Our focus instead is on the penalties assessed when stated requirements are not met.

6. More precisely, only those participants within the reach of American authority, and operating in a context where other substitutes for the production lever are insufficient, should be subject to such liability.

7. One could also advance arguments about exceptions provided by GATT's Article XX(b) and the Agreement on Sanitary and Phytosanitary Measures (WTO 1994), both of which address health and safety concerns. We omit these because the exception in GATT XX(d) is more appropriate for this situation and, in any event, to the extent the other exceptions might apply the reasoning would be quite similar to our discussion of GATT XX(d).

8. Indeed, one of the reasons the production lever works poorly for imports is that the trading rules generally do not allow importing states to demand specific production methods.

9. Importantly, to be compliant with the trading rules, the use of discriminatory regulation must be used only when other alternatives are not available. Thus, for example, if reliance on foreign regulatory systems will achieve a state's safety objectives, discriminatory regulation may well be forbidden by WTO rules. Similarly, if the safety of domestic production is determined by outcome-based regulation, and if that outcome-based regulation can be applied to foreign production, there is no justification for discriminatory regulation under either our proposal or the rules of international trade. Discrimination in penalties would not be "necessary" in that context.

References

Agence France-Presse (2007) "U.S. Senator Calls for Inspection of All Imported Chinese Toys." *Industry Week,* August 15.

ASTM International-Standards Worldwide (ASTM) (2008) "ASTM F963-08: Consumer Safety Specification for Toy Safety." http://enterprise.astm.org/REDLINE_PAGES/F963.htm.

Bamberger, Kenneth A. (2006) "Regulation as Delegation: Private Firms, Decisionmaking, and Accountability in the Administrative State." 56 *Duke Law Journal* 377–468.

Bamberger, Kenneth A. and Andrew T. Guzman (2008) "Keeping Imports Safe: A Proposal for Discriminatory Regulation of International Trade." 96 *California Law Review* 1405–46.

Bardach, Eugene and Robert A. Kagan (1982) *Going by the Book: The Problem of Regulatory Unreasonableness.* Philadelphia: Temple University Press.

Barrionuevo, Alexei (2007) "Food Imports Often Escape Scrutiny." *New York Times,* May 1, sec. C.

Berinato, Scott (2008) "Data Breach Notification Laws, State by State." *CSO,* February 1.

Clarke, Donald C. (2004) "The Enforcement of United States Court Judgments in China: A Research Note." George Washington Legal Studies Research Paper No. 236, Washington, D.C. http://ssrn.com/abstract=943922.

Coglianese, Cary (2002) "Reducing Risk with Management-Based Regulation." Columbia/Wharton-Penn Roundtable on Risk Management Strategies in an Uncertain World. http://www.ldeo.columbia.edu/chrr/documents/meetings/roundtable/pdf/notes/coglianese_cary_note.pdf.

Coglianese, Cary and David Lazer (2003) "Management-Based Regulation: Prescribing Private Management to Achieve Public Goals." 37 *Law & Society Review* 691–730.

FDAnews (2008) "More Inspectors a Top Priority for FDA." *MQN Weekly Bulletin,* March 14. FDCH Regulatory Intelligence Database (2004) "California Company To Pay $200,000 Civil Penalty for Importing and Selling Illegal Children's Toys." FDCH Regulatory Intelligence Database, January 12.

———. (2001) "California Man Charged in Illegal Toy Importation Case." FDCH Regulatory Intelligence Database, May 17.

Gunningham, Neil, Robert Kagan, and Dorothy Thornton (2004) "Social License and Environmental Protection: Why Businesses Go Beyond Compliance." 29 *Law & Social Inquiry* 307–42.

———. (2003) *Shades of Green: Business, Regulation, and Environment.* Stanford, Calif.: Stanford University Press.

Harris, Gardiner and Walt Bogdanich (2008) "Drug Tied to China Had Contaminant, F.D.A. Says." *New York Times,* March 6. http://www.nytimes.com/2008/03/06/health/06heparin.html.

HHS Task Force on Drug Importation (2004) *Report on Prescription Drug Importation.* http://archive.hhs.gov/importtaskforce/Report1220.pdf.

Interagency Working Group on Import Safety (IWGIS) (2007a) "Action Plan for Import Safety: A Roadmap for Continual Improvement." http://www.importsafety.gov/report/actionplan.pdf.

———. (2007b) "Protecting American Consumers Every Step of the Way: A Strategic Framework for Continual Improvement in Import Safety: A Report to the President." http://www.importsafety.gov/report/report.pdf.

Kaufman, Marc (2008) "FDA Says It Approved the Wrong Drug Plant." *Washington Post,* February 19, sec. A.

———. (2007) "FDA Scrutiny Scant in India, China as Drugs Pour into U.S. . . ." *Washington Post,* June 17, sec. A.

Keeton, W. Page, Dan B. Dobbs, Robert E. Keeton, and David G. Owen, eds. (1984) *Prosser and Keeton on the Law of Torts,* 5th ed. Eagan, Minn.: West.

Public Citizen (2007) "Santa's Sweatshop: 'Made in D.C.' with Bad Trade Policy." Public Citizen's Global Trade Watch. http://www.citizen.org/documents/Santas%20Sweatshop.pdf.

Schwartz, Paul M. and Edward J. Janger (2007) "Notification of Data Security Breaches." 105 *Michigan Law Review* 913–84.

Sparks, Ron (2007) "Food Safety Editorial." Alabama Department of Agriculture and Industry. http://www.agi.state.al.us/press_releases/2007may06?op=makePrintable;pn=2.

U.S. Bureau of the Census (2008) *Foreign Trade Statistics.* http://www.census.gov/foreign-trade/balance/c0015.html#2008.

U.S. Congress. House Committee on Energy and Commerce (2008) *Science and Mission at Risk: FDA's Self Assessment: Hearing of the Oversight and Investigations Subcommittee.* 110th Cong. http://energycommerce.house.gov/index.php?option=com_content&view=article&id=633&catid=31&Itemid=58.

U.S. Consumer Products Safety Commission (CPSC) (2009) "Frequently Asked Questions." http://www.cpsc.gov/about/faq.html.

U.S. Department of Agriculture (USDA) (1996) "Pathogen Reduction: Hazard Analysis and Critical Control Point (HACCP) Systems." 61 *Federal Register* 38,806.

U.S. Food and Drug Administration (FDA) (2008) "FDA's Evaluation of the Seafood HACCP Program for Fiscal Years 2004/2005." http://www.fda.gov/Food/FoodSafety/Product-SpecificInformation/Seafood/SeafoodHACCP/ucm111059.htm.

———. (2001) "Food and Drugs." 21 *Code of Federal Regulations* §§ 207.20, 207.37, 207.40, 210.1.

———. (1995) "Procedures for the Safe and Sanitary Processing and Importing of Fish and Fishery Products." 60 *Federal Register* 65,096.

World Trade Organization (WTO) (2001) European Communities-Measures Affecting Asbestos and Asbestos-Containing Products. WT/DS135/AB/R (Appellate Body Report).

———. (2000) Korea-Measures Affecting Imports of Fresh, Chilled and Frozen Beef. WT/DS161/AB/R, WT/DS169/AB/R (Appellate Body Report).

————. (1994) Agreement on the Application of Sanitary and Phytosanitary Measures (SPS) (April 15). Marrakesh Agreement Establishing the World Trade Organization, Annex 1A, pmbl., Legal Instruments, Results of the Uruguay Round. 1867 U.N.T.S. 493.

Cases, Regulations, Statutes, and Treaties Cited

Consumer Product Safety Improvement Act of 2008 (2008) PL 110–314.
Federal Meat Inspection Act (2000) U.S. Code, title 21, sec. 604.
General Agreement on Tariffs and Trade (GATT) (1947) 30 Oct., 61 Stat. A-11, 55 U.N.T.S. 194.
Poultry Products Inspection Act (2000) U.S. Code, title 21, sec. 455.

Chapter 11
Bonded Import Safety Warranties

Tom Baker

Consumers increasingly confront serious safety risks from imported products. Contaminated heparin, adulterated pet food and candy, lead-painted toys, and lead-filled children's jewelry are only some of the more vivid examples. U.S. and European regulators are working on ways to stimulate improvements in manufacturing and testing processes in source countries, but regulators in one country can only do so much to affect the health and safety practices of businesses located in another. With the expansion in international trade, the lengthening of the product supply chain, and the vast numbers of importers and exporters, government regulators in importing countries simply cannot solve the problem on their own.

This chapter proposes a framework for import safety warranties that would supplement the regulatory efforts described in other chapters. The warranties would be bonded, meaning that importers would enter into contracts with insurance companies that would guarantee payments due under the warranties. The warranties would create a private enforcement mechanism to stimulate demand for compliance with existing health and safety standards throughout the global product supply chain. Significantly, this enforcement mechanism would not dictate how product suppliers would meet these standards, nor would it require governmental actors to coordinate action beyond their borders. Thus, bonded warranties may pose less threat to trade relations than other potential responses to import safety problems. Moreover, they have the potential to harness far more resources to address import safety than any country could realistically allocate to a more centralized regulatory response, especially in light of the current financial crisis.

Like other risk-shifting approaches to regulation, import safety warranties would provide a decentralized supplement to more traditional command and control approaches (Baker and Moss 2009, forthcoming).

Although the warranties would have extraterritorial regulatory impact —indeed, that is the goal—the entities delivering that impact will be private parties: warranty holders enforcing warranty rights, and insurance companies deciding which importers and products to bond and at what price. Significantly, the warranty standards derive from existing health and safety regulations, which apply equally to domestic and imported goods. The program simply creates a new enforcement mechanism for imported goods, which are produced beyond the reach of domestic health and safety inspectors and thus may justifiably be subject to different health and safety enforcement procedures than domestic goods.

In that sense, the bonded import safety warranty program bears much in common with the import safety penalties proposed by Kenneth Bamberger and Andrew Guzman in chapter 10. Indeed, the statutory damages I propose for breach of the warranty can be understood as an example of the type of administrative penalties that they propose. The idea I present here would create what they call "outcome-based" consequences for products that are produced beyond the reach of domestic "process-based" regulation. Whereas they present a more fully elaborated justification for outcome-based consequences for imported goods, I present a more fully elaborated enforcement mechanism for those consequences, as well as a more concrete approach to setting the dollar amount of those consequences.

This chapter, however, elaborates a concept; it does not develop a fully worked out legislative proposal. My aim is to stimulate creative thinking about risk-shifting supplements to traditional approaches to import safety regulation. As a result, I seek to sufficiently describe the concept of bonded import safety warranties so that they can be debated by experts with the necessary institutional knowledge about health and safety standards, suretyship, payment procedures, and civil enforcement. Whether the concept introduced here is eventually adopted or not, a serious consideration of it can nevertheless help us better understand the incentives and constraints surrounding the import safety problem.

The General Framework

The warranty program would work as follows. Importers and sellers of imported food, medicine, toys, and other designated products would have a statutory obligation to warrant that the products meet established health and safety standards adopted in the jurisdiction and do not contain undisclosed substances in a quantity that poses a threat to human health or safety. Breach of this warranty would lead to statutory liability, which would be based on three factors: the retail price of the products, the seriousness of the risk, and the role and success of the responsible parties in discovering the breach and recalling affected products. Much as with claims under the U.S. Fair Credit Reporting Act (2008), the statutory liability for breach of the import safety warranty would not need to depend on the showing of actual harm resulting from the breach and, thus, would be amenable to aggregate resolution (meaning that the damages could be determined on a class action basis rather than through an individualized claim resolution process).

As a condition to importing products covered by the warranty, importers would be required to post a bond equal to the retail value of the goods. Consumers purchasing products covered by the warranties would have the option to assign their warranty rights to a warranty enforcement organization, with such assignment being the default option. This would mean that consumers would assign their warranty rights to the default organization, unless they elected to assign the rights to another organization, or to opt out of the assignment process. Organizations would compete to be designated as default warranty enforcers through an auction or other process administered by a designated national agency. To further facilitate private enforcement of the warranty, there would be subsidies available for individuals and small businesses that wish to test whether an imported product meets health and safety standards, with the subsidies funded in part by a tax on payments made pursuant to the warranties.

The Basic Warranty

The import safety warranty itself would have two parts, neither of which would impose a new substantive obligation on importers or sellers of imported goods. Indeed, the first part of the warranty would be entirely derivative of existing government health and safety standards. Under this part, importers and retailers would warrant that imported products meet existing health and safety standards in the jurisdiction adopting this program. Because importers already are obligated to meet these standards, it is easy to see that this aspect of the warranty simply represents a new enforcement mechanism.

Under the second part of the warranty, importers and retailers would warrant that imported products do not contain any undisclosed substances in a quantity that poses a threat to human health or safety. Significantly, this part of the warranty would not be more demanding than the warranty of merchantability that already applies to products in the United States under the Uniform Commercial Code (UCC). Under the UCC, a merchant in goods warrants that the goods "are fit for the ordinary purposes for which such goods are used" and are of at least ordinary quality (ALI 2008: sec. 2-314). So, for example, a retailer that sold a product that failed to perform as promised will have breached the UCC but will not have breached the import safety warranty unless the product contained an undisclosed substance in a quantity that poses a threat to human health or safety (or failed to meet a health or safety regulatory standard).

Statutory Damages

The amount of the statutory damages would be a function of three factors: the retail price of the products sold by the importer in breach of the warranty, the seriousness of the health and safety risk posed by the breach, and the role and success of the responsible parties in recalling products sold in breach of the warranty (and refunding to consumers the purchase price plus associated costs). The first factor links the damages to the revenue from the product. The second factor addresses the deterrence objective of linking the damages to the risk of harm. The third factor provides an incentive for sellers to quickly remove unsafe products from the market. The application of these factors would not require any claimant-by-claimant adjudication, with the result that both liability and damages may be determined on a class action basis, with the allocation of the award to individual warranty rights holders according to ordinary class action procedure.

The statute establishing the warranty program would also establish minimum and maximum damages in relation to the three factors and would direct a designated agency to promulgate a regulation creating an easily applied formula to be used to calculate the damages in any particular case. For example, the statutory minimum damages imposed in a minimal risk case in which the importer itself first detected, and then promptly reported, the breach of warranty might be 200 percent of the retail price of all products sold in breach of the warranty and not returned by consumers for refund or otherwise documented as destroyed. The statutory maximum damages imposed in a high risk case, or a case in which the importer stalled or tried to cover up the breach of warranty, might be three times that minimum amount, with an additional multiple in any cases involving a combination of high risk and noncooperation.

In addition to the statutory damages, the responsible parties would be liable for the attorneys' fees and other costs associated with a successful breach of warranty action. As noted, the amount of the damages would not depend on the harm actually caused or the level of fault on the part of the responsible parties, and there would be no punitive damages. Harm- and fault-based damages already are available under state law, and would remain available, as discussed in the subsection on preemption below.

The Bonding Requirement

A surety bond is a contract that guarantees the financial responsibility of a "principal" with regard to specified obligations that the principal has to another person, often called the "beneficiary" (Andrews and Millett 2008; Gallagher 2000). The "surety" (the entity issuing the bond) agrees to pay the beneficiary when the principal defaults on a contract. In the case of an import safety warranty, the bond would guarantee the payment of statutory damages to entities holding the warranty rights.

One kind of surety bond is already widely used in international trade: performance bonds (Andrews and Millett 2008). Performance bonds typically guaranty the performance of contracts for the sale of goods. They often are written by banks on a "demand" basis, meaning that the bank serving as the surety must pay the beneficiary whenever the beneficiary demands to be paid, whether the principal is in fact in default on a contract with the beneficiary or not (Andrews and Millett 2008: 575). Import safety warranty bonds would differ from these performance bonds in at least one key respect. The obligation of the surety to the beneficiary would be contingent upon the principal's breach of the import safety warranty. It would not be enough for the warranty rights holder simply to assert that the warranty was breached; rather, the breach would have to be proven.

Sureties ordinarily have a right of indemnity against principals, meaning that a surety may recover from a principal the money that it pays to a beneficiary, unless the surety contract provides to the contrary (Andrews and Millett 2008: 398; Shaninian 2000). It is worth considering whether the indemnity rights of the surety against the principal in the import safety context might be subject to a "best practices" defense. Such a defense would allow the importer to avoid the obligation to indemnify the surety by proving that it had adopted and complied with import safety best practices. This approach would provide greater incentive to the importer to adopt such practices; doing so would not only reduce the likelihood of breaching the warranty, it would also insulate the import from financial responsibility in the event that the warranty is breached.

In addition to enhancing the financial responsibility of the bonded entities, bonding requirements may also reduce the likelihood that the bonded event takes place. Companies that issue bonds conduct examinations of the applicants for bonds and strive to issue the bonds to applicants who are unlikely to incur the liability protected by the bond. As a result, a statement that a bonding company is willing to issue a

bond on a contractor's job, for example, signals that the bonding company's expert underwriters have determined that the contractor has the
financial capacity and experience to get the job done (Duke and Anderson 2000). Moreover, prices for the bonds generally reflect the issuer's
assessment of the risk that the principal will incur the liability protected by the bond (along with the insurer's assessment of the principal's ability to repay the liability) and, thus, the prices encourage bond
purchasers to reduce that risk (Duke and Anderson 2000). These risk
reduction pathways reflect the fact that companies issuing the bonds
have an incentive to reduce the chance that they will have to pay out on
the bonds (Baker and Griffith 2007).

Requiring importers to obtain a bond would make consumer health
and safety risks a visible and explicitly priced part of the product supply chain. In addition, the companies issuing the bonds would demand
that importers maintain detailed records of the sources of all of the ingredients and components of the goods being imported, facilitating the
accountability process that would ensue when bonding companies enforce their subrogation rights in the event of a claim under the bond.[1]

Clearly, there would be start-up costs for the companies issuing the
bonds. Nevertheless, for some types of products, such as food, a network of private inspection services already exists. In those industries,
bonding companies would be building on an existing institutional base,
not starting from scratch. Moreover, existing large and high-quality exporters already possess substantial quality and exporting expertise that
could be combined with the financial expertise of bonding companies
through joint ventures or other forms of investment.

Default Assignment to Warranty Enforcers

Under the default warranty rights assignment part of the program, consumers would automatically assign their warranty rights to a designated
warranty rights enforcement organization whenever they purchased
products covered by the warranty, unless they had chosen to opt out of
the default assignment. Default warranty rights enforcement organizations would be selected through a governmentally administered process
that designated a warranty enforcer for each type of imported product. This means that a consumer who did not elect otherwise would
automatically transfer her warranty rights to the enforcement organization designated for the product in question. Consumers could choose
to transfer their rights to another organization or they could opt out of
the assignment process.

The assignment of legal rights is very common in contemporary society. People regularly give insurance companies, banks, and other com-

panies the right to do certain things—such as paying doctors, reviewing medical records, verifying transactions, and selling their mortgages or other loans. The warranty rights assignment simply applies this common practice to a new realm.

There are at least three reasons the transfer of warranty rights would ordinarily be in a consumer's interest. First, the enforcement organization would be in a better position to enforce the rights and, thus, the assignment would increase the health and safety incentives provided by the warranty. In economic terms, helping consumers to assign their rights to enforcement organizations would address the collective action problem that results from the fact that an individual purchaser—especially one who is not actually harmed by an unsafe product—is unlikely to be able or willing to enforce the warranty. An organization that owns a large fraction of the warranty rights has more to gain from enforcing the rights and, thus, more incentive to test the products, to advertise for information relating to unsafe products, and to bring enforcement actions when products fail to meet the standard.

Second, because the statutory damages formula provides a strong incentive for sellers to recall defective products and to provide full refunds to consumers, consumers would not, as a practical matter, be giving up a significant claim on future compensation when they assign their rights. Consumers who are seriously injured by a product retain the right to bring a state law product liability claim, so they are not adversely affected by the assignment. And a consumer who is not injured at all will still be able to get a refund. To obtain more than a full refund, a consumer who opted out of the assignment process would have to (a) decide not to take the seller's refund offer, (b) keep track of the warranty enforcement proceeding, and (c) remember to submit a claim to the court or claims service organization that is managing the disbursement of the statutory damages to the owners of the warranty rights. Most people would likely prefer the easier, quicker refund route. Moreover, a warranty rights enforcement organization that is doing a good job will engage in public information campaigns that encourage people to transfer their warranty rights.

Third, consumers who transfer their warranty rights may derive a psychological benefit from knowing that they are contributing to overall consumer protection, similar to the benefit that many people draw from voluntary conservation and recycling. Indeed, it is easy to imagine warranty rights enforcement organizations emphasizing this benefit when they compete for selection as consumers' chosen warranty rights enforcer.

This final benefit points toward a substantial difference between a default assignment and a mandatory assignment or a government enforcement mechanism. While it is undoubtedly the case that a direct auction of the enforcement rights, without consumer involvement, or a government enforcement process would reduce some transaction costs, there are significant advantages to involving consumers. Allowing consumers the opportunity to opt out of the warranty assignment sets the stage for public debate over the import safety warranty program. Importers would be free to join together to conduct public information campaigns urging consumers to, in effect, vote against the import safety warranty program by opting out. This would encourage warranty enforcement organizations to conduct their own public information campaigns promoting the program. In addition, warranty enforcement organizations would engage in public information campaigns to compete for consumer assignments.

Among existing organizations, logical candidates to compete for the warranty enforcement responsibility include: consumer groups (U.S. examples include the Consumers Union and the American Association of Retired People); law firms with consumer class action or products liability practices; public interest advocacy groups (U.S. examples include Public Citizen and the Center for Science in the Public Interest); and perhaps even government agencies (U.S. examples include the Consumer Product Safety Commission, the Food and Drug Administration, the U.S. Department of Agriculture, and state attorneys general or consumer protection agencies). In order to promote the kind of diversity and competitive pressure that leads to cost and quality improvements in other areas of the economy, the government agency or ministry with overall responsibility for overseeing the warranty program could select a variety of warranty rights enforcement organizations to receive the default assignments. The designation as a default enforcement organization could be for a limited period so that organizations would need to compete for renewal. One option would be to make government agencies the default warranty enforcement organizations for all products at the inception of the program, allowing private organizations to earn the right to become eligible for default assignments for specific categories of products only after they have demonstrated their capacity by obtaining and enforcing consumer-elected assignments.

Banks and credit card companies would be logical choices to administer the opt-out process through which consumers could choose a warranty enforcer other than the default organization. The credit card, check, or debit card transaction would provide the means for connecting the sales to the appropriate warranty enforcement organization, and the relationship between the payment organization and the consumer would provide the means for the consumer to choose something other than the default assignment option. Supermarkets and other large retailers also could administer consumer choices through their customer loyalty programs, though there may be some concerns about conflicts of interest because the retailers themselves would be liable for breach of warranty.

There would be important details to work out with all these procedures: for qualifying organizations to serve as warranty enforcers, for designating the default enforcement organization(s), and for consumer choice. Working out these details would require care and creativity, but so does managing a global supply chain.

Testing Subsidies

The testing subsidy element of the proposed warranty program also addresses the import safety collective action problem. Absent a subsidy, an individual purchaser who wished to have goods tested would have to incur the full costs of the test but would not be able to obtain the full benefit of the test. Indeed, most of the benefits of the test would go to other consumers. A test indicating that the product is safe would increase the security of all purchasers of the product, and a test indicating that the product is unsafe would trigger warranty payments and corrective action that would also benefit other purchasers of the product.

Providing discounts for tests ordered by consumers and small wholesale purchasers would help address this collective action problem, and it would also create a decentralized testing environment that would be more difficult for an unscrupulous importer to corrupt. The government would negotiate prices for tests with qualified testing companies and would issue coupons that eligible purchasers could use to obtain discounted prices on the tests. The coupons could be packaged with the imported products, put on a rack in a supermarket in the case of unpackaged food items, and also made available on the Internet. Experience and experimentation over time would allow the sponsoring agency and the testing organizations to arrive at the right mix of price and subsidy to encourage an appropriate amount of testing for different kinds of products. Initially the testing subsidies would need to be funded from general revenues. Over time, the subsidies could be funded by a tax on payments made to warranty enforcement organizations.

Preemption

Contract, tort, and consumer protection law in the United States presently provides consumers some recourse for damage from unsafe imported goods. Because of high transaction costs, however, consumers cannot in fact exercise their contract and tort law rights unless they are very seriously injured or the defendant's conduct was so outrageous that there may be a possibility of punitive damages. Very few people will hire a lawyer to recover a $100 claim. But someone with a $100,000 claim may well be able to find a lawyer willing to take the case on a contingent fee basis.

As this suggests, the question of preemption—whether the federal warranty right will replace existing contract and tort law rights—will arise as a practical matter in individual cases only when a consumer is seriously injured or there is a possibility of a substantial punitive damages award. In such cases, strong considerations counsel against preemption. In the case of a serious injury, the damage to the consumer will greatly exceed the amount that would be paid under the new warranty program, and the consumer will most likely have assigned the warranty rights in any event. As a result, if a federal warranty right were to preempt other options, the compensation and deterrence objectives of state tort, contract, and consumer protection law would not be satisfied by the warranty rights enforcement procedure, nor would the corrective justice objectives of state tort law. In a punitive damages case, the warranty rights enforcement procedure would not have satisfied the punishment objective of punitive damages.

By contrast, there are stronger arguments in favor of the preemption of class actions based on state contract or consumer protection law in cases in which a recovery is available under the import safety warranty. The objectives of, and remedies available under, the warranty enforcement program more nearly match those of a consumer class action. Moreover, if the behavior of the company was sufficiently egregious to justify punitive damages under state law, parties can proceed through individual actions, perhaps with the assistance of informal aggregation methods that lawyers have developed in personal injury litigation.

Bonded Import Safety Warranties in Action: A Toy Recall Scenario

To illustrate some of the ways that bonded import safety warranties would improve existing liability law, consider how a recent imported toy recall might have proceeded differently had the warranty program been in effect. In June 2007, the company that sold Thomas the Tank Engine trains announced that it was recalling 1.5 million Thomas and Friends wooden railway toys sold between January 2005 and June 2007 because the products contained lead paint (CPSC 2007). According to news reports, the company, now called Learning Curve, discovered the problem in 2007 through internal testing procedures (Barboza and Story 2007). The company at first offered to give consumers a replacement toy and a free train only if customers mailed back the toy at their own expense. The company later agreed to refund the postage and, in settlement of a consumer class action, to provide consumers with a cash refund.

How might the bonded import safety warranty have affected this situation had it been in place? First, there are a variety of ways that the warranty program might have caught the problem sooner. These include: the prequalification and quality assurance procedures required by the bonding company; more frequent or thorough testing procedures implemented by Learning Curve as a result of the deterrent incentive of the program; the use of discount coupons for lead testing provided by the testing subsidy part of the program; testing by the default warranty rights enforcement organization assigned to Learning Curve toys; and testing by another warranty rights enforcement organization selected by consumers as an alternative to the default. Given the serious adverse harms from lead poisoning, and the fact that young children put toys into their mouths, substantial and obvious public health benefits would have been derived from any effort to detect more quickly the lead paint in the Thomas the Tank Engine trains.

Second, regardless of whether the program would have identified the lead paint sooner, the recall would have proceeded more quickly and more completely if the warranty rights program had been in effect, which would have significantly reduced the opportunity for children to put the toys in their mouths. The statutory damages formula treats the total retail value of the goods not returned, or documented as destroyed before consumption, as the base damages number to which the applicable multiplication factor is applied. Because of this formula, Learning Curve would have had a strong incentive to immediately and aggressively publicize the recall, offer to provide consumers a cash refund, and develop procedures to maximize the number of refund requests. In addition to reducing Learning Curve's statutory damages, the publicity would have reduced the likelihood of lead poisoning. The Thomas and Friends recall eventually did receive widespread publicity, but this appears to have been in spite of the company's efforts. According to contemporary news accounts, Learning Curve initially provided very little information, perhaps because earlier recalls by the same company received little publicity (Barboza and Story 2007).

Third, the warranty rights enforcement organizations would have begun enforcement proceedings immediately, placing additional pressure on Learning Curve to mount an effective recall. At first, there may have been competing enforcement actions filed by different organizations, but these actions would have been consolidated in a single court (through procedures that would be specified in the authorizing legislation or implementing regulations). Discovery in the enforcement proceeding would identify all the information needed to apply the statutory damages formula: the number of toys affected, their retail price, efforts undertaken by Learning Curve to affirmatively discover and publicize the problem, whether there had been any effort to cover up the problem or delay the announcement, and the extent of the health hazard posed by the paint in the toys.

Finally, all of this information would have been publicly disclosed as part of the resolution of the enforcement proceeding, in marked contrast to what actually occurred in the Thomas and Friends case. Despite the momentary period of intense media attention, today no official report exists documenting what occurred in the Thomas and Friends litigation. The website that was set up to facilitate the recall has been shut down (and web archiving organizations apparently were not permitted to archive the site). And the press has since lost interest in the story.

Responses to Potential Objections

There are a number of potential objections to the warranty rights program I have proposed. Explicitly considering these objections helps to better understand the concept itself, as well as the incentives and market structure that produce the import safety problem. The objections can be classified into four groups: trade barriers, ineffectiveness, cost and administrability, reluctant bonding companies, and the potential for industry capture of the warranty rights enforcement organization assignment and enforcement processes.

Trade Barriers

International trade rules limit the ability of nations to discriminate in trade between domestic and imported products or among products imported from different countries. Countries are permitted to enforce regulations to protect health and safety, but under the General Agreement on Tariffs and Trade (GATT), they must do so in a manner that is not discriminatory.

As discussed earlier, the bonded import safety warranty does not create new substantive standards, but only provides new incentives for complying with existing law. Indeed, the warranty standards are less demanding than the existing law on the implied warranty of merchantability. Thus, as a matter of substantive law, the bonded import safety program would not discriminate between imported or domestic goods, or among goods from different countries. The program does create a new enforcement mechanism, however, and that enforcement mechanism is targeted at imported goods.

Whether, and to what degree, international trade law prevents a country from adopting different enforcement mechanisms for imported goods presents an interesting and important question that is beyond the scope of this chapter. However, as with Bamberger and Guzman in chapter 10, I believe there are strong public policy reasons supporting an alternative health and safety standard enforcement mechanism for imported goods, primarily because the foreign sources are beyond the jurisdiction of domestic health and safety regulators. Thus, even if the bonded warranty program were found to be a violation of obligations under the GATT's most-favored-nation or national treatment provisions, it may be justifiable under Article XX(b) as necessary to protect human health (GATT 1947).

If it turns out that the enforcement mechanism proposed here violates international trade law, one simple solution would be to subject domestic goods to the same mechanism. By the time that any trade dispute arising from the adoption of the bonded import safety warranty program was resolved, there would be substantial experience with the program and some evidence regarding its effectiveness. That experience could well justify the extension of the program to domestic goods. Concerns about international trade law should thus not be an insurmountable obstacle to adoption of the program.

Effectiveness

The main concern here is that it will be too difficult to prove that a product does not meet the warranty standard. Proof problems seem especially likely to affect food and, to a lesser extent, medicine, because consuming food and medicine may destroy essential evidence of contamination. As a practical matter, consumers will not be able to link imported food with an illness unless they have saved some of the food (or can get more from the same source), suspect that the food might have caused the illness, and have sent the food out for testing. Even with a subsidized testing program and vigorous warranty rights enforcement organizations, most foods and medicines are unlikely to be tested unless and until there is some reason to suspect a problem, most likely after someone gets sick, presenting the same kind of proof of causation problems that have affected the use of product liability law to promote food safety (Buzby et al. 2001).

One possible solution is to extend the subsidized testing program to include free stool sampling to anyone suffering intestinal distress and to establish a centralized test analysis and information management system, perhaps under the auspices of the U.S. Centers for Disease Control and Prevention (CDC). Illnesses caused by imported food will not be limited to just one or two consumers, and, thus, a widely used testing program would allow the CDC to identify problems and track them down, perhaps with the assistance of warranty rights enforcement organizations. The same food safety and proof of causation problems affect domestic food, as the recent problems with peanut butter, pistachios, and spinach in the United States have demonstrated. Thus, it is certainly worth considering whether the same warranty and subsidized testing program ought to apply to domestic food producers as well.

Cost and Administrability

Adopting a bonded import safety warranty seems likely to increase somewhat the *price* of imported goods, at least in the short term. It is by no means clear, however, that this increase in price would reflect an increase in social *costs*. At present, the social costs of unsafe and unhealthy imported goods fall largely on the affected consumers, not importers. Shifting these costs from consumers to importers does not increase the total social costs, even though the shift may increase some prices. Indeed, shifting these costs to importers could lead to safer imported products, thereby reducing social costs in the long run (as long as the transaction costs are not too large).

It is important to keep in mind that the import safety warranty simply requires imported products to meet established domestic health and safety standards. Thus, there is no concern that the import safety warranty will force consumers to buy "too much" safety (a concern that is sometimes voiced with regard to strict products liability). If the standards are too strict, the answer is to change the standards, not to allow importers to evade them. By the same token, if the standards are too weak or unclear, creating this new enforcement mechanism will not fix those problems.

Concerns about administrability of the program are information management concerns. Implementing the program will require setting up information management systems that connect consumers and transactions to warranty rights enforcement organizations and that enable importers and bonding companies to track sources of supply and compliance with bonding procedures. Setting up these systems clearly will take effort, but it will not require new technology. Credit card companies already engage in similar consumer and transaction tracking, and high-quality food manufacturers already maintain similar source-tracking systems. The main concern for the warranty rights enforcement system is to connect consumer-tracking systems with source-tracking systems, a connection that supermarkets and other high-volume retailers like Walmart already are beginning to make.

Reluctant Bonding Companies

Some readers may wonder whether insurance companies would be willing to issue the import safety warranty bonds at a price that importers would be willing to pay. There is no definitive answer to this question, other than to observe that the import safety bonds are similar to other financial services that are currently available and that the financial services industry is among the most innovative industries.

As already noted, the import safety bonds are similar in significant ways to the performance bonds that already are widely used in international trade. They are also similar in significant ways to the construction bonds used all over the United States and in some other countries. Both of these existing financial services have provided financial institutions with substantial experience in assessing the financial capacity of companies seeking to purchase bonds.

Admittedly, the health and safety warranty aspects of the bonds differ from the financial and political risks presented by the international trade performance bonds, as well as the construction risks presented by construction bonds. Nevertheless, the global insurance industry already has substantial experience with these same kinds of health and safety risks, and also with the assessment of the global food and product supply chain (Swiss Re 2008). Large importers to the United States already face substantial product liability risks and they are able to obtain liability insurance covering those risks.[2] In addition, insurance companies already offer product recall coverage, which reimburses manufacturers for the costs of recalling a defective product (Zinkewicz 2008).

The import safety warranty risks would be similar to the risks insured by these existing forms of liability insurance. In addition, the limited amount of damages available for breach of the warranty, the ability of importers to reduce those damages through prompt recalls, and the ability of bonding companies to obtain indemnity from importers are all likely to make import safety bonds much easier to price than products liability insurance coverage. Accordingly, there are good reasons to conclude that insurance companies would be willing to sell import safety warranty bonds.

Industry Capture of the Warranty Rights Assignment and Enforcement Processes

Some may worry that interests hostile to consumer protection could gain control over the warranty rights assignment and enforcement processes, turning warranty enforcement organizations into paper tigers that sell out consumer protection. One answer to this concern is to prohibit warranty enforcement organizations from receiving revenue from any source other than enforcement actions (or limiting the percentage of revenue that they could receive from other sources, such as contributions), thereby increasing the incentive to bring enforcement actions. In addition, the warranty enforcement qualification process could reduce the risk that industry-supported groups would compete for warranty rights assignments and pursue strategies of nonenforcement. For example, the license to operate as a warranty rights enforcement organization could be issued for a limited time only, and the renewal process could involve a determination by the responsible government agency that the organization was actively engaged in enforcement activities.

Conclusion

It is clear that a bonded import safety warranty program would facilitate the enforcement of established health and safety standards to imported goods. Importers would be required to post a bond that would cover their warranty obligations. Consumers would have the option of assigning their warranty rights to qualified warranty rights enforcement organizations, with such assignment being the default option. Warranty rights enforcement organizations would compete in a government-administered selection process to receive default assignments, and they would compete through public information campaigns to become consumers' enforcement organization of choice. The damages assessed for breach of the warranty would give importers an incentive to engage in prompt recalls that provide full refunds to consumers. In addition, the government would administer a decentralized subsidized testing program that would facilitate the detection of warranty breaches.

Of course, important details need to be addressed. Nevertheless, the components of the concept are sufficiently similar to existing practice that effectiveness, cost, and administrability concerns should not pose insurmountable challenges. What is needed is for the basic concept to be subjected to the strong debates and challenges of the political process.

Acknowledgments

I extend my thanks to the editors of this volume and to the participants in the May 2009 import safety workshop for very helpful comments and suggestions, and to Edwin Greenlee for timely research assistance.

Notes

1. Subrogation is the term used for the right of an insurance company to recover from a responsible third party the amount that it paid to or on behalf of a beneficiary. For example, health insurance companies that pay for medical expenses attributable to automobile accidents regularly receive reimbursements from the liability insurance company of the responsible driver. In the import safety warranty context, a bonding company could bring a subrogation action against the company that supplied the defective goods to the importer for whom the bonding company issued the bond.

2. Product liability insurance for pharmaceutical products is less widely available, but these availability concerns relate to problems in pricing the liability, which would not be presented in the case of import safety warranties.

References

American Law Institute (ALI) (2008) *Uniform Commercial Code.* Philadelphia: ALI.

Andrews, Geraldine and Richard Millett (2008) *Law of Guarantees,* 5th ed. London: Sweet & Maxwell.

Baker, Tom and Sean Griffith (2007) "Predicting Corporate Governance Risk: Evidence from the Directors' and Officers' Liability Insurance Market." 74 *University of Chicago Law Review* 487–544.

Baker, Tom and David Moss (2009) "Government as Risk Manager." In *Principles of Regulation,* edited by John Cisternino and David Moss. Cambridge, Mass.: The Tobin Project.

Barboza, David and Louise Story (2007) "RC2's Train Wreck." *New York Times,* June 19, sec. C.

Buzby, Jean C., Apul d. Frenzen, and Barbara Rasco (2001) *Product Liability and Microbial Foodborne Illness.* Agricultural Economic Report 799. Washington, D.C.: USDA.

Duke, Stewart R. and Mary Jeanne Anderson (2000) "How Contract Surety Bonds Are Underwritten." In *The Law of Suretyship,* edited by Edward G. Gallagher. Chicago: American Bar Association.

Gallagher, Edward G., ed. (2000) *The Law of Suretyship.* Chicago: American Bar Association.

Shaninian, Armen (2000) "The General Agreement of Indemnity." In *The Law of Suretyship,* edited by Edward G. Gallagher. Chicago: American Bar Association.

Swiss Re (2008) "Food for the Mind." Swiss Re Center for Global Dialogue. http://www.swissre.com/resources/daaaf1804bfff8828ffa8f8467939c1e-Foodforthemind_final.pdf.

U.S. Consumer Product Safety Commission (CPSC) (2007) *RC2 Corp. Recalls Various Thomas and Friends Wooden Railway Toys Due to Lead Poisoning Hazard.* Washington, D.C.: CPSC, Office of Information and Public Affairs.

Zinkewicz, Phil (2008) "Insuring Recalls of Unsafe Products." *Rough Notes* 96–98 (January).

Statutes and Treaties Cited

General Agreement on Tariffs and Trade (GATT), October 30, 1947, 61 Stat. A-11, 55 U.N.T.S. 194.

U.S. Fair Credit Reporting Act, 15 U.S.C., sec. 1681n (2008).

Chapter 12
Private Import Safety Regulation and Transnational New Governance

Errol Meidinger

The world is awash in complex systems of private regulation, many of which are highly innovative and dynamic. This chapter discusses the current and potential role of private regulatory systems in ensuring import safety. Using recent developments in food safety regulation as a primary example, it argues that private regulatory institutions can provide valuable control and learning capacities for an effective import safety regulatory system. However, significant institutional developments are needed to adequately take into account the full range of interests that must be accommodated in global production systems. Safety regulation is currently spread out among a large number of public and private organizations, often with overlapping or competing roles, which can be thought of as constituting "regulatory ecosystems." Regulatory actors will have to develop new strategies for maximizing the effects of these polycentric authority structures. Moreover, most private safety regulation currently faces northward. It protects developed country ("northern," hereafter) interests, and has only haltingly and partially incorporated the voices and interests of developing country ("southern," hereafter) producers and publics. To achieve effective and sustainable transnational governance, private import safety regulation will have to pioneer significant new ways of incorporating the interests of southern countries and coordinating them with the interests of northern ones.

Private Safety Regulation

"Regulation" is simply formalized social control that aims to establish a desired level of order in a given field of human activity. It typically defines the duties of different kinds of actors through rules or standards and uses credentialed experts to enforce them (Black 2008: 139; Meidinger 2007: 121). "Private" regulation refers to regulatory programs that are not created or managed primarily by governments. Nongovernmental actors engage in every facet of safety regulation, from standard-setting and adoption through inspection, monitoring, and enforcement. As we will see, most private regulatory programs are nonetheless deeply intertwined with governmental and intergovernmental regulatory structures. Moreover, many have developed increasingly "public" dimensions in that they seek to incorporate the concerns of all interested parties, operate with a high degree of transparency, and implement standards that claim to be in the public interest. Thus, the term "private" must be understood critically.

Safety is a long-standing focus of regulation, and safety regulation has long involved major elements of private regulation. In the United States, for example, private safety regulation became important in the 1890s as one of the first companies to make a business out of product safety testing and standard-setting, Underwriters Laboratories (UL), started to conduct thousands of laboratory tests of products such as arc lamps, circuit breakers, fuses, heaters, lamp adjusters, and rheostats (UL 2009). Testing necessarily implied standards, and within a decade UL had gotten into the business of writing and publishing standards. UL was not alone in the product-testing and standard-setting business. Many such organizations, some for-profit and others not-for-profit, emerged during the same period, multiplying, merging, and redefining themselves in a dizzying spiral of development (Cheit 1990; Krislov 1997; Schepel 2005).

The drivers of private safety regulation have been partly public and partly private. One main public influence has been tort liability. Simply put, manufacturers have a powerful and abiding interest in showing that their designs and production processes entail due care; widely accepted production standards and testing programs have been highly valuable in that effort. Another important public driver has been government procurement, particularly defense procurement, which led to the creation and implementation of many safety standards beginning at about the time of World War II. A final important public driver that endures today is the desire to forestall government regulation by demonstrating adequate self-regulation.

On the private side, the most important force has been the insurance industry, which has had a powerful and sustained interest in controlling the risks that it was insuring against. UL's rise was largely propelled by the insurance industry, which funded UL's early development and often required insured parties to use UL certified products. Other important private incentives included businesses' reliance on available product standards to reduce transaction costs and the competitive value of having a reputation for safe products.

Today the universe of safety standard-setting and implementation bodies includes thousands of businesses, trade associations, and scientific and technical associations, as well as government agencies (Krislov 1997). Many are involved in a global federation of standard-setting bodies, the International Organization for Standardization (ISO). It is impossible to know exactly how many product safety standards exist, yet we do know they number in the many thousands. Any complex product capable of causing injury is likely to involve dozens of safety standards, some for the product as a whole and some for individual components.

Moreover, for many products there are multiple, often competing regulatory programs. Some may be private, others public. This regulatory complexity is sharply amplified by international trade. Both producing and importing countries are likely to have their own safety programs, sometimes also competing, and products that flow from one to the other may be subject to all of them. No government regulatory body has jurisdiction over the entire supply chain. For many technically complex or risky modern products, standards and assessment procedures are constantly changing as new technologies and unanticipated problems steadily emerge.

In sum, international product safety regulation consists of a profusion of standards made and implemented by a multitude of private and public bodies, none of which necessarily has the final say. The products and problems involved are highly complex and changeable, requiring a great deal of adaptation and innovation.

The most dynamic field of international product safety regulation at present is food. Although it may seem technologically simple, food production is often highly complex and involves many biological and chemical components that can change and interact quickly. Food is also a sensitive issue, since it is both essential and ingested. The enormous growth of transnational food supply chains in recent years has combined with multiple food scares (Knowles et al. 2007) to make food a major focus of innovative and sometimes controversial import safety regulation.

The major recent developments in food regulation have occurred in nongovernmental organizations (NGOs). At the same time, the roles of private and public regulators across national boundaries are highly interconnected and fluid. This chapter thus examines food safety regulation as a major field of transnational "new governance," and uses research on new governance generally to analyze the promise and peril of this major example of private safety regulation.

Transnational New Governance

New governance scholarship focuses on several broad ongoing changes in policy making and regulation. These include decentralization of authority, networked governance structures, public-private partnerships, transparency, stakeholder participation, increased reliance on "soft law," stress on policy experimentation and learning, and implementation through a wide array of mechanisms that include general standards and rules, contracts, independent monitoring, benchmarking, and institutionalization (Lobel 2004).

Decentralized (or perhaps better, polycentric) authority structures and efforts to institute experimentation and learning are the key features of new governance for purposes of analyzing import safety regulation. Decentralization involves the increasingly broad distribution of governance functions among a wide array of social actors, including government bodies, business firms, trade associations, professional organizations, and activist NGOs. Decentralization also involves various types of cooperation and competition among all of these types of actors. The ideas of networked governance and private-public partnerships follow more or less directly. The concept of network is important because many emerging governance systems manifest complex mechanisms of coordination (or sometimes, a worrying lack of coordination). Decentralization is driven by many factors, including shrinking state capacity, the increasing complexity of governance problems, and the expanding regulatory capacity of nonstate institutions, as well as broad changes in contemporary thinking about regulatory institutions (Lobel 2004).

Experimentation and learning are critical to new governance because of the high degree of complexity, uncertainty, and rapid change that characterizes most regulatory arenas and the consequent need to constantly assess progress, adjust policies, and learn from other arenas of governance. The use of soft law methods, such as recommendations, principles, voluntary standards, benchmarking practices, and the like, follows from the difficulty of imposing mandatory requirements and the value of retaining experimentation and learning. The same is true for expanded stakeholder participation and transparency (Dorf and Sabel 1998).

New governance offers several important practical lessons for import safety regulation. First, different regulatory organizations are likely to have different comparative advantages, and should be utilized according to those advantages. Some may be better positioned to set standards, while others may be better at monitoring, inspection, or enforcement functions. Second, each organization observes and learns from other organizations, since there is experience and knowledge to be gained. Third, information sharing is consequently critical to new governance arrangements. Fourth, in thinking about how to maximize its effectiveness with the available resources, each regulatory agency must necessarily consider how best to coordinate with others.

Transnational new governance is distinctive mainly because the difficulties of achieving intelligent and legitimate regulation are much greater across national borders than within them, and because the variability of regulatory problems and practices is compounded. Thus, the difficulty of orchestrating transnational governance institutions is enormous (Abbott and Snidal 2009). At the same time, as elaborated below, the growth of transnational trade and communication increases the need for transnational governance, with the consequence that a great number of innovative governance institutions are constantly being established, tested, and revamped (Abbott and Snidal 2009; Meidinger 2008a).

Recent Growth in Private Safety Regulation

Private safety regulation is booming for many reasons, among them the limitations of government regulators and the distinctive capacities and interests of private regulators. Private regulators also appear to have been particularly nimble in developing transnational regulatory programs, both in safety regulation and in other areas such as environment and labor (Abbott and Snidal 2009; Meidinger 2008a, b). Private regulators can have a variety of motives, but one of them is almost always to facilitate transactions, since it is that capacity that induces the participation of firms. Like much public regulation, expansions in private regulation are often driven by public scares, such as food safety, or other perceived risks, such as destruction of the world's rainforests. In recent years, private regulatory programs have also become central to corporate branding.

Regulatory programs can be broken down into several basic functions, including standard-setting and rule-making, adoption, implementation, inspection and monitoring, and sanctioning (Henson and Humphrey 2008). Over the years certain institutional patterns have become common in private regulation for each of these functions, and they bear many similarities to government regulation.

Private standard-setting processes have gradually moved from relying primarily on technical expertise to combining such expertise with expanded participation, transparency, and multistakeholder decision making. Ideally, standard-setting bodies include representatives of all relevant interests and seek to operate by consensus (ISO/IEC 1994; WTO/TBT 2000).

In private regulation the adoption of standards is usually distinct from their development. Adoption can be done either by an authoritative legislature or agency, or by a firm or group of firms.

Implementation is carried out primarily by firms, and hence is sometimes overlooked in conceptions focusing primarily on external regulators. This is a serious oversight because firms' capacity to implement regulatory standards is essential to regulatory success and because those capacities are rapidly expanding in some cases, due to advances in supply chain management, discussed below.

External inspection and monitoring have also become a standard part of private regulation. The general assumption is that inspections will be conducted by third-party experts accredited in a separate process and organizationally independent of the firm. In most cases producers receive formal certification of compliance with the standard, and often their products can be so labeled. Inspectors are generally chosen and paid by the firms seeking certification, so they face complex pressures to please the client while also retaining their reputation for integrity (Havinga 2006: 526). The only formal sanction in most private regulatory systems is the loss of the certifying organization's approval, or the threat of that loss. This is important to the degree that it entails a loss of business or revenue, which will occur because important buyers value the certification. NGO activists can also leverage sanctions by pointing to lack of certification as an indicator of poor corporate citizenship.

While substantive product quality or performance standards were long the *sine qua non* of private regulatory programs, they are increasingly being displaced or absorbed by management or system standards. Whereas performance standards focus on assessing measurable qualities of the product, system standards seek to assess the quality of the production and distribution system. They recognize the complexity and variability of risks by institutionalizing processes of searching for and reducing them.

Supply Chain Regulation

As noted earlier, supply chain control has become a major factor in the effectiveness of private regulation. The rapid development of supply chain management over the past two decades, and its integration into operations management, has meant that powerful actors along the supply chain—often but not always retailers—can assert enormous control over the quality of products received by consumers (Bozarth and Handfield 2006; Vandenbergh 2007). New production, transportation, communications, and information technologies have allowed vast consolidation of control over production, processing, transportation, and retailing. This can be achieved regardless of whether the firms carrying out these functions are part of the same organization.

Global supply chains bring both the possibility of greatly increased value and new sources of risks in the form of different producers, production practices, physical conditions, and institutional structures (Roth et al. 2008). The brunt of these risks most often falls on retail firms, which may be legally liable for product defects and which risk reputational damage well beyond legal liability. Thus, actors at different stages of the supply chain become increasingly dependent on each other as it becomes increasingly possible to trace problems to their sources and as the economic viability of the producers depends on the success of the retailers.

In some cases this interdependence extends across different supply chains in the same sectors. A case of peanut butter food poisoning, for example, may affect all manufacturers and distributors of peanut butter, not just the culpable producers. These interdependent actors thus become "hostages of each other" in highly sensitive industries (Rees 1996). This condition, in which an entire industry is dependent on effective regulation, can give rise to rapid development of private regulation under certain conditions, or calls for public regulation if effective industry-wide private regulation is too difficult to achieve, as has recently been the case in the food industry.

Private Food Safety Regulation

The main engine of private food safety regulation over the past two decades has been the European retail sector, and British retailers in particular. The food scares that began in the late 1980s severely undermined public trust in the reliability of the European food supply, which in turn threatened the profitability of the large retailers. The UK seems to have been the driving force of regulatory innovation for two primary reasons. First, the UK retail sector is large and highly concentrated. Four supermarkets control 70 percent of the market, and ten control 85 percent. Moreover, the UK food retail sector has a high propensity for private labels, making retailers highly vulnerable to safety failures (Gow 2008). Second, the British Food Safety Act of 1990 imposed a form of strict liability on providers of food injurious to health (as defined under European Union, or EU, law) (FSA 1990), but also allowed a defense for those who "took all reasonable precautions and exercised all due diligence to avoid the commission of the offense by himself or by a person under his control" (FEPA 1985: sec. 22).

Consequently, to minimize both legal liability and brand risk, British retailers embarked on intensive efforts to establish quality control systems that could identify their products' sources and conditions of production. Given that much of the British food supply is imported, these systems were inherently transnational. It soon became apparent that there was great duplication of effort, since many producers sold to multiple retailers and each retailer was visiting and monitoring virtually every producer. Treading carefully around the edges of antitrust laws, some retailers began discussing a harmonized approach and converged on the idea of creating a common standard for good agricultural practices (GAP) for fruits and vegetables. They then established a membership group, the Euro-Retailer Produce Work Group (EUREP), to move the project forward, soon named EUREPGAP (Bell and Shelman 2009).

EUREP successfully recruited other large retailers from a half-dozen European countries, greatly aided by the 1996 discovery of mad cow disease in Britain, and continued work on the fruit and vegetable standard. For the first several years EUREP consisted solely of retailers; producers groups declined to be involved. After the retailers accumulated enough strength to persuade many producers that standards for agriculture were going to change with or without their active participation, a significant number joined and EUREP was restructured to become an equal partnership between retailers and producers.

EUREPGAP followed best practices for standard setting by convening a Technical Standards Committee with wider stakeholder representation, including retailers, consumer groups, agro-science, agro-industry, environmental groups, other related NGOs, government agencies, and producer organizations (Campbell 2005). The GAP standard for produce was completed in 2001, and incorporated a variety of best management practices techniques such as integrated pest management and hazard analysis and critical control point (HACCP) management systems. HACCP systems involve proactively searching for and analyzing safety hazards, identifying critical control points where the hazards can be managed or eliminated, establishing preventive measures with critical limits for each control point, monitoring the control points, taking corrective actions where critical limits are exceeded, keeping good records, and regularly verifying that the system is working properly. The EUREPGAP standard centered on the HAACP strategy, and created a number of predefined critical control points. These were divided into "major musts" for which 100 percent compliance was required, "minor musts," for which 95 percent compliance was required, and recommended control points, leaving significant but constrained discretion to producers (Campbell 2005).

Soon thereafter, at the request of retailers, EUREP produced standards for coffee, tea, ornamental plants, livestock, and aquaculture. EUREP also began using ISO accredited third-party certifiers to conduct inspections, issue certificates, and conduct annual audits. Members committed to pushing their suppliers to become certified and by 2004 the number of certified producers had reached the tens of thousands (Bell and Shelman 2009).

Reflecting global trading patterns, EUREPGAP steadily went global and changed its name in 2007 to GLOBALGAP. Its standards now include not only requirements directly related to food quality, but also environmental protection and worker health and safety, thus encompassing both consumption and production externalities. GLOBALGAP has also sought to address the disadvantages faced by small producers (a producer certification can cost anywhere from several hundred to several thousand dollars) by creating a group certification program, whereby small producers can combine under a unified management regime and certification can be achieved by sampling some of the producers (Bell and Shelman 2009).

While GLOBALGAP has been the leading edge of private food safety regulation, the field is full of other players and contenders for leadership. Small and large producers, retailers, and governments are all part of the mix. The UK Assured Food Standard, for example, was developed by a coalition of producer organizations and grants rights to use the "Red Tractor" symbol. Red Tractor standards are distinguishable from, but also evidently partially derivative of, the GLOBALGAP ones (Assured Food Standards 2009).

There are also other major global players. As the EUREPGAP effort began to take off in 2000, the Food Business Forum, the world's most powerful association of major food retailers, established the Global Food Safety Initiative (GFSI) to "promote convergence among food safety standards through maintaining a benchmarking process for food safety management schemes" (Food Business Forum 2008). Unlike GLOBALGAP, GFSI concentrates solely on food safety and excludes quality, environmental, and social concerns. GFSI is governed by an appointed board of nine retailers, three manufacturers, and one food service. The board currently includes officers of Coca-Cola, Hormel, Walmart, and the China Resources Vanguard Company, among others (Food Business Forum 2008).

ISO also recently entered the fray with its 22000 standard, intended to provide an "internationally recognized standard for a food safety management system that can be applied to any organization in the food chain" (ISO 2009). Relying primarily on the ISO's management system approach and using an HACCP framework, the 22000 standard leaves great policy discretion in the company developing the system. Serious companies are therefore likely to have strong systems, less serious ones less strong systems.

In sum, the world of private food safety regulation is currently made up of a multitude of large and small regulatory systems. Some focus solely and narrowly on safety issues; others include safety in a larger set of food quality, environmental, and social concerns. All rely to a great extent on the HACCP strategy of proactively searching for potential problem areas and trying to control the risks in advance. For the most part they are competing to achieve market acceptance, but governments will also play an important role in determining the fates of these regulatory programs.

Government/Private Relations

Private safety regulation has long been deeply intertwined with government safety regulation, both through the legal liability system and through more complex relationships between government and private regulatory agencies. In recent years private safety regulatory programs seem to have grown in importance in both Europe and the United States. Moreover, the relationship between public and private regulation may be shifting. Rather than government agencies either "delegating" or "dominating," they are more often coexisting in complex fields of highly dynamic private regulatory initiatives.

Today, governments regularly find themselves competing with private safety regulatory programs for authority. In food safety, for example, the rise of private regulatory programs was partly driven by a loss of public faith in government due to its failure to avert major food problems such as those that arose with the mad cow debacle (Ansell 2006: 332). While governments have regained some of that authority, they cannot take it for granted—nor should they. Governments do not have the capacity to protect public safety all on their own, and they should not expend resources to carry out functions that private regulatory actors can perform within the cost structures of their products. The question is: What regulatory roles do and should governments play?

There are two helpful ways of envisioning modern fields of safety regulation: the ecosystem model and the orchestra model. In the ecosystem model, different regulatory programs occupy "niches" they have found in production systems and compete with each other for the nutrients of resources and public acceptance. For example, Iizuka and Borbon-Galvez (2008) describe the variety of regulatory functions—from standard-setting to sanctioning—carried out by various public and private actors in the Chilean salmon fishing and Mexican fresh agricultural produce industries. These actors range from industry associations, private purchasers, and independent standard-setting bodies to regional and national government regulators and foreign governments, and they often perform similar or overlapping functions. Most of the varied regulators in an ecosystem seek to expand their ranges to increase their likelihood of survival. They also develop many kinds of exchanges that are stable to the degree that the environment is stable and none of the competitors obtains a major infusion of resources or a new technology. This seems to describe much transnational safety regulation today, where government and private actors carry out many similar activities and overlap, cooperate, compete, feed off, and sometimes mimic each other.

The orchestration model acknowledges similar complexity, but envisions a "conductor" to get the various regulatory actors to perform reasonably efficiently and in concert (Abbott and Snidal 2009). But which actor can serve as the conductor? The advantages of the coercive capacity of government are considerable, but not always decisive. The transnational nature of the regulatory field means that there will always be at least two governments involved, together with multiple agencies.

Still, the governments of wealthy, northern countries have considerable capacity to regulate the entire supply chain, subject mainly to important constraints imposed by the World Trade Organization (WTO). While these constraints are detailed more fully in chapter 4, it is important here to understand that the Sanitary and Phytosanitary Measures Agreement (SPS) puts special burdens on governments to justify mandatory food safety standards stricter than those of the Codex Alimentarius Commission (Codex) (SPS 1994: arts. 3.1, 5, Annex A, para. 3[a]) and that the Technical Barriers to Trade (TBT) Agreement requires governments adopting nonfood safety standards to give special consideration to existing international standards (TBT 1994: art. 2.4). Thus, governments will have to be particularly sophisticated to effectively orchestrate the standards they are encouraged to follow.

To date, few government agencies seem to be acting as conductors—or if they are, they are doing so only in a relatively weak sense. Both the United States and the European Union (EU) are increasing their promotion of private regulatory programs. The United States has required use of HACCP systems in meat and poultry plants since 1996 (USDA 1996), and has repeatedly called for greater use of voluntary third-party food safety programs in recent years (USDA/ERS 2007). Congress is also in the process of mandating much greater use of private regulatory systems in food import safety bills. But it will be a considerable challenge for legislation to give a government agency the kind of flexible, adaptive mandate necessary to orchestrate complex, competitive, and highly dynamic regulatory domains of the kind described above. Moreover, to meet the challenges of fairness and legitimacy, such an agency would have to develop an uncommonly high level of consideration for the legitimate expectations and needs of other countries, particularly southern ones.

Private Safety Regulation and International Trade

It is increasingly common for northern retailers to require southern producers to meet private certification standards in order to access northern markets (Maertens and Swinnen 2007, 2009). The attendant costs are often seen as trade barriers by southern countries.

However, the evidence on trade barriers is complex. Although it seems clear that it would be cheaper for any given producer to meet only home country standards and not pay for certification, often the only way for southern producers to sell into northern markets is to meet standards accepted by northern consumers. There is some research that private certification facilitates that access, effectively serving as a market maker rather than a market breaker (Henson and Jaffee 2008; Maertens and Swinnen 2007, 2009). By clarifying requirements and offering standardized conformity assessment mechanisms, private regulatory programs can reduce transactions costs and serve as bridges between northern consumers and southern suppliers. They may also improve northern consumer confidence, thereby increasing demand. There is also some evidence that private regulatory programs may improve efficiency in southern enterprises, thus increasing their market competitiveness (Henson and Jaffee 2008; Maertens and Swinnen 2007, 2009). Evidence is limited, however, and further research is needed.

Regardless of the effects of individual private regulatory programs, there is a significant debate regarding how many there should be. One view holds that standards should be widely harmonized: "certified once, accepted everywhere," as a recent SPS document puts it (WTO/SPS 2008: 5). A more stringent version of that view is that private food regulatory standards are suspect whenever they are stricter than Codex standards. An alternative view is that the SPS Agreement was never meant to reach so deeply into private market relations. Rather, there must be allowance for different private standards because consumers in different parts of the world inevitably have different values (Epps 2009) and because the food safety regime should be given equal stature to the international trade regime (Wouters et al. 2008).

What effect the WTO will have on the degree of consistency among private regulatory programs is quite unclear at present. While SPS Article 13 directs governments to "take such reasonable measures as may be available to them to ensure that nongovernmental entities within their territories . . . comply with the relevant provisions" of the SPS Agreement, the meaning of compliance is still to be worked out (Epps 2009). Currently the SPS Committee is undertaking a general study to compare private standards with international and official requirements (WTO/SPS 2008). Regarding nonfood safety standards, the TBT Agreement is even less directive, although the TBT Committee interprets it as encouraging good governance practices in the setting of standards (WTO/TBT 2000).

Assessing Private Import Safety Regulation

Successful regulatory regimes must meet minimum standards of effectiveness, fairness, accountability, and legitimacy, among others. The following discussion offers some preliminary assessments of private safety regulation programs and indicates key questions yet to be answered.

Effectiveness

Although it is impossible to draw conclusions about the effectiveness of private safety regulatory programs in general, it is clear that they can be remarkably effective. As suggested earlier, a major reason is the growing ability of powerful firms to manage information and control the operations of extended and complex supply chains. When these capacities are harnessed to appropriate incentives, private regulatory programs can be enormously effective. There is reason to believe that the British Food Safety Act of 1990 established good incentives for effectiveness. The combination of strict liability with a demanding due diligence defense prompted British retailers to implement highly effective private regulatory systems to deal with highly variable production conditions. Moreover, the practices thus established seem to have had network effects, as other European food certification systems operating under less rigorous liability systems developed similarly stringent requirements. Over time, moreover, it is likely that practices adopted to control risks will become institutionalized in taken-for-granted routines of regulated organizations.

Private food safety regulation also embodies a considerable capacity to learn and adapt because it is centered on HACCP management systems that require constant searching for hazards and control points. While this capacity can be constrained by the incentives of firms to take advantage of it, even in cases with relatively weak incentives HACCP systems can lead to reductions in risks (Coglianese and Lazer 2003: 724). Where there is both legal and market accountability, HACCP systems can be expected to yield considerable risk reduction benefits. Effectiveness can be enhanced through appropriate legal liability mechanisms, as well as the use of information to focus risks upon firms capable of controlling them.

Because private regulatory programs compete with each other for consumer trust and commercial acceptance, they also have systematic interests in learning. There is considerable evidence of competing regulatory programs adopting standards and practices from each other where they work, and also differentiating themselves from one another in hopes of achieving improved results or acceptance. In general, private regulatory systems can adapt to changed circumstances much more quickly than government ones.

Government regulatory programs can maximize their own effectiveness by maximizing the effectiveness of private regulatory programs. They will thus be most successful when they seek to align the incentives of organizations capable of imposing significant supply chain control with the public interest. They can facilitate coordination across regulatory ecosystem niches by strengthening rules and incentives for information production and sharing. They should also focus on finding possible weaknesses of private regulatory systems and either recommending or requiring changes as appropriate. In the case of the United States, this will require significant change. Government agencies will need greater authority with greater discretion, upgraded expertise capable of monitoring and assessing complex safety management systems, and changed attitudes in which private safety regulation is seen as a valuable but shifting and difficult-to-monitor asset (Coglianese and Lazer 2003; May 2007).

Fairness

Private import safety regulation typically relies on the market power of northern retailers. By imposing management and product standards on foreign producers, northern retailers presumably increase the value of the supply chain, but it also seems likely that northern retailers or consumers will retain most of that value. Still, there is little reason to think that producers are worse off than they otherwise would have been, since they retain or obtain access to desired northern markets, and avoid the same risks of catastrophic market loss that retailers avoid. Thus, private import regulation is likely to satisfy the criterion of Pareto improvement in most cases. Nonetheless, fairness, or distributive justice, may pose significant challenges over time. If northern interests are retaining most of the surplus generated by private safety regulatory systems, southern interests—especially in large economies such as China, India, and Brazil—will have an incentive to create competing programs and brand identities to take some of that surplus back (Henson and Humphrey 2008: 16). Thus, private import safety regulators will have to attend carefully to questions of distributive justice if they hope to persist.

There is also an important question of the fairness of private regulatory systems to small producers. Management system and record-keeping requirements, like most regulatory requirements, are generally more difficult for small enterprises to implement, and certification fees are relatively more burdensome. Some ameliorative steps have been taken through programs such as the GLOBALGAP's group certification program. Moreover, some research indicates that agricultural programs do not necessarily disadvantage small operators (Maertens and Swinnen 2007, 2009). But these effects are highly context dependent, and private safety regulation must be closely scrutinized for its ability to treat small operators fairly.

"Rent seeking"—that is, the construction of rules to favor some interests over others (Tullock 1967)—is a problem in all regulatory programs, public and private. Competition among regulatory programs may reduce this problem, as different interests commit to programs that do not unfairly disadvantage them, and programs thus have incentives to adapt in order to attract a wider array of interests.

Equally important is the political distribution of regulatory authority. Reliance on standards generated largely by northern interests can remove considerable regulatory power from southern countries, and they often express concern about that fact. While some of this problem may be alleviated by the legitimacy strategies discussed later in this chapter, it is also important to note that researchers have recently found that southern countries experience benefits in using regulatory standards developed in the north. In their studies of the Chilean salmon and Mexican fresh produce industries, Iizuka and Borbon-Galvez (2008) find that the availability of working packages of private standards and implementation institutions benefits resource-strapped southern countries because they can avoid expending resources on those functions and instead devote them to communicating policies, adapting agency practices, and supporting local businesses. While the benefits and costs of using such packages will undoubtedly be weighed differently in different contexts, trade-offs do exist.

Accountability and Legitimacy

Accountability arrangements are far more complex and multidimensional than is commonly understood (Scott 2000). Accountability takes multiple forms and runs in multiple directions in private safety regulation. Nonetheless, the dominant accountability in current import safety regulation is to northern interests. Northern retailers are accountable largely to northern consumers, and northern governments to northern citizens.

The widespread emergence of transnational supply chains puts this accountability structure in question. To whom should private regulators be accountable? There is of course no straightforward answer. Northerners interested in import regulation are primarily concerned with ensuring that participants in foreign supply chains keep risks to consumers down to an acceptable level. However, private safety regulatory regimes also have very significant effects on southern producers, as well as their employees, and on southern consumers because the quality and prices of products may be affected. Moreover, private regulatory programs have incentives to consider southern interests, since failure to do so might undermine the programs' long-term viability.

The food safety programs have begun to incorporate representatives of producer and southern interests, thus expanding their accountability. But it is not clear how far this expansion of stakeholders will go; at present decision making appears likely to remain dominated by retailers and producers, usually relatively large ones. The interests of many other constituencies (e.g., southern consumers, laborers, northern workers) are not well represented, and that could turn out to be a major problem. On the other hand, it is possible that the regulatory programs' need to achieve broad legitimacy will make up for this limited accountability structure.

To survive and thrive, private import safety programs must achieve a significant level of legitimacy—that is, acceptance that they are the appropriate agencies to carry out their functions and that the requirements they stand for deserve adherence. Legitimacy is essential to effective regulation; without it the costs of monitoring and enforcement are too high. The ecosystem structure of modern safety regulation suggests that there are multiple publics with multiple legitimacy standards. It may indicate that a new kind of system legitimacy is under construction. Most constituencies are satisfied by one regulatory program or another, but there is no single legitimacy structure (Black 2008). It may also be that continuities from one program to the other create a kind of mutually reinforcing legitimacy dynamic. If this arrangement holds, it may signal a significant new development in legitimacy structures.

Just as there is no single accountability framework for the regime as a whole, so also is there no single legitimacy structure. Instead, there is a patchwork of legitimacy that will add up to system legitimacy if enough of the individual pieces maintain sufficient acceptance with their relevant constituencies. This is a very rough, inelegant conception of legitimacy, but it may be emblematic of the present era in new transnational governance. Assessing it will require looking not only at the individual regulatory programs, but also at how they interact with each other and how they add up. Analyzing it may be aided by Scharpf's (1970) equally rough concepts of "input" and "output" legitimacy. Input legitimacy refers to the procedural pedigree of a policy, including the degree of participation by affected interests and the quality of openness and deliberation that goes into forming it. Output legitimacy refers to a policy's substantive acceptability, and includes its success in addressing the social problem to which it is addressed.

On the input side, we see that most private safety regulatory programs involve limited but expanding stakeholder participation, still dominated by northern interests but with growing southern representation. Overall, they also seem to show a growing amount of transparency and public deliberation. Private import safety programs thus seem to be developing considerable input legitimacy, sometimes comparable to that of public agencies.

On the output side, well-managed private safety regulation programs have the capacity to significantly improve the control of risks to safety. They may also improve the positions of affected stakeholders if properly constructed. Effectiveness and fairness can thus be seen as augmenting output legitimacy. Moreover, by competing to attract ever larger constituencies, private regulatory programs may potentially be adumbrating a new kind of anticipatory democracy, one in which they attempt to predict and implement the kinds of standards and regulatory institutions that emerging constituencies will eventually desire (Meidinger 2008b).

However, these prospective legitimacy gains remain deeply contingent. Significant failure in one portion of the regulatory ecosystem has the capacity to undermine the legitimacy of programs in other portions. Thus, each program has an interest in preventing catastrophic failures in other nearby ones while still competing with them. Whether they will manage to so coordinate themselves remains to be seen.

Regulatory Legitimacy in a New Era

Today's transnational safety regulatory system is made up of a multitude of competing, yet partially interdependent, public and private regulatory programs in which most regulatory functions are carried out by both government and private entities. While this regulatory pluralism has considerable advantages, individual actors in the system also face major challenges in determining how to relate to other actors and the regulatory ecosystem as a whole. Doing so will probably require much more improvisational, adaptive, and cooperative strategies than many regulators—particularly government agencies accustomed to relative monopolies—are accustomed to. In trying to protect the public interest, government agencies will have to find ways to take advantage of useful private regulatory practices and curb problematic ones. They will also have to foster accountability structures wherein the interests of powerful private regulators are aligned with larger public interests and the full range of interests along the supply chain is accounted for satisfactorily.

Ultimately, the existence of multiple public and private regulators means that there is an ongoing contest for regulatory legitimacy, and governments will have to both foster effective private regulation and partially "ride" the legitimacy of private regulatory organizations if they are to have a chance of effectively orchestrating the relevant actors.

Acknowledgments

The author thanks Barry Boyer, Cary Coglianese, Adam Finkel, and Colin Scott for their comments on earlier drafts of this chapter. The chapter also benefited from comments by participants at the Penn Program on Regulation workshop at the University of Pennsylvania Law School and the annual meeting of the Law and Society Association, Denver, May 27–31, 2009.

References

Abbott, Kenneth W. and Duncan Snidal (2009) "Strengthening International Regulation Through Transnational New Governance: Overcoming the Orchestration Deficit." 42 *Vanderbilt Journal of Transnational Law* 1–80.

Ansell, Christopher (2006) "The Asymmetries of Governance." In *What's the Beef? The Contested Governance of European Food Safety*, edited by Christoper Ansell and David Vogel. Cambridge, Mass.: MIT Press.

Assured Food Standards (2009) "The Standards." http://www.redtractor.org .uk/site/REDT/Templates/GeneralStandards.aspx?pageid=6&cc=GB.

Bell, David E. and Mary Shelman (2009) *GLOBALGAP: Food Safety and Private Standards.* Harvard Business School Case Study 9-509-004, January 5. Boston: Harvard Business School.

Black, Julia (2008) "Constructing and Contesting Legitimacy and Accountability in Polycentric Regulatory Regimes." 2 *Regulation and Governance* 137–64.

Bozarth, Cecil C. and Robert B. Handfield (2006) *Introduction to Operations and Supply Chain Management.* Upper Saddle River, N.J.: Pearson Education.

Campbell, Hugh (2005) "The Rise and Rise of EurepGAP: European (Re)Invention of Colonial Food Relations?" 13 *International Journal of Sociology of Food and Agriculture* 1–19.

Cheit, Ross (1990) *Setting Safety Standards: Regulation in the Public and Private Sectors.* Berkeley and Los Angeles: University of California Press.

Coglianese, Cary and David Lazer (2003) "Management-Based Regulation: Prescribing Private Management to Achieve Public Goals." 37 *Law and Society Review* 691–730.

Dorf, Michael and Charles Sabel (1998) "A Constitution of Democratic Experimentalism." 98 *Columbia Law Review* 267–473.

Epps, Tracey (2009) "Demanding Perfection: Private Food Standards and the SPS Agreement." In *International Economic Law and National Autonomy*, edited by Meredith Lewis and Susy Frankel. Cambridge: Cambridge University Press.

Food Business Forum (2008) "Global Food Safety Initiative Frequently Asked Questions." Comité International d'Entreprises à Succursales (CIES). http://www.ciesnet.com/pfiles/programmes/foodsafety/GFSI-FAQs.pdf.

Gow, Hamish (2008) Global agrifood industry development and private standards. Paper presented at the International Workshop on Globalization, Global Governance and Private Standards, University of Leuven, Leuven, Belgium, November 4–5.

Havinga, Tetty (2006) "Private Regulation of Food Safety by Supermarkets." 28 *Law and Policy* 515–33.

Henson, Spencer J. and John Humphrey (2008) Understanding the complexities of private standards in global agri-food chains. Paper presented at the International Workshop on Globalization, Global Governance and Private Standards, University of Leuven, Leuven, Belgium, November 4–5.

Henson, Spencer and Steven Jaffee (2008) "Understanding Developing Country Strategic Responses to the Enhancement of Food Safety Standards." 31 *World Economy* 1–15.

Iizuka, Michiko and Yari Borbon-Galvez (2008) Compliance with the private standards and capacity building of national institutions under globalization: New agendas for developing countries? Paper presented at the International Workshop on Globalization, Global Governance and Private Standards, University of Leuven, Leuven, Belgium, November 4–5.

International Organization for Standardization (ISO) (2009) "Introduction to ISO 22000." http://www.22000-tools.com/free-iso-22000-powerpoint.html.

International Organization for Standardization/International Electrotechnical Commission (ISO/IEC) (1994) *Guide 59: Code of Good Practice for Standardization.* Geneva: ISO.

Knowles, Tim, Richard Moody, and Morven G. McEachem (2007) "European Food Scares and Their Impact on EU Food Policy." 109 *British Food Journal* 43–67.

Krislov, Samuel (1997) *How Nations Choose Product Standards and Standards Change Nations.* Pittsburgh: University of Pittsburgh Press.

Lobel, Orly (2004) "The Renew Deal: The Fall of Regulation and the Rise of Governance in Contemporary Legal Thought." 89 *Minnesota Law Review* 342–470.

Maertens, Miet and Johan F. M. Swinnen (2009) "Trade, Standards, and Poverty: Evidence from Senegal." 37 *World Development* 161–78.

———. (2007) "Standards as Barriers and Catalysts for Trade, Growth and Poverty Reduction." 4 *Journal of International Agricultural Trade and Development* 1–15.

May, Peter (2007) "Regulatory Regimes and Accountability." 1 *Regulation and Governance* 8–26.

Meidinger, Errol (2008a) "Multi-Interest Self-Governance Through Global Product Certification Programs." In *Responsible Business? Self-Governance in Transnational Economic Transactions,* edited by Olaf Dilling, Martin Herberg, and Gerd Winter. Oxford: Hart.

———. (2008b) "Competitive Supra-Governmental Regulation: How Could It Be Democratic?" 8 *Chicago Journal of International Law* 513–34.

———. (2007) "Beyond Westphalia: Competitive Legalization in Emerging Transnational Regulatory Systems." In *Law and Legalization in Transnational Relations,* edited by Christian Brütsch and Dirk Lehmkuhl. London: Routledge.

Rees, Joseph (1996) *Hostages of Each Other: The Transformation of Nuclear Safety Since Three Mile Island.* Chicago: University of Chicago Press.

Roth, Aleda V., Andy A. Tsay, Madeleine E. Pullman, and John V. Roth (2008) "Unraveling the Food Supply Chain: Strategic Insights from China and the 2007 Recalls." 44 *Journal of Supply Chain Management* 22–39.

Scharpf, Fritz W. (1970) "Economic Integration, Democracy, and the Welfare State." 4 *Journal of European Public Policy* 18–30.

Schepel, Harm (2005) *The Constitution of Private Governance: Product Standards in the Regulation of Integrating Markets.* Oxford: Hart.

Scott, Colin (2000) "Accountability in the Regulatory State." 27 *Journal of Law and Society* 38–60.

Tullock, Gordon (1967) "The Welfare Costs of Tariffs, Monopolies, and Theft." 5 *Western Economic Journal* 224–32.

Underwriters Laboratories (UL) (2009) "UL Historical Timeline." http://www.ul.com/global/eng/pages/corporate/aboutul/history/.

U.S. Department of Agriculture/Economic Research Service (USDA/ERS) (2007) "Food Safety: Private Market Mechanisms and Government Regulation." http://www.ers.usda.gov/briefing/foodsafety/private.htm. (Accessed May 6, 2009).

Vandenbergh, Michael (2007) "The New Wal-Mart Effect: The Role of Private Contracting in Global Governance." 54 *UCLA Law Review* 913–70.

World Trade Organization/Committee on Sanitary and Phytosanitary Measures (WTO/SPS) (2008) "Private Standards—Identifying Practical Actions for the SPS Committee—Summary of Responses." G/SPS/W/230. Geneva: WTO.

World Trade Organization/Committee on Technical Barriers to Trade (WTO/TBT) (2000) "Second Triennial Review of the Operation and Implementation of the Agreement on Technical Barriers to Trade." G/TBT/9. Geneva: WTO.

Wouters, Jan, Axel Marx, and Nicholas Hachez (2008) Public and private food safety standards and international trade law: How to build a balanced relationship. Paper presented at the International Workshop on Globalization, Global Governance and Private Standards, University of Leuven, Leuven, Belgium, November 4–5.

Regulations, Statutes, and Treaties Cited

Agreement on the Application of Sanitary and Phytosanitary Measures (SPS), April 15, 1994, Marrakesh Agreement Establishing the World Trade Organization, Annex 1A, pmbl., Legal Instruments—Results of the Uruguay Round, 1867 U.N.T.S. 493.

Final Act Embodying the Results of the Uruguay Round of Multilateral Trade Negotiations, April 15, 1994, Agreement on Technical Barriers to Trade (TBT), Annex 1A, Legal Instruments—Results of the Uruguay Round, 33 I.L.M. 1125.

Food and Environment Protection Act (FEPA) (1985), c. 48 (Eng.).

Food Safety Act (FSA) (1990), c. 16 (Eng.).

U.S. Department of Agriculture (USDA) (1996) *Pathogen Reduction; Hazard Analysis and Critical Control Point (HACCP) Systems*, 61 Federal Register 38805 (July 25).

Part V
The Way Forward

Chapter 13
Delegated Governance
Consumer Safety in the Global Marketplace

David Zaring and Cary Coglianese

As the world's consumers increasingly enjoy the benefits of open trade, the challenges of protecting them from harmful products have grown. The goods they consume are now regularly produced abroad or are sourced with ingredients or parts from an array of countries. The expanding reach of international supply chains means that many producers of goods, or of components of goods, do not bear the costs incurred by those injured by what they sell, that liability and reputational sanctions are difficult to impose, and that private accountability remains low. At the same time, regulators simply are unable to interdict all potentially dangerous goods at the border or through inspection. What can be done? Any solution will require new ways of thinking about regulatory governance in a globalized economy. In this concluding chapter, we propose the concept of *delegated governance* as one way to think about how import safety is currently practiced and about the kinds of innovative policies suggested in this book that engage both the public and private sectors.

This book reflects a collaborative effort to think broadly about global consumer protection across several types of borders. These borders include the jurisdictional and cultural ones through which imports must pass. But they also include intellectual borders demarcating separate policy and research domains. For too many years, government officials and scholars have worried about the safety of food, drugs, and consumer products as discrete problem areas. The contributors to this book have instead engaged with, and cut across, the borders that have traditionally defined each of these issue areas. This book has also crossed the disciplinary boundaries of law, social science, statistics, engineering, and policy analysis in order to consider how sensible and creative regulatory solutions can be brought to bear on the problem of unsafe imports.

This book encourages both policy makers and analysts to look beyond traditional regulatory solutions and consider new forms of governance. The chapters in this book suggest that, to address the import safety problem adequately, the private sector must be engaged, contract and tort law must be deployed and reconfigured, renewed efforts at smarter regulation must be pursued, and carefully designed multinational cooperation must be part of any palette of governmental responses. Together, the chapters indicate a need for varied solutions to a large and multi-faceted problem—but of course not every conceivable solution will be appropriate. The contributors are generally skeptical of the global community's ability to create new, formal multilateral institutions with direct regulatory authority. Instead they seek ways to create incentives for the private sector to protect consumers, or for nations to police more effectively the quality of imports entering their borders. They are also concerned with providing information to consumers as well as to manufacturers wanting to manage their complex supply chains.

This book suggests to us the need for a model of global consumer safety—one we call delegated governance—whereby consumer protection is achieved by combining targeted public action with private inspections, public and private standard-setting, and ultimately a degree of *caveat emptor*. With delegated governance, the public regulatory role is one that relies at least as much on coordination and the provision of information as it does on direct monitoring and control; the processes of standard-setting, benchmarking, and global capacity-building are also necessarily disaggregated. Delegated governance may be imperfect—although some forms of it are less so than others, and in any case there are always ways to improve anything—but it is nevertheless an appropriate acknowledgment of the necessary limitations of completely centralized, preventative regulation of the entire, vast, and rapidly changing array of products exchanged in the global economy.

The contributors have tackled the import safety problem by addressing two critical aspects of any solution to it: institutional structure and policy design. Institutional structure focuses on the regime level, considering the totality of a regulatory system, such as the entirety of a single country's import safety apparatus or of multinational regulatory and trade systems. Policy designs are those more concrete strategies that can be adopted by any variety of national or international institutions, be they nations such as China or the United States or international entities such as the European Union (EU) or the World Trade Organization (WTO). Policy design choices range from the novel, such as bonded import safety warranties, to a repurposing of the more familiar, such as the use of risk analysis and forecasting to help regulators act in smarter, more targeted ways.

An analysis of both policy designs and institutional structures for enhancing import safety suggests a growing need to combine public-sector oversight with private participation by importers and producers of goods, and even consumers themselves. And no wonder. Private action is surely a crucial part of any solution to the import safety problem, simply because this problem is bigger than the capacity of even the most effective public regulators acting by themselves.

New Institutions

The institutional design contributions in this book both support and qualify the perception that consumer protection around the world reflects the different tastes for safety that different countries and cultures appear to embrace (Inglehart and Welzel 2005). China, for example, has prioritized the provision of low-cost exports to safe products, which reflects a certain kind of rough balancing of competing preferences. The People's Republic has been a predominant source of adulterated food and dangerous toys, and appears to be among the largest providers of counterfeit drugs in the world (see chapter 2). By contrast, Europeans seem almost to be safety fanatics. They have frequently found themselves before the WTO with their concerns about the adulteration of foreign foods with hormones, steroids, and the like; and they have lived through a number of outbreaks of bovine spongiform encephalopathy, or "mad cow disease," as well as foot-in-mouth epidemics that have decimated herds (Ansell and Vogel 2006: 48).

The European response for ensuring the safety of imported food is a rapid response network. The network coordinates the food safety regimes of the EU members in a way that makes them responsive to emergencies and protective of sovereignty, while utilizing already extant and elaborate bureaucracies when either internal or external food crises require rapid response (Alemanno 2007). The Rapid Alert System for Nonfood Consumer Products (RAPEX), with its fast and public reporting, may be reflective of peculiar European commitments, including the high value that Europeans put on safe food and other products.[1] But it may also be the sort of mechanism that other federal jurisdictions, or multilateral entities, should consider adopting.

Rather than seeking to impose their safety standards on manufacturers outside their borders, perhaps the best way for Europeans and others concerned about the safety of their imports is to cajole exporting countries such as China to tie product safety to other priorities that matter to decision makers and domestic publics. This might require making a fundamental conceptual tie between safety and other goals, such as increasing export volume, and perhaps offering other incentives to contribute to reinforce such a connection between safety and self-interest. Alternatively, perhaps another strategy would be to encourage the Chinese government to look to the European coordination and rapid response model as a way of building capacity for addressing import safety—and potentially creating, as a by-product, some changed cultural tastes for safety.

Ultimately, the question is how varied preferences for consumer safety can be translated into a global baseline that provides for the level of safety demanded by consumers (and voters) in importing countries without also overly discouraging trade from exporting countries with different safety standards. The WTO might seem to be an ideal vehicle for harmonizing demands for consumer protection around the globe. The WTO already regulates international trade in most goods and comes equipped with years of experience dealing with import safety. Its Agreement on the Application of Sanitary and Phytosanitary Measures presumably signals an effort to harmonize domestic health and safety standards—and implicitly acknowledges that those standards might be necessary barriers to the trade in goods (WTO 1994).[2] Moreover, the WTO has charged other international bodies of regulators, including the Codex Alimentarius Commission, with responsibility to develop health-related standards that it will deem compliant with the WTO's rules (WTO 1994: art. 3[a]). The WTO represents the potential of international cooperation to leverage resources, build capacity, and harmonize standards, which could counteract a race to the bottom.

Yet as much as cultural differences help explain the differences in national regulatory regimes that give rise to the need for harmonization, they also contribute to an overall skepticism about the ability of a single international institution such as the WTO to address the import safety problem. At worst, the WTO may be subject to capture and politicization, which has little to do with good import safety regulation (Mattli and Woods 2009). At best, the WTO does more to constrain, rather than encourage, the kind of coordination and creative response that global consumer protection demands. As it currently exists, the WTO appears not to be the place to look for innovation in import safety; it may be only a vehicle for all-but-intractable conflict on the issue, as Mark Pollack and Greg Shaffer have suggested may have been the case with genetically modified food (Pollack and Shaffer 2009).

If the WTO is unlikely to be the salvation for import safety, perhaps it might be worth considering more sweeping alternatives. Perhaps a new regime to protect consumer safety should be supported with a small global duty on goods, which could finance a global consumer protection authority. Creating a globally applied duty would represent in one sense just an extension of welfare economics, by addressing market failures through taxes; however, such a tax and any corresponding multinational administrative regime it funded would also be an unprecedented step toward something like worldwide government.

At the other extreme, perhaps there is need to consider a "global" strategy to support local economies. A transnational consumer movement could possibly foster a safety vision that would, to the extent possible, seek to reverse the tide of globalization and encourage "locavores," that is, those who make consumption choices reflect intimate supply, personal knowledge, and local community values (Pollan 2007). Further thought would obviously be needed to fill out how such a movement could be created and whether it would be worthwhile, but at the moment at least some individual consumers appear to find it attractive.

In all likelihood, though, the most viable international institutional responses to the import safety problem will lie somewhere between the radical extremes of localism and worldwide government. Global network-based solutions might be one such alternative (Raustiala 2002; Slaughter 2004), as would a mix of international and national, public and private solutions. However structured, a viable global regime of consumer safety protection will likely be complicated. Such a regime will undoubtedly involve a mix of domestic strategies, with international innovations created through treaties or some other institutional form, combined with national regulatory strategies and private-sector efforts. Importing countries might potentially learn to share and coordinate regulatory resources, dividing the exporting world up and, through mutual recognition, accepting each other's inspections as their own. One might ask, for example, if it is the best use of scarce regulatory resources to have inspectors from both the United States and the EU visit the same facilities in China and other exporting countries, when a greater number of facilities could be inspected if the United States and the EU coordinated and relied on each other's inspections. In addition, exporters and exporting countries may over time develop their own internal approaches to product safety and risk management. The variety of possible responses suggests that attending to the details of policy design will be at least as important, if not more important, than institutional structures in creating solutions to the problem of unsafe imports.

Public Policy and the Private Sector

Rather than urging wholesale change in trade or regulatory institutions themselves, contributors to this book have proposed policy reforms that could be adopted by either existing or new institutions. Most of these ideas either require or encourage the involvement of the private sector, even though all of them envision a continued role for government.

One facet of policy design would focus on ways of executing traditional government regulation better: more inspections, greater border interdiction, increased product recalls, and faster response when import injuries occur. In principle, increased government resources and more effective bureaucratic practices could indeed help reduce import safety problems.

Despite their obvious appeal, proposals for bigger government do not dominate the pages of this book. In large part this is simply because it is difficult to see how the public sector alone might be capable of policing the vast and increasing volume of international trade—even if government capacity were significantly expanded. After all, even if resources for border inspections were doubled or tripled, this would only mean that somewhat *less* of a small percentage of imported goods would be inspected. It still would be a small percentage, and hardly a process on which consumers could confidently and exclusively rely. It is precisely because of the mismatch between the scale of the problem and the limited availability of public-sector resources that the government needs to use statistical and risk analysis in order to deploy its scarce resources more efficiently and effectively. At the very least, data-driven modeling calls for data collection, and the government may be well suited to undertake the critical baseline work that would assist both private and public safety efforts.

Even with smarter government inspections, other alternatives will be needed. The tort system, including class action litigation, remains an important, although imperfect, backstop in any defective products regime. The public sector's role in disseminating and managing information is also vital. Information dissemination is the major purpose of the RAPEX system in the EU, where coordination is achieved through the rapid dissemination of product risk information identified by its members. The Hazard Analysis and Critical Control Point (HACCP) program in the United States is also an information-oriented regime, as it institutionalizes risk assessment, data collection, and continuous monitoring, although much of the responsibility for these tasks is delegated to the importers themselves

In none of these approaches is the government meant to act alone in curbing import safety abuses. As such, these approaches are consistent with the so-called new governance approach to regulatory problems. That approach is not always easy to specify, but at its core it suggests the need to merge the public and private sectors in a common regulatory enterprise, chiefly by contracting out some public duties to private actors.[3] Such proposals disaggregate government; at their best fostering a "new form of government" that enables "citizens ... to utilize their local knowledge to fit solutions to their individual circumstances" (Dorf and Sabel 1998: 267).

In keeping with the new governance model, several of the chapters in this book have proposed solutions that would depend only on a modest role for the public sector, including bonded import safety warranties that require only an initial mandate from the government and some management in the background. In essence, a bonded warranty system is a private insurance scheme that would create a resource pool to compensate those who are injured by unsafe imports, and an aggregation process that could encourage the prosecution of breaches in the warranties. This creative approach is thus both an insurance plan and a novel enforcement scheme; the latter has a lineage with those who welcome a set of "private attorneys general" that permit the legislature to "vindicate important public policy goals by empowering private individuals to bring suit" (Karlan 2003: 184; see also Meltzer 1988).

The private sector could also play a role by encouraging importers to take responsibility for injuries incurred further up the supply chain, and far away from the importing country. U.S. Food and Drug Administration (FDA) and U.S. Department of Agriculture (USDA) inspectors cannot easily regulate extraterritorially; private parties, on the other hand, can much more easily transcend borders through business relationships. For example, it is generally much easier—and perhaps more effective—for the large purchaser simply to cancel a contract with a supplier if a question arises about its product's safety. Blurring together private and public actions to ensure import safety fits within an emerging, new-governance literature that accepts as inevitable, and values as useful, such a blending of the public and private roles.[4]

In addition to the variety of potential solutions contained in the chapters in this book, there surely are other variations that could be added to the possible mix. Some additional solutions might focus on interdiction, others on consumer education, and others on the government response to hazards and outbreaks. Enforcement reforms, for example, could include enlisting private third-party inspectors, much as the accounting industry audits compliance with tax requirements. If they hope to respond quickly to outbreaks and other incidents, as well as learn from them, importing countries will almost certainly need a much better global trace-back system for all kinds of consumer goods. Perhaps the U.S. hazardous waste "cradle-to-grave" manifest system could provide a model for tracking imports, one that today could take advantage of modern information technology.

Another option would be to place more emphasis on signaling potential risk or safety through labeling and other "right-to-know" measures (Fung et al. 2007). This would in effect let consumers assess risky products at the point of sale, "regulating" products by what consumers purchase and what they eschew. Recent ideas to improve consumer right-to-know include:

- Establishing a system of country-of-origin labeling
- Creating a body akin to Underwriters Laboratories to put its seal on approved imports
- Mandating product labeling that would show if a product has been refused entry into the United States, so as to prevent re-introduction
- Taking advantage of the Internet to post the names of retail establishments that have sold products that have been subject to recall
- Creating an online database of pending and completed investigations by the FDA, USDA, Consumer Product Safety Commission (CPSC), and other safety regulators, so consumers would not have to piece together information from media coverage

As with informational strategies in other contexts, there are possible downsides to labeling requirements. Labeling can sometimes place additional burdens on businesses, such as in the time and effort needed to gather information and prepare the necessary forms. Consumers may ultimately misunderstand or ignore information on labels—or worse yet, they might misconstrue and thereby amplify public fear. It is also possible for the public to suffer "information overload" in which too many warnings become tantamount to too few warnings (Twerski et al. 1976).[5]

An alternative, but complementary, approach to many of the innovations discussed in this book would be to develop domestic institutions capable of responding more quickly and effectively *after the fact*, once unsafe imports enter the stream of commerce. Response strategies would seek to contain the damage, prevent recurrences, and redress harms. Appropriate strategies would include empowering domestic agencies with mandatory recall authority they can easily use. Another possibility, much akin to Baker's in chapter 11 of this book, would be to promulgate requirements that, before exporters receive certification, they must post a surety bond that they can lose if they default on a judgment in a U.S. court (Popper 2008).

Many of these solutions to the import safety problem have a post-bureaucratic flavor. In this they are certainly not alone. Other scholars have recently sought to identify how the public sector might encourage private industry to act more responsibly (Coglianese and Nash 2006; Salamon 2002: 156–85). Among government officials themselves, decentralized, public-private partnerships have been in vogue for the past decade or more (Osborne and Gaebler 1993).[6]

Cooperative, private-sector solutions are "new" governance approaches in that they are consistent with a new literature. But they also have a rich tradition.[7] In product safety, there have long been third parties such as liability insurers and seal-of-approval private standard setters, such as Underwriters Laboratories (Cheit 1990).[8] More skeptical theories of regulation, such as capture theory (the idea that regulators may do the bidding of regulated entities), blur the distinction between public and private in their own way.[9] Accordingly, the general idea of public-private collaboration reflected in some of the chapters in this book is neither unprecedented nor completely unproblematic; however, we believe attention to business-government interaction is an essential part of any serious approach to ensuring safe imports.

Import safety is a problem that undoubtedly vexes government regulators at least as much as any other. In the 1960s and 1970s, American courts and agencies began to grapple with a similarly vexing problem: mass justice, where fair treatment was to be delivered to vast numbers of new entitlement holders. The dilemmas of reconciling due process, individualized protections, and massive bureaucracies perplexed designers of the regulatory state at that time. Those early efforts addressed welfare and disability payments, benefits that affect "mere" millions. Reconciling the demands of justice and administrative efficiency has proven to be even harder in the United States with health care, a good that every citizen consumes. But all of these early mass justice challenges pale in comparison to the import safety problem. The safety of food, drugs, and consumer products involves transactions that literally every individual makes multiple times every day. In this sense, it is the most significant of all mass justice problems. At the same time, as government officials seek to protect consumer safety, deliver cost-effective regulatory services, and deal with the politicization that accompanies international trade, they must also deliver fair treatment to the providers of food, drugs, and consumer products.

The scope of the problem could not be broader. Perhaps that is one reason so many proposed solutions seek to leverage private industry and rely to some degree on self-regulation, with government oversight and enforcement as a backdrop. Import safety, in other words, is almost certainly too big a problem for the public sector to solve alone.

Delegated Governance

In Europe, food safety and health scares have resulted in what has been called "contested governance," which stems from a "pervasive sense of distrust that challenges the legitimacy of existing institutional arrangements" (Ansell and Vogel 2006: 10). In contested governance, Ansell and Vogel argue, substantive policy disputes between interested parties spill over into differences over who should make the decisions and how they should be made. The problem is even more acute on a global stage, where there has always been an anarchic world order (Waltz 1979), and never broad agreement on what the institutions of consumer protection should look like, or even whether it is realistic to think about a single model in a diverse global regulatory environment.

Nonetheless, this book indicates that there may be the beginnings of a new organized approach to import safety regulation; it is the organization itself that is different. The model emerging is one of disaggregated governance, one driven in part by two large, functional difficulties of regulating imports, and in part by implicit choices driven by those difficulties. The two functional difficulties are the size of the problem of regulating imports, which dwarfs the public resources available to oversee them, and the problem of the world's legal and political multipolarity.

These difficulties may have contributed to the contested governance scheme in Europe, but it is also possible to envision that global governance could become less contested if it were more delegated. Global governance of consumer protection appears increasingly to rely in large measure on delegation away from the national regulator, a phenomenon that we term *delegated governance*. To be sure, governance has long involved delegation—whether from citizens to their representatives, or from representatives to unelected bureaucrats (Epstein and O'Halloran 1999; Flinders 2008). Delegation per se is not new; rather, what is new is the increasingly explicit recognition that government regulators' roles are inevitably limited and therefore must involve working with and relying upon the regulatory efforts of others. Instead of trying to bear the entire burden of consumer protection on their own shoulders, government regulators are working harder and more self-consciously to manage the overall system, including trying to affect the roles played by "surrogate regulators." Some have applied the label "meta-regulation" to the challenges associated with having regulators manage or cultivate the work of other "regulators" (Parker 2002).

Delegated governance may apply not only to the problems of safe imports, but also to other public goods on the consumer level that must be coordinated globally, including environmental and workplace protection and perhaps the provision of safe and sound financial services. Each of these problems crosses borders and interacts with complex social and economic systems, and such problems will continue to arise with still greater interdependent effects in the future. But at least for some aspects of import safety, delegation to an *international* institution such as the WTO is, as we have seen, likely to be fraught with problems. On the other hand, as contributors to this book have made clear, *national* governments cannot adequately police imports alone. The result is that there has been a search for new and different delegates who can help national governments solve a global problem.

Delegated governance, at least as it currently exists, relies significantly on the private sector to do much of the policing of safe products—particularly on the producer side. Leveraging the private sector is not easy, but at its best it may result in much more bang for the public-sector buck by internalizing the compliance process in the companies that import and export goods (Coglianese and Nash 2005). Encouraging that internalization in a useful way is one of the challenges of delegated governance, and many of the policy proposals in this book deal with this challenge.

Delegated governance also leaves consumers themselves with a great deal of responsibility for ensuring that the products they buy are safe. For better or worse, consumers themselves are some of the delegates charged with taking responsibility for determining whether their foods are safe, for cooking or using them properly, and for making price versus quality trade-offs. However, if consumers elsewhere are like the Americans surveyed by Jonathan Baron (see chapter 3), they may not fully accept this responsibility, preferring instead to blame the government for failing to protect them.

Even if necessary, broad delegation of responsibilities to private actors—consumers, nongovernmental organizations, suppliers, manufacturers, and retailers—is hardly uncontroversial or unproblematic. Reliance on the private sector to perform or assist in regulatory tasks raises questions about transparency and accountability—other types of public "goods" that the private sector typically does not provide in abundance. Even though food and product consumption are laden with deeply held values, it still may be difficult, in a delegated regime, for members of the public to articulate the values they hold and see that they are well represented. If the public's traditional regulatory delegate—national government—cannot address import safety adequately, and if the private sector is unable to protect the public sufficiently, serious questions about regime legitimacy are likely to arise. Again, as Baron's results suggest, the government will still receive the blame if a delegated governance system breaks down.

But governments have little choice. The emerging global import safety regime—multipolar, semi-private, and imperfect—seems necessary, even if it is only a second-best regime. Second-best regimes are increasingly common in international regulation, and, as Robert Keohane (2000) has suggested, they can be structured in ways that mitigate some of the problems of democracy and accountability. In the end, sometimes the second-best is really the only best there is (Bennear and Stavins 2007), and the challenge may simply be to try to infuse delegated governance with a greater degree of transparency and oversight by publicly accountable entities and appropriately motivated non-governmental organizations (Braithwaite and Drahos 2000).

New Directions

The only way to meet that challenge and make better decisions about the problem of import safety is to know more about decision makers' choices and the effects of different policy designs. Broadening efforts like those represented by the European RAPEX solution will be critical not only to inform policy responses, but also to facilitate future research. In an aggregated world, where millions of consumers are interacting with millions of products, product-by-product and item-by-item monitoring is almost surely impossible. However, broader trends can be observed and must be consciously studied in order to develop a better picture of emerging problems and the efficacy of alternative solutions. More data on the "near misses," the cases of unsafe products that were caught before anyone was harmed, are critical—but obviously they are harder to study and therefore not as well understood.

More generally, our very picture of the problem of import safety can benefit from further elaboration and characterization. We still do not know how much of the import safety problem stems from situations of momentary and unintentional lapses in product quality, or how much stems from gross negligence or deliberate tampering by bad actors. It may also be that, scanning across all products, the biggest health and safety threats to consumers stem from domestically sourced products. Or perhaps the biggest threats come not from contaminated or defective products that could otherwise be safe, but from new types of technologies—such as certain applications of nanotechnology—that are inherently risky no matter where such products are made. The vast scope of international supply chains means that inevitably both new and old dangers, as well as both negligent and intentional actions, pose risks to consumers. These dangers could come from any ingredient or any part, from any supplier. As such, there are perhaps an infinite variety of ways a consumer could get sick or injured from food, drugs, or consumer goods. Both researchers and policy decision makers need to understand better which of these ways are the most significant. The import safety problem is, at base, an informational problem.

Given the current lack of precise ex ante knowledge about which pathway of a seemingly infinite number of pathways to consumer harm is most likely, perhaps the most crucial, immediate role for governments arises after the fact, acting in response to incidents as much as preventing them from ever occurring. The most compelling implication of this book, in other words, may be that regulatory governance in the global economy needs to be reactive as much as proactive. Since regulators cannot anticipate or guard against every possible pathway of consumer harm from global trade, they need to build a better capacity for monitoring harms when they do arise, responding nimbly to mitigate the damage, and disseminating information to warn others to check their products for similar hazards. Delegated governance of import safety needs, in short, to be responsive governance, in the sense that regulatory officials must closely monitor for problems and disseminate information when they arise.

The European RAPEX system provides a model of such a responsive approach. Not only does the RAPEX system provide a warning to European customs officials and consumers, it also provides information that manufacturers can use to monitor their own supply chains. A food manufacturer, for example, faces the dilemma of discerning which of any number of possible contaminants to test its product for—as any ingredient could have been tampered with or contaminated by innumerable harmful chemicals. Once RAPEX sounds the alarm about contamination from one harmful chemical found in a given food product in Europe, manufacturers around the world know to test for the presence of that chemical in their products. RAPEX illustrates one important way that governments can work to create an informational infrastructure that can lead to positive spillovers, in terms of the mitigation of identified risks, actions to prevent future risks, and ultimately improved research and policy analysis.

By providing information, as well as incentives and oversight, government will continue to play a critical role in a system of delegated governance. But, as with RAPEX, the best solutions for government will be those that support and encourage private actors to meet their responsibilities for protecting consumers. Import safety in an era of global trade is a problem markedly different from those that national regulation has traditionally addressed, and the solutions considered in this book point the way forward to delegated forms of governance that can be used to address, and hopefully enhance, consumer protection in a globalized economy.

Acknowledgments

The authors thank all the contributors to this book, as well as the other participants at the Penn Program on Regulation's workshop on import safety; this chapter was stimulated by the insights they have provided throughout this book. In addition, we greatly thank Adam Finkel for his collaboration on this book and his comments on an earlier draft of this chapter, both of which have helped immeasurably.

Notes

1. As Alemanno explains, RAPEX is the EU rapid alert mechanism that deals with nonfood and nonpharmaceutical products (see chapter 9). The system enables greater and quicker exchange of information between EU member countries and the European Commission to speed up any actions taken to address products found to be dangerous. There is also a RAPEX-CHINA online system that attempts a similar level of information flow on dangerous products between the EU and China (EU 2009). If RAPEX is reflective of a European taste for high levels of protection, it could be, of course, that this taste has been encouraged by, or at least combines well with, an inclination toward protectionism by its agricultural and manufacturing sectors.

2. Robert Howse (2000: 2330), for example, has argued that WTO tools such as the Agreement on the Application of Sanitary and Phytosanitary Measures (SPS Agreement) can be "understood not as usurping legitimate democratic choices for stricter regulations, but as enhancing the quality of rational democratic deliberation about risk and its control."

3. Another principal strain of new governance research recommends running government more like a business. For example, David Osborne and Ted Gaebler's influential book *Reinventing Government*—a title used by the Clinton administration to brand its efforts at bureaucratic reform—argued for an entrepreneurial form of government that would delegate a great deal of authority to street-level officials (Osborne and Gaebler 1993). But Osborne and Gaebler were writing during a period of considerable private-sector expansion; it is far from clear how their suggestion that governments encourage and rely on private-sector risk-taking would be received today, following an economic crisis triggered in part by imprudent business decision making.

4. William Simon and Charles Sabel (2006: 399), for example, suggest that "new governance . . . [works] through explicitly provisional and incomplete legislative frameworks that set the terms for diffuse groups of stakeholders to elaborate in particular applications, which will then be reviewed at the center with an eye toward revision of the frameworks." Orly Lobel (2005) puts forward certain Occupational Safety and Health Administration (OSHA) initiatives as examples of a shift to a new governance model based on "cooperative compliance and coercive enforcement."

5. We thank Adam Finkel for providing the basis for the preceding paragraphs on information disclosure.

6. Indeed, in the wake of the expansion in the role of decentralized private institutions in the function of governance, scholars are increasingly asking how these institutions themselves might be managed and held accountable (Freeman 1997, 2003; May 2007).

7. Private parties have played a role in most elaborate regulatory systems for decades. In financial regulation, it is lawyers, accountants, and rating agencies that have provided, since the beginning of the twentieth century, a segment of the palette of market oversight.

8. One such organization is the Underwriters Laboratories (UL). Founded in 1894, UL evaluates products and product inputs, allowing those that passed certain specifications to carry a UL certification mark (UL 2009).

9. Capture theory suggests that interest groups and political groups can pressure the government to manipulate laws and regulations so that they benefit private interests rather than public interests (Bernstein 1955; Huntington 1952; Stigler 1971).

References

Alemanno, Alberto (2007) *Trade in Food: Regulatory and Judicial Approaches in the EC and the WTO*. London: Cameron May.

Ansell, Christopher K. and David Vogel (2006) *What's the Beef? The Contested Governance of European Food Safety*. Cambridge, Mass.: MIT Press.

Bennear, Lori S. and Robert N. Stavins (2007) "Second-Best Theory and the Use of Multiple Policy Instruments." 37 *Environmental and Resource Economics* 111–29.

Bernstein, Marver (1955) *Regulating Business by Independent Commission*. Princeton, N.J.: Princeton University Press.

Braithwaite, John and Peter Drahos (2000) *Global Business Regulation*. Cambridge: Cambridge University Press.

Cheit, Ross (1990) *Setting Safety Standards: Regulation in the Public and Private Sectors*. Berkeley and Los Angeles: University of California Press.

Coglianese, Cary and Jennifer Nash (2006) *Leveraging the Private Sector: Management-Based Strategies for Improving Environmental Performance*. Washington, D.C.: Resources for the Future Press.

Dorf, Michael C. and Charles F. Sabel (1998) "A Constitution of Democratic Experimentalism." 98 *Columbia Law Review* 267, 354.

Epstein, David and Sharyn O'Halloran (1999) *Delegating Powers: A Transaction Cost Politics Approach to Policy Making Under Separate Powers*. Cambridge: Cambridge University Press.

European Union (EU) (2009) "Rapid Alert System for Non-Food Consumer Products (RAPEX)." http://ec.europa.eu/consumers/safety/rapex/index_en.htm.

Flinders, Matthew (2008) *Delegated Governance and the British State: Walking Without Order*. Oxford: Oxford University Press.

Freeman, Jody (2003) "Extending Public Law Norms Through Privatization." 116 *Harvard Law Review* 1285.

———. (1997) "Collaborative Governance in the Administrative State." 45 *UCLA Law Review* 1, 7.

Fung, Archon, Mary Graham, and David Weil (2007) *Full Disclosure: The Perils and Promise of Transparency*. New York: Cambridge University Press.

Howse, Robert (2000) "Democracy, Science, and Free Trade: Risk Regulation on Trial at the World Trade Organization." 98 *Michigan Law Review* 2329.

Huntington, Samuel (1952) "The Marasmus of the ICC: The Commission, the Railroads, and the Public Interest." 61 *Yale Law Journal* 467–509.

Inglehart, Ronald F. and Christian Welzel (2005) *Modernization, Cultural Change, and Democracy: The Human Development Sequence*. New York: Cambridge University Press.

Karlan, Pamela S. (2003) "Disarming the Private Attorney General." 2003 *University of Illinois Law Review* 183.

Keohane, Robert O. (2000) "Governance in a Partially Globalized World." 95 *American Political Science Review* 1–13.

Lobel, Orly (2005) "Setting the Agenda for New Governance Research." San Diego Legal Studies Paper No. 07-28. http://ssrn.com/abstract=724561.

Mattli, Walter and Ngaire Woods (2009) "In Whose Benefit? Explaining Regulatory Change in Global Politics." In *The Politics of Global Regulation*, edited by Walter Mattli and Ngaire Woods. Princeton, N.J.: Princeton University Press.

May, Peter J. (2007) "Regulatory Regimes and Accountability." 1 *Regulation & Governance* 1–21.

Meltzer, Daniel J. (1988) "Deterring Constitutional Violations by Law Enforcement Officials: Plaintiffs and Defendants as Private Attorneys General." 88 *Columbia Law Review* 247.

Osborne, David and Ted Gaebler (1993) *Reinventing Government: How the Entrepreneurial Spirit Is Transforming the Public Sector.* New York: Plume.

Parker, Christine (2002) *The Open Corporation: Effective Self-Regulation and Democracy.* Cambridge: Cambridge University Press.

Pollack, Mark A. and Gregory C. Shaffer (2009) *When Cooperation Fails: The International Law and Politics of Genetically Modified Foods.* Oxford: Oxford University Press.

Pollan, Michael (2007) *Omnivore's Dilemma.* New York: Penguin.

Popper, Andrew F. (2008) "Unavailable and Unaccountable: A Free Ride for Foreign Manufacturers of Defective Consumer Goods." 36 *Product Safety & Liability Reporter* 1–11 (March 3).

Raustiala, Kal (2002) "The Architecture of International Cooperation: Transgovernmental Networks and the Future of International Law." 43 *Virginia Journal of International Law* 1.

Sabel, Charles F. and William H. Simon (2006) "Epilogue: Accountability Without Sovereignty." In *Law and New Governance in the EU and the U.S.*, edited by Gráinne de Búrca and Joanna Scott. Oxford: Hart.

Salamon, Lester M., ed. (2002) *Tools of Government: A Guide to the New Governance.* Oxford: Oxford University Press.

Slaughter, Anne-Marie (2004) *A New World Order.* Princeton, N.J.: Princeton University Press.

Stigler, George (1971) "The Theory of Economic Regulation." 2 *Bell Journal of Economics & Management Science* 3–21.

Twerski, Aaron, W. A. Donaher, H. R. Piehler, and A. S. Weinstein (1976) "The Use and Abuse of Warnings in Products Liability: Design Defect Litigation Comes of Age." 61 *Cornell Law Review* 495–540.

Underwriters Laboratories (UL) (2009) About UL. http://www.ul.com/global/eng/pages/corporate/aboutul/.

Waltz, Kenneth (1979) *The Theory of International Politics.* Boston: McGraw-Hill.

Agreement Cited

World Trade Organization (WTO), Agreement on the Application of Sanitary and Phytosanitary Measures. (1994). http://www.wto.org/english/docs_e/legal_e/15sps_01_e.htm.

Contributors

Alberto Alemanno

Alberto Alemanno is Associate Professor of Law at HEC Paris, where he teaches European and WTO law. He previously worked as a Legal Secretary at the European Court of Justice. He holds LLM degrees from Harvard Law School and the College of Europe as well as a PhD in International Law and Economics from Bocconi University. He is the author of *Trade in Food: Regulatory and Judicial Approaches in the EC and the WTO*.

Tom Baker

Tom Baker is William Maul Measey Professor of Law and Health Sciences at the University of Pennsylvania Law School. His work explores insurance, risk, and responsibility in a wide variety of settings, using methods and perspectives drawn from economics, sociology, and history. He is the author of *The Medical Malpractice Myth* and *Insurance Law and Policy: Cases, Materials and Problems*, and a contributing editor of *Embracing Risk: The Changing Culture of Insurance and Responsibility*.

Kenneth A. Bamberger

Kenneth A. Bamberger is Assistant Professor of Law at the University of California, Berkeley. His research focuses on the allocation of governance decisions among institutions, both public and private, on the role of corporate compliance in regulatory implementation, and on questions of technology in governance. Bamberger is affiliated with the Center for the Study of Law and Society and with the Berkeley Center for Law, Business and the Economy.

Jonathan Baron

Jonathan Baron is Professor of Psychology at the University of Pennsylvania. He holds a BA from Harvard and a PhD in psychology from the

University of Michigan. His main research interest is in moral judgments about public policies. More generally, he is interested in judgment and decision making. He is author of a major textbook on that topic, past president of the Society for Judgment and Decision Making, and editor of its journal.

Richard Berk

Richard Berk is a professor in the Departments of Criminology and Statistics at the University of Pennsylvania. Professor Berk is an elected Fellow of the American Association for the Advancement of Science, the American Statistical Association, and the Academy of Experimental Criminology. He works on various topics in applied statistics including causal inference, machine learning, and methods for evaluating social programs.

Vicki Bier

Vicki Bier holds a joint appointment as a professor in the Departments of Industrial Engineering and Engineering Physics at the University of Wisconsin, Madison, where she has since 1995 directed the Center for Human Performance and Risk Analysis (formerly the Center for Human Performance in Complex Systems). She received a PhD in Operations Research from the Massachusetts Institute of Technology in 1983, and a BS in Mathematical Sciences from Stanford University in 1976.

Tim Büthe

Tim Büthe is Assistant Professor of Political Science at Duke University. His current work focuses primarily on regulatory issues as well as public and private modes of setting standards for international product and financial markets. His other work on the governance of the global economy focuses on foreign direct investment and competition policy (antitrust enforcement and merger review) in the EU and the United States.

Cary Coglianese

Cary Coglianese is Deputy Dean for Academic Affairs, Edward B. Shils Professor of Law, and Professor of Political Science at the University of Pennsylvania, where he is also Director of the Penn Program on Regulation. He has taught at Harvard University's John F. Kennedy School of Government and at the Stanford Law School, and he served as a founding editor of the international, peer-reviewed journal *Regulation & Governance*.

Jacques deLisle

Jacques deLisle is Stephen Cozen Professor of Law at the University of Pennsylvania Law School. An expert in contemporary Chinese law and politics, he is Director of the Asia Program at the Foreign Policy Research Institute, Director of the Center for East Asian Studies at the University of Pennsylvania, and a member of the National Committee on U.S.-China Relations.

Tracey Epps

Tracey Epps lectures on the Faculty of Law at the University of Otago, New Zealand. She has a BA/LLB (Hons) from the University of Auckland and an LLM and SJD from the University of Toronto. Her research interests largely concern the tension between domestic regulatory autonomy and trade liberalization in the international trading system. She is the author of *International Trade and Health Protection: A Critical Analysis of the WTO's SPS Agreement.*

Adam M. Finkel

Adam M. Finkel is Executive Director of the Penn Program on Regulation and Professor at the UMDNJ School of Public Health. A leading expert in quantitative risk assessment and cost-benefit analysis, he was a senior regulatory and enforcement official at the U.S. Occupational Safety and Health Administration from 1995 to 2005. He wishes to acknowledge the inspirational example of his uncle, Louis Fink, DVM (1912–2009), who was the chief food safety officer for the Panama Canal Zone from 1952 to 1970.

Andrew T. Guzman

Andrew T. Guzman is Professor of Law, Director of the Advanced Law Degree Programs, and Associate Dean for International and Executive Education at the Boalt Hall School of Law, University of California, Berkeley. Professor Guzman holds a JD and PhD (economics) from Harvard University. He has written extensively on international trade, international regulatory matters, foreign direct investment, and public international law. He is the author of *How International Law Works* and *International Trade Law.*

Errol Meidinger

Errol Meidinger is Professor and Vice-Dean of Law for Research and Faculty Development at the State University of New York, Buffalo, and also an Honorary Professor at the University of Freiburg, Germany. His current research focuses on innovative institutional arrangements for promoting environmental protection, social equity, and public safety.

Kevin Outterson

Kevin Outterson is Associate Professor at Boston University School of Law. His academic work focuses on legal issues in global pharmaceutical markets and appears in both legal journals and peer-reviewed medical and health policy journals. He has testified on pharmaceutical marketing issues before legislative and regulatory bodies at both the state and federal levels of government.

Michael J. Trebilcock

Michael J. Trebilcock is University Professor and Professor of Law and Economics at the University of Toronto. He was awarded the Owen Prize in 1989 by the Foundation for Legal Research for his book *The Common Law of Restraint of Trade*. He is also the author of *The Limits of Freedom of Contract*, coauthor of *The Regulation of International Trade* (3rd edition), and coauthor of *The Law and Economics of Canadian Competition Policy*.

Lorna Zach

Lorna Zach is a scientist at the Center for Human Performance and Risk Assessment at the University of Wisconsin, Madison. She received a PhD in chemical engineering from the University of Canterbury, New Zealand, and an MS in food science and a BS in chemical engineering from the University of Wisconsin, Madison. She has more than fourteen years' experience in the food processing and agriculturally related industries in addition to experience in environmental consulting and risk analysis.

David Zaring

David Zaring is Assistant Professor of Law at the Wharton School of Business and a faculty affiliate of the Penn Program on Regulation. His research focuses on international economic regulation and administrative law. He served as a law clerk on the U.S. Court of Appeals for the District of Columbia Circuit, worked at the U.S. Department of Justice, and was educated at Harvard Law School and Swarthmore College.

Index

tion, 74–79, 84; SPS Agreement and, 79–81; TBT agreement and, 77, 80, 83; third-party certification, 74, 80–82, 84; U.S., 69–70, 73–85; world and, 69; WTO import safety rules and, 78–80, 84–85. *See also* Food and Drug Administration; Hazard Analysis and Critical Control Point; import risk prevention; Interagency Working Group on Import Safety

import safety regulation: consequences for violation, 10–11; decisions, 10; delegated governance, 266–68; domestic product regulation and, 12–13; export/import jurisdictional border and, 10–11; global consumer protection system and, 13–16; GMOs and, 12; governments/WTO and, 69; HACCP systems and, 13; along import safety causal chain, 9; import safety warranties and, 215–16; international food safety standard differences and, 11; international mechanisms for, 9–10; international trade and, 69–85; preventive regulation and, 10, 12; regulatory networks and, 15; transnational new governance and, 236–37. *See also* European import safety regulation; import safety warranties; private import safety regulation; public import safety regulation; risk-based import safety regulation

import safety regulation solutions: importer product safety regulation mechanism, 202–6; legislative proposals/state-regulator-centered approaches, 200–202

import safety research, 6. *See also* import safety parochialism research

import safety rules: ensuring working, 83–85; generic drug markets and, 110–24. *See also* import safety reform proposals; WTO import safety rules

import safety solutions, 12–13, 14–15; institutional structures in, 258, 259; labeling in, 12; new directions, 268–69; new governance regulation and, 261–65; other, 263–65; policy design in, 258–59, 262; private/public sectors merging in, 262–65, 270nn3–4, 270nn6–7, 271nn8–9; public policy in, 261–65; public sector in, 261–65

import safety warranties: importer product safety regulation and, 209–10; import safety regulation and, 215–16. *See also* bonded import safety warranties; import safety regulation

industries: different regulation for different, 6; domination of Codex, 94, 104, 106n7; import safety across different, 6–7; import safety and, 6. *See also* private sector

institutions: global consumer protection/safety new, 259–61; selection in international regulatory delegation, 99–102, *101*; status quo ante in international food safety standards, 96–99; structures in import safety solutions, 258–59. *See also* international institutions

intellectual property (IP): border enforcement and, 112–13, 123; generic drugs and, 112–13; import safety and, 113; industries and TRIPS, 111; rights/rules and global trade negotiations, 110–11. *See also* Agreement on Trade-Related Intellectual Property

Interagency Working Group on Import Safety (IWGIS), 200–201, 211n4; import safety reform proposals and, 74, 79, 81; risk-based food import safety regulation, 154

international, networks, 15

International Consumer Product Safety Caucus, 15

international food safety standards: benefits of, 88–89; Codex, 89–90, 92, 94, 103, 104–5, 105n3, 152; developed countries and, 92; developing countries and, 92, 93, 101, 106n14; EU and, 92–94, 101, 105n5; GATT and, 88; GATT Uruguay Round and, 89–92, 100, 103, 105n4; governance issues and, 88–89; import safety regulation and differences over, 11; institutional status quo ante in, 96–99; international regulatory delegation and, 91–93; IOs and, 90–91; policy implications, 102–5; SPS agreement and, 89–92, 94, 99, 100–102, 103–4, 105nn2–4; U.S. and, 92–93, 105n5; WTO and, 89, 105n1. *See also* IO food safety standards

international institutions: import safety problem and, 266; trade, 67, 69–124

networks: international, 15. *See also* regulatory networks

new governance, 258, 262. *See also* transnational new governance

new governance regulation: import safety solutions and, 261–65; private/public sectors merging in, 262–65, 270nn3–4, 270nn6–7, 271nn8–9

NHTSA. *See* National Highway Traffic Safety Administration

nontariff barrier to trade (NTB), 99–100

northern countries. *See* developed countries

NRC. *See* National Research Council

NTB. *See* nontariff barrier to trade

Obama, Barack, 74

OECD. *See* Organization for Economic Cooperation and Development

Organization for Economic Cooperation and Development (OECD): food safety standards, 96, 98, *101*; SPS Agreement and, 100. *See also* IO food safety standards

outcomes regulation, 211n2; challenges in globalized world product safety regulation, 197–98; CPSC, 195; domestic consumer safety regulation, 195–96; product regulation, 194

Panama, 3

parochialism: bias/framing and, 51–52; definition of, 50–52; different groups and, 51–52; domestic job protection and, 50–51; protectionism and, 51; trade policy and, 51. *See also* import safety parochialism

parochialism research, 51–52. *See also* import safety parochialism research

peanut products, 5, 137–39, *138*

People's Republic of China (PRC), 23. *See also* China

pharmaceuticals. *See* drugs

pharmaceutical industry: import safety and, 6

policy: design in addressing import safety problems, 258–59, 262; implications of international food safety standards, 102–5; rent-seeking and health, 110. *See also* import safety policy; public policy; regulation

politics: global trade and food safety, 88–105; ideology and risk perception, 50

PRC. *See* People's Republic of China

prevention. *See* import risk prevention

preventive regulation: global consumer protection and, 15; import safety regulation and, 10, 12

private food safety regulation: Europe and, 239–41; HACCP and, 241; ISO and, 241–42

private import safety regulation: accountability/legitimacy, 248–50; developed countries and, 233; developing countries and, 233; effectiveness, 245–46; fairness, 246–48; food safety regulation, 233; public import safety regulation and, 259, 263; transnational new governance and, 233

private regulation: government regulation and, 234; international product safety regulation and, 235, 250; product regulation, 235; public regulation and, 233–34, 250; safety regulation and, 233–34. *See also* private safety regulation

private safety regulation, 233–36; government safety regulation and, 242–44; international trade and, 244–45; private drivers, 234–35; public drivers, 234; recent growth, 237–38; tort liability and, 234; U.S., 234. *See also* private food safety regulation; private import safety regulation

private sector: delegated governance of, import safety and, 267; in import safety solution, 261–65; import safety solution and merging of public and, 262–65, 270nn3–4, 270nn6–7, 271nn8–9; involvement in import safety reform proposals, 74, 79–80, 84; leveraging, 191, 193–250, 267; new governance regulation and merging of public and, 262–65, 270nn3–4, 270nn6–7, 271nn8–9; WTO import safety rules and, 80

production regulation, 211n3; challenges in globalized world product safety regulation, 198–200; domestic consumer safety regulation, 196–97; drug import safety and, 197; drug regulation and, 199; imported drugs and, 199;

Acknowledgments

This project was conceived a little over a year ago, not long after the global crisis emerged over melamine in milk products. Moving from a nascent idea to a published volume in such a short time can only occur with help provided by many people whose names do not appear on this book's cover.

At the outset, we thank Ron Daniels, who served as the provost of the University of Pennsylvania at the time this project first took root. This book grows out of his vision for bringing university research to bear on significant problems facing the global society. When the Penn Program on Regulation convened its workshop in the spring of 2009 to discuss the drafts of this book's chapters, Ron had already gone on to assume the presidency of Johns Hopkins University, but his intellectual finger-prints can still be found on this volume. We are grateful not only for the mark he left on this project but for the many other ways his leadership enhanced the University of Pennsylvania's strength and vitality.

We owe exceeding thanks, obviously, to the authors of the book's chapters. Their role has already been acknowledged in the usual way, but they deserve a still further word of appreciation for their diligence and conscientiousness. Thanks to their cooperation, we have been able to move this project forward on a time frame that should enable the ideas in this book to make an impact not only on future academic in-quiry, but also on contemporary policy deliberations. Our colleagues' intellectual energy and professional dedication have made this project most gratifying for us as editors.

We also gratefully acknowledge the role played by several other col-leagues in providing feedback on the draft chapters at our workshop, in particular Corinna Colatore, Marsha Echols, Doug Grob, David Plun-kett, Ted Ruger, and Mike Taylor. We appreciate as well the feedback the chapter authors gave each other. In addition, Sandra Hoffmann provided an insightful commentary on all the papers at the conclusion of the workshop, and Marion Nestle opened the event by delivering an outstanding keynote address. Elliot Posner offered valuable comments when portions of this book were presented at the 2009 American Political Science Association Meeting.

Many staff members at the University of Pennsylvania Law School played instrumental roles. Anna Gavin handled with aplomb all the arrangements for the workshop and then continued to play a key coordinating role in preparing the final manuscript. Her many hours of effort have not only made this book possible, they have made it better in innumerable ways. Other members of the Law School's faculty support team, including Silvana Burgese, Eric Dillalogue, and Nesha Patel, contributed significantly to the completion of this volume, while Rod Afshar helped manage key file conversions as we prepared the manuscript. The reference librarians at the Biddle Law Library, in particular Tim von Dulm, provided crucial research support. We are enormously grateful to Ben Meltzer, who devoted untold hours—sometimes at all hours of the day—cite-checking under tight time constraints.

We wish to express our deep appreciation to Dean Mike Fitts of the University of Pennsylvania Law School for his generous support of the Penn Program on Regulation from its inception. A cross-disciplinary project such as this one owes much to Mike's extraordinary leadership at Penn Law and to his wisdom in encouraging integrative legal scholarship. We also greatly appreciate the financial support of this project provided by the University's Office of the Provost, now under the able stewardship of our valued colleague Vince Price.

We could not have asked for a better publisher to work with than the University of Pennsylvania Press. Director Eric Halpern and Editor-in-Chief Peter Agree readily saw the need for a book such as this to be issued in a timely manner, and Bill Finan's great skill as an editor made our vision a reality—in what seemed to us a remarkably seamless process.

We also note our appreciation to Erin Graham for joining us for the workshop and supporting the project, and to Peggy Gordon, Debra Schiff, and their colleagues for their assistance with copy-editing and typesetting. Hope Steele also contributed her editorial acumen at the final stage of production.

The usual caveat absolves all of the above-named individuals for responsibility for scholarly errors and omissions, as well as for any implication that they necessarily agree with all of the views expressed in these pages. That said, in the event this book succeeds in helping improve consumer protection in the global economy, even in a small way, we happily share the credit with all who have helped make this volume possible.